OPERA

Dead or Alive

OPERA

Dead or Alive

Production, Performance, and Enjoyment of Musical Theatre

RONALD E. MITCHELL

The University of Wisconsin Press

MADISON, MILWAUKEE,
& LONDON

Published 1970
The University of Wisconsin Press
Box 1379, Madison, Wisconsin 53701

The University of Wisconsin Press, Ltd.
27–29 Whitfield Street, London, W.1

First printing

Printed in the United States of America
Kingsport Press, Inc., Kingsport, Tennessee

ISBN 0-299-05811-5; LC 73-121772

To those who buy tickets and go

ACKNOWLEDGMENTS

Grateful acknowledgments are made to the Graduate School of the University of Wisconsin, to Mark Ingraham and Edwin Young, former deans of the College of Letters and Science, and to the former chairman of the Department of Speech, Frederick W. Haberman. Their practical assistance, intercession, and encouragement helped to bring this book to completion.

It would be ungracious not to mention the friendly interest of many of the School of Music faculty over the years. Especially rewarding has been a working association with Karlos Moser, director of the Opera Workshop.

Although my interest in the subject and my musical theatregoing date back nearly half a century, the impetus for the written study was provided by a Fulbright grant awarded me in 1960.

I wish also to express my gratitude to my wife and children, who have long humored my enthusiasms, the first-mentioned having cheerfully endured the most.

Contents

Illustrations

ILLUSTRATIONS IN TEXT

Introduction

This book about lyric drama is intended neither for beginners nor for specialists, but for that large and important group of people who constitute the bulk of audiences for opera, operetta, and musical comedy. The members of these audiences are mostly generalists. They will have preferences and prejudices, but for the most part they cannot lay claim to any specialized knowledge of vocal music, instrumental music, dramatic theory, scene design, costume design, stage lighting, choreography, acting, directing, or business management. Nevertheless it is they who decide upon the success or failure of a new work or a revival. It is they who, by attending and applauding, have kept Giuseppe Verdi's *Rigoletto* going for well over a century and who do not insist upon a revival of Horatio Parker's *Mona*. It is they who have seen *The Merry Widow* into its second half-century, while permitting *The Belle of New York* to languish. It is they who decreed that *Oklahoma* and *My Fair Lady* should delight millions, that *The Mikado* should fill theatres more readily than *Fra Diavolo*, and *Madam Butterfly* more readily than *Wozzeck*.

Specialists may berate them for acclaiming worthless trifles while neglecting masterpieces, but the facts remain. The musical theatre cannot exist, much less prosper, without its public, and a theatre operated for specialists is likely to have discouragingly thin audiences and, after a while, extremely high prices. There are simply not enough specialists, and some of them are impecunious.

If this book has a missionary purpose it is to increase the curiosity, interest, and appreciation of the generalist audience, to make that audience more critical, yet more understanding of the many problems attending the various musical theatre forms, to stimulate audience attention, both visual and aural, and to improve audience behavior. Improvement of management and production will take care of itself the moment audiences have learned to be more demanding, more discriminating, more sympathetic, and altogether more aware of the complex nature of the kind of theatre they are attending.

It is hoped that there will also be some specialists in these audiences. Their observations may be of considerable value to managers, performers, and the generalists. It is the specialist who is likely to notice shoddy scenery, faulty intonation, acting mannerisms, slackness of rhythm, careless costuming, poorly planned lighting, inferior diction, the imminence of vocal disability, or unimaginatively arranged movement. The generalist will accept much of that which is painful and distracting to the specialist, and even the specialist out of his own field, of course, is a generalist.

The strength of the real generalist lies in his impartiality, his weakness in his ignorance. A specialist knows far more about one aspect or a few aspects of the finished production, but it is harder for him to see the work as a whole. If those with special interests can be induced to broaden their interests and all generalists be induced to broaden their experience, the first steps will have been taken to the signal improvement of audiences. As soon as audiences become better, better pieces have to be done and the pieces have to be better done. It means a great deal more work. Is it worth it? It is not only worth it; it is imperative.

ON STAGE WITH MUSICAL THEATRE

I

Audiences and Theatres

The appeal of musical theatre is of extraordinary breadth, and its length is greater than that of civilization. The ancestor of the ecstatic or marrow-freezing high note so treasured in our opera houses from the expensive fifth-row-center orchestra seat to the standing place at the back of the topmost gallery was probably the ecstatic or marrow-freezing yell which accompanied the human sacrifice on pagan altars. It is no accident that the serious drama, especially intensified by song, should be concerned with the propitiation of the forces governing the universe and with the familiar phenomena of life and death. It is just as natural that less serious drama, similarly made more festive by song, should be concerned with the delights of living and with the familiar phenomenon of sex.

A theatre is anywhere. An audience is anyone. The threshing floor at one side of a Greek hill is a theatre and the watchers clustered above are the audience. A cathedral or a country church is a theatre in which the elaborate statuary or the simple carvings, the stained-glass windows or the crude wall paintings, seem to come miraculously alive when the priests assume their appearances at Christmas or at Easter and the congregation watches and listens. When village festivities included "ballets," carols, wooing dialogues, and *pastourelles* and in addition to singing them acted them out, whoever was present was the audience, and as in a party game, audience became performer and the performer became audience. In the marble courtyard at Versailles in 1676 there was staged the *Alceste* of Quinault and Lully with the royal court as the audience, and at Falaise in Normandy *vaudevilles* were performed on trestle booths

3

a few feet from the cattle market with a sword fight in progress ten rows from the edge of the stage.

Until recently (for they have, regrettably, abandoned opera) one could sit in a Cleveland, Ohio, settlement house called Karamu (Swahili for a place of communal recreation) and participate as an audience member in a vital production of an opera, with no conductor and no orchestra but a single pianist to provide the only music which was not sung. Today one may attend a spectacle in an enormous Roman amphitheatre in Verona. One may find oneself trapped in a side loge in the Vienna Staatsoper with an excellent view of the backs of the front row of the next loge but no view of the stage. One may sit on cane seats in the Bayreuth Festspielhaus and see no orchestra, but hear its music surging up from a dim space between the front row and the stage. One may experience musical comedy from expensive seats in a Broadway theatre or in a high school auditorium in Nevada, on the first night of the opening run or during a single performance of a thirty-year-old success. A seat for musical theatre may cost anything from thirty-five cents to thirty-five dollars. The audience may contain a seven-year-old girl who is seeing a work of the musical theatre for the first time in her life, or a seventy-year-old gentleman who has seen two thousand and conducted two hundred performances.

Some members of the audience have come knowing the work, musically and dramatically. Others, if the work is an opera in Italian, French, or German, have only the haziest notion of what is going on. Music is so persuasive, so enjoyable to listen to, that it is easy to let it take over, to accept the general idea emotionally without bothering to investigate the specific idea intellectually. Many of us are attracted to musical theatre by the sound of it, only discovering later that some sense is involved also. The industrious who have studied the works and the music are in the minority. When the work is a musical comedy or an operetta in English there are no such problems and, depending upon the interest in the script, we pay attention to what is happening and to whom it is happening.

The first-night audience at a Broadway musical is quite different in composition from the fortieth-night audience at the same production. If the production is a highly publicized success, the fortieth-night audience is quite different from the fortieth-night audience for a musical that has announced its closing with the fiftieth night. The audience at the Metropolitan during the first week of the season, or for a new production or the debut of a European discovery already read about and heard on records, is vastly different from a Saturday-night audience halfway through the season or from an audience of opera-loving Italians in Brooklyn or from an operetta audience in Regensburg or Graz.

In the days before the opening of the first public opera house (Venice, 1637), it was a privilege to be invited to an expensive entertainment, and ever since that date it has been prestigious to be able to afford to support the opera by possessing keys to a box, or simply by buying the best tickets.

Since the seventeenth century there has been a fashionable public for opera and the fashionable public still exists, as the opening notices of the Metropolitan Opera and Covent Garden and La Scala testify. This public, which has given a certain class dignity to the art as well as itself gaining prestige by attending it, has in many instances done great service in supporting opera financially. A segment of it, it is true, cares nothing for music or the theatre, and the members of that segment go to the opera to be seen in the best seats and in the bar and the foyer and on the grand staircase. In the last century their comments helped to provide jokes for the authors of drawing-room plays. It is not correct, however, to assume that all the wealthy and fashionable who attend opera care nothing for it. Many of them have attended a very large number of works for years and have profited by doing so. As befits their station they are generally well mannered.

The placard-carrying, button-wearing voice fanciers are less well behaved and are sometimes a serious nuisance. They are more interested in stirring up factions in and out of the theatre than in the work to be performed. They argue as they wait for curtain time, and in the theatre itself their energies are devoted to applauding, forcing and counting curtain calls, hissing rival singers, and generally turning an art form into a contest. When they are not doing harm they are performing their one good deed of enlivening many a production which would otherwise collapse from sheer boredom on both sides of the proscenium. The interruption is less distressing than demise from inanition.

There are genuine voice fanciers who may be teachers or young singers themselves, and they naturally have opinions based upon technical knowledge, but they are generally quieter than those who have no knowledge but who have managed to pick up a deal of jargon on vocal matters.

Many audience members enjoy the music and can afford the extra excitement of attending productions where the audience, the live orchestra, and the scenery and costumes can make the dull passages seem less dull and somewhat shorter. At home, when there is a broadcast, they turn on the radio but they occupy themselves with other activities; they do not give their full attention to the music, and no attention at all to the text which interested the composer long enough to make him spend a great deal of time and energy writing music for it.

An increasing number of audience members, it is to be hoped, are taking a more comprehensive interest than ever before. Among them, expectably, are students of singing, of the theatre, and of all manner of subjects, but students with a particular interest in opera and music drama. Some of these deny themselves the pleasure of being interested in operetta and musical comedy. Some are frank to express their dislike of the lighter, more popular forms. Yet others enjoy these forms as welcome relaxation but find the more ambitious works of musical theatre too taxing. The subject matter is often serious, sometimes depressing, the music is more difficult to grasp, and the works are frequently performed in foreign languages.

There is no need to place opera in English and opera in the original language in the context of a debate. The advantages of each are obvious, and much time has been wasted favoring one in opposition to the other. Both are necessary, just as large theatres and small theatres are necessary and sopranos and basses are necessary. They perform different functions.

For the inexperienced playgoer, opera in English is essential, and the faster he can rid himself of prejudice against it the better. For the experienced theatregoer, opera in the original language is just as essential. Those who heard and saw *Il Trovatore* in English before they heard and saw it in Italian may now prefer it in Italian, but they cannot deny that hearing it in English, if English is their only fluent language, was helpful to understanding. The mistake is to indulge the prejudice by acquiring a taste for the emotional pleasure to be derived from hearing the music, without making the effort to understand what is happening, who the characters are, and why the music is fast or slow, soft or loud, turbulent or gentle. If opera in English can precede opera in the original language, an adjustment can be smoothly made. It is when understanding a part or the whole of a text impedes enjoyment by surprising us with the meaning that we are tempted to succumb to the easier pleasure of simply allowing ourselves to be bathed in a generalized emotion. All this presupposes clear English diction on the part of the singers, since a token performance in English with foreigners struggling to enunciate the unfamiliar English sounds is even more frustrating than a performance wholly in a foreign language.

The French hear most of their opera in French before they hear opera in Italian, English, German, or Russian. The Germans hear their Verdi in German and the Italians hear their Wagner in Italian. There is an occasional exception in Vienna, where such works as *Figaro, Don Giovanni,* and *Così fan Tutte* are frequently sung in Italian and *Faust* has been done in French. There have been Wagner and Strauss productions in the German language at La Scala, since the cast has almost entirely been imported for the occasion. Usually, however, the language of the opera is the language of the audience. In England it is possible to grow up hearing opera in English for a number of years before hearing international artists at Covent Garden singing Verdi in Italian, Wagner in German, and Gounod in French.

In America there are so few opera companies performing in English that Italian-Americans hear their Italian opera in Italian at the Metropolitan, the San Francisco Opera, the Chicago Lyric Opera, and elsewhere, while operas in French and German are more frequently to be encountered than those in English. Not many years ago a Metropolitan *La Bohème* in English was quickly withdrawn, and the more familiar Italian was sung at the remaining performances of the season. Over the remainder of the country, listeners are so accustomed to the Metropolitan broadcasts and to recordings in the original language that an English translation comes as a rude shock.

The main support for the prejudice against opera in English may be attributed to old-fashioned and incompetent translations, many of them so poor that they cause unintentional laughter in the theatre. While such translations are seldom performed today and much better ones by John Gutman or Ruth and Thomas Martin are offered instead, the recollection of awkward phrases and ill-chosen words remains. "To a little light give access" from Violetta's deathbed is likely to occasion a ruinous flurry of audience amusement, while in *Don Giovanni* "Why quits the rose thy pallid cheek? So, I spy it. I spy the truth, sly hussy! Wouldst deceive me and mean you I should not see the what hath passed between you?" is certain to be protested by the Masetto who has to enunciate it, as well as jeered by the audience who has to listen to it.* The cause for at least some opera in English is lost if versions such as these are performed. Even a translation which seemed good a dozen years ago should be carefully scanned for necessary revisions today.

The problems of translation are overlooked by those who have never had to cope with them. It is difficult enough to translate a prose play without losing much of its original flavor. In translating a piece which is not only in verse but also set to music, the words have to fit the notes, the assemblage of English consonants must not be awkward, and the vowel sounds must be singable according to pitch. Ideally, a singer ought to be able to sing every vowel on every note of his or her compass, but many excellent sopranos cannot comfortably sing "Siegfried" on high notes. Since the first syllable is likely to be the high one, "ai" as in "high" is often substituted so that what one hears is "Seigfried" or "Säägfried." Sieglinde and Brünnhilde must sing this syllable above the staff.

Difficulties in the originals occasioned by composer indulgence or forgetfulness (and even Mozart is not blameless in this regard) are comparatively rare. A careful translator tries not to increase the number of difficulties but, as he strives for the exact sense or strug-

* Translations from *Authentic Librettos of the Italian Operas*, New York, 1939, pp. 137, 409.

gles for a rhyme that is appropriate, his judgment may fail him. If he favors the sense he may cause the singer difficulty. If he considers the singer he may distort the sense, or, in trying to give equal attention to sense and singer, he may produce a characterless phrase which the audience finds vapid. The audience accustomed to but not understanding much French, German, or Italian will ignore the vapid phrases in the original texts, while appreciating the librettist's choice of words for sound alone. This is more likely to satisfy listeners in serious drama than in comedy. One may wallow in the sheer sound of *Simon Boccanegra* or *Die Frau ohne Schatten* with only the haziest notion of what the characters are saying as well as singing (and both operas are difficult to follow in any language), but *The Secret Marriage*, *Fra Diavolo*, and *The Barber of Baghdad* can be frustrating experiences for audiences who are totally baffled by Italian, French, and German, respectively, especially if the productions are sparkling and dexterously acted and other members of the audience are clearly enjoying the comedy or pretending to do so. With operetta and musical comedy there is no such problem, since these forms are invariably performed in the language of the audience.

From early times in the public theatres audiences have sat or stood in different-priced sections according to social position or immediate financial condition. The most fashionable seats have not always been the best seats, although they are often the most comfortable. Box seats near the sides of the stage are good to be seen in and looked at but poor both visually and aurally. A slanting view of the scenery and groupings and, on one side, the proximity of the tympani do not reduce the price of such seats, but they certainly reduce the pleasure provided by a musical-dramatic performance. Custom has decreed the main-floor seating to be more prestigious than seats in balconies, but the first few rows, often the most expensive, are too close for musical comfort, and visually one is more aware of makeup and glottal movements than is pleasurable. If the floor is not adequately sloped and the seats are immediately behind each other, a tall man or a high feminine hair arrangement can easily place an opaque oval in the middle of the rectangle in which all the action takes place.

Musically and choreographically the best places are in the middle rows of the first balcony, center section, with some second balconies almost as good. Other second balconies, if closer to the stage, are too high. Third and fourth balconies and the sides of balconies are for the temporarily or permanently impoverished. The side box or loge in many European theatres is visually good only in the front row, fair in the second row, and impossible in the third. The seating chart should be consulted. Aurally, a loge may be adequate in front, with somewhat smothered sound at the rear. Center loges are excellent, both visually and aurally, the rear seats once again being somewhat too boxed in for good sound. In a small theatre of eighteenth-century design, the center loge seats are the best seats (the royal box is often there), but in a large theatre they seem rather far back, and for visual rather than aural reasons an orchestra seat may be preferable.

The size of the theatre is of significance not only to the members of the audience who see and hear the work being staged but to the actors and singers who are performing in it. For a play or a musical piece, an adequate stage and space for an adequate audience are necessary.

There is some correlation between the size of a theatre and the work performed in it. The space may be enlarged and the number of seats for the audience increased until the point is reached where the space required is too large for the singers to project vocally and physically without strain and for the audience in the rear to see and hear comfortably. Pergolesi's *La Serva Padrona* and Mozart's *The Impresario* are easily projected in a small theatre and may well seem distant and trivial in a large one. *Aida* and *Turandot*, in addition to requiring a large stage in order to accommodate the chorus and some grandiose scenic effects, require the distance in order to avoid the imputation of noisy vulgarity. A small theatre building, however, does not necessarily mean a small stage. Many European theatres built in the eighteenth century have a large stage attached to a small auditorium. The Drottningholm Slottsteater (Figure 1 and Plate 3), a summer palace theatre near Stockholm built in 1766, was originally intended only for the royal family, members of the court, and invited guests. The auditorium is therefore quite small. The depth of its stage, however, is 62 feet, the fourth-deepest in the whole of Sweden, the other three being twentieth-century buildings.

A private theatre in a monarchy can afford the large stage–small auditorium ratio. Even public, unsubsidized theatres two hundred years ago tended to be small until, late in the eighteenth century with middle-class and working-class audiences crowding the theatres, the buildings were altered to bring in more money. In 1762 London's Drury Lane Theatre was remodelled in order to increase the number of seats and therefore the amount of money taken in at a single performance. It was altered a second time in 1780 and a dozen years later was rebuilt to contain over 3600 people. Covent Garden, not yet an opera house, was similarly enlarged to 2800 in 1808. In the later years of her career the actress Sarah Siddons, whose splendor of voice struck shop assistants with panic, complained that the huge auditorium was too hard on her equipment. It is generally accepted that the combination of the large auditorium and the inadequate gas lighting was in part responsible for the broad, unsubtle acting characteristic of the nineteenth century from about 1820 to about 1860, and for the broad, unsubtle plays which were successful under these theatre conditions.

A similar phenomenon may be noted in the musical theatre of the present. It is fortunate that opera houses, operetta houses, and theatres in which musical comedies are performed vary widely in size, so that we are accustomed to adjusting from theatres holding over 3000 to theatres holding less than 500. High production costs and increasing salaries for performers make the operation of large theatres less unprofitable and generally more manageable than small theatres. If singers are to be hired at high fees in a theatre seating over 3000, the management may hope, with ticket costs at an average of $6 a seat, to take in $18,000. A theatre of half the size must charge a $12 average if it is to clear the same amount before expenses. If, instead of a single performance, it has to stage two in order to avoid angering the community, the members of which always seem to remember disappointments, it will lose money unless it raises the prices above $6, for singers do not sing two performances for the price of one, and other costs increase by performance, labor costs especially.

From the commercial point of view the larger the theatre the better. From the audience and performer point of view there is a point of diminishing returns, a point which is often seriously over-reached in the international opera houses of the greatest fame. A state-subsidized repertory opera house need not bewail its lack of size. In most instances the repertory opera house has also to be a spoken drama house, and even though we have better stage lighting than they had in the eighteenth century, no one wishes to return to a spoken theatre in which the auditorium seats more than 3000 and all subtle effect is made impossible. The repertory opera house therefore seldom exceeds a capacity of 1500, with the Théâtre de la Monnaie in Brussels exactly that size and the Stockholm Royal Opera only a little over 1200, replacing the smaller one in which King Gustav III was murdered in 1792. Some German theatres in which both plays and operas are performed are below 1000 in capacity—for example, the theatres at Kassel, Coburg, and Kiel a little over 900, and Wuppertal in the 800–900 category. Hannover and Frankfurt are in the 1400–1500 category and Cologne, Wiesbaden, and Düsseldorf between 1300 and 1400, much the same size as several university theatres in the United States. Even the Hamburg Staatsoper seats fewer than 1700, and the Vienna Staatsoper is under 2000. In Vienna, works suitable to a smaller opera house are performed at the Volksoper and at the refurbished Theater an der Wien. Many German theatres in the 1200–1500 category operate an intimate theatre of two or three hundred, and there is a suitable distribution of productions according to size, intimate operas going into the smaller theatre while Shakespeare and Schiller take the larger one.

A similar arrangement was attempted in Gatti-Casazza's 1909–1910 season at the New York Metropolitan, when several works suitable for a smaller auditorium, *Fra Diavolo, Stradella,* and *Werther,* were given at the New Theatre. This excellent idea was quickly abandoned.

Not every large auditorium, of course, poses hearing difficulties, though it can scarcely avoid posing some seeing difficulties. The Chicago auditorium, designed by Dankmar Adler and Louis Sullivan, dedicated in 1889 and having a capacity of 4000, has close to the best acoustics in the world. With its unenclosed boxes, a sharply rising floor, and a shrewd avoidance of straight lines, the hall flares out from the stage in the shape of a flattened gramophone horn of the old-fashioned kind. It was some years ago saved from total destruction and taken over by Roosevelt University, and it has recently been restored to its former glory.

Among the world's largest opera houses are the Paris Opera, the Metropolitan Opera House in Lincoln Center (the old Metropolitan was built to seat 3045), La Scala in Milan, the Colon in Buenos Aires, and the Liceo in Barcelona. The Liceo, seating 3500, was built in 1847 when Barcelona had fewer than 175,000 inhabitants, and it was for many years considered too big.

Covent Garden, under 2200 in recent years, is somewhat larger than the Vienna Staatsoper but only two-thirds the size of the biggest opera houses. It is not necessary to have a large voice to sound to good advantage in the opera house, but a large voice has far more chance of doing so than a small one, however clear. Elisabeth Schumann and Bidu Sayao were able to be heard in spaces where voices of greater heft sounded weak, but they were exceptions. Ordinarily the larger the voice, the more likely it is to be welcomed in opera houses of 2500 capacity or more. This tends to make what is now called the jet circuit consist of a small number of highly paid singers ($5000 and up for a single performance in some establishments), most of them with large voices. When all the costs of a singer's education are considered, together with the amount of pleasure singers give, the quantity of publicity they engender, the amount of money they bring to the theatres in which they sing, and the possibility that their triumph will be all too short-lived, they deserve every dollar.

There are, however, many singers and actors who sound and look better in the 1500-capacity theatres. Among them are many who would prefer to stay in the smaller theatres of the repertory system, even if they had the opportunity to become international celebrities. Others, understandably, would eagerly trade the milder benefits of the repertory system for the heady excitement of international fame.

Where there is a sound repertory system there is no harm in adding to it the excitement and color of international opera, as long as the public does not come to demand the celebrities exclusively and fail in its support of the steady but less stellar operation. A well-educated public has no difficulty in making the proper distinctions and enjoys both. Those, however, accustomed only to a large opera house leaning heavily for support upon the engagement of the most sensational and well-publicized singers are going to lose their taste for daily bread and want nothing but rich cake with quantities of cream. With this goes the mistaken opinion that singers with smaller voices are not as good singers and that all opera must be "grand." While the ample voice may find the large houses not so very trying, acting in works calling for swiftness and delicacy is invariably coarsened, and the pointing of comedy becomes difficult.

Most works of the musical theatre are more adaptable than spoken plays and can be successfully performed in a wide range of space. A small theatre presents problems for the *Ring,* but it is most unlikely that a really small theatre will attempt it. Several medium-sized theatres in Germany have staged it. *Così fan Tutte* and *The Secret Marriage* have been staged in Hamburg (over 1600), but the theatre seems large for *opera buffa.* Both have been staged at the old Metropolitan. In the 1922 production of *Così* an attempt was made to offset the huge space by placing an inner stage upon the real stage, with old-fashioned lamps along the inner curtain line to be lighted by liveried footmen before the performance. Two chandeliers were also lighted in the effort to supply the much-missed intimacy, but moving the inner stage back from the audience was the very opposite of what the work cries out for—to be brought right into the audience, which would have been impractical. In the 1951 English-language production the problem was partly solved, with some stylistic loss, by the inventiveness of Alfred Lunt, the stage director. The 1937 production of *The Secret Marriage* lasted only two performances. Both works are popular in small and medium-sized European opera houses.

In the future, opera houses, both stage and auditorium, will undoubtedly be constructed to expand and contract so that the proper size for each production and assemblage can be readily attained. Primitive attempts to cut down the size of houses by closing off certain sections have obtained for half a century or more, and significant advances have recently been made. Until an efficient system which is not at the same time ruinously expensive can be devised, however, opera houses must choose with care in order to avoid productions which seem disproportionate, or must adapt them with skill to the conditions of the building.

In addition to the tangible considerations of size and the somewhat less tangible ones of sightlines (in a full house, not an empty one) and acoustics (also in a full house), there are the quite intangible considerations of audience relationship to theatre, of the composition of audiences, of their reasons for coming, and of their mental and emotional attitude toward the building, the productions, and even toward each other. An opera house audience, although it is never exactly the same on two successive evenings, does much over the years to give an opera house a sequence of associations which, combined with the quality of the productions staged there, produces an ambiance not readily describable but strongly felt. The bricks, wood, stone, glass, concrete, and interior decorations of a theatre are not easily separable from what takes place there, from those who perform there, and from those who go there to watch and to listen and to grow fond of being there.

The new Metropolitan Opera House in Lincoln Center and the new opera house in Santa Fe will in time acquire their respective atmospheres and sets of associations, but at present their predecessors have the advantage, and the grief was genuine when the first was demolished and the second burned.

The first Metropolitan Opera House was opened on October 22, 1883, with Charles Gounod's *Faust,* sung in Italian. From that night until the 1966 closing, the old Metropolitan staged 217 operas, of which 25 were world premieres. Gustav Mahler, Arturo Toscanini, Tullio Serafin, Fritz Busch, and Bruno Walter were five of its many conductors. The singers, from Marcella Sembrich's debut in the opening season to a decade beyond the Maria Callas *Norma,* included most of the international celebrities. There was a Caruso era of nearly two decades, and there was a Flagstad-Melchior seven-year domination until 1941.

For many Americans it was the only opera house in the world, the only one they ever attended. It was not even, of course, the only opera house in the United States, but many who attended opera at the Metropolitan were never inside the opera houses of Boston, Chicago, and San Francisco. The New York opera house for much of its eighty-three-year life stood as the symbol of opera in America, a distinguished but lonely outpost of international opera performing its repertory in the language of the original text and taking a long time to encourage opera in English, a long time to encourage a proportionate number of American singers instead of imported ones, and a long time to encourage American composers.

Although the Metropolitan had heard *Lohengrin* in Italian and *Carmen* and *Aida* in German, it was 1936, in the first season of Edward Johnson's management, that an opera written in French, German, or Italian was performed in an English translation. The first happened to be an Italian one and, sensibly enough, a comedy, *Gianni Schicchi*. Before this, when a translation was used it had been for the benefit of the cast, not for the audience. The Russian opera *Boris Godounov* was given its first Metropolitan production in 1913 in Italian. When Chaliapin sang Boris there in 1921 he sang in Russian, while the remainder of the cast sang in Italian, before an audience most of whom did not know either language. When another Russian opera, *Pique Dame*, first appeared at the Metropolitan, it was sung in German.

An American soprano, Alwina Valleria, sang in the first week of the first season (Leonora in *Trovatore*), but while Lillian Nordica and Geraldine Farrar advertised the fact that Americans also sang, it was not until the Johnson regime that the proportion rose to a noticeable amount.

Horatio Parker's *Mona* received four performances between March 14 and April 1 in 1912, never to be performed there again. In the previous season Converse's *The Pipe of Desire*, the first American opera to be produced at the theatre, had the doubtful distinction of two performances, the first following *Pagliacci* and the second preceding *Cavalleria Rusticana*. The history of American operas at the Metropolitan has been a melancholy one. It is customary to attack the conservatism of the managers, but the managements have been for the most part strikingly progressive in the face of the apathy and downright opposition of audiences, and much money has been lost in ventures which many applaud in spirit without attending in person.

An established opera company needs a well-equipped theatre with the space in which to operate a complex repertory. This the Metropolitan finally achieved in 1966. An equally good thing to have is sharp rivalry, or a number of complementary theatres. This the Metropolitan has, to some extent, in the New York City Opera Company and in the nearby Broadway theatre, which stages the musical comedies not suited to the Metropolitan and overlaps the repertory only occasionally with an operetta revival. The Metropolitan could profit from more. What it needs most is a faithful yet demanding audience, an astute audience which can discriminate between a music drama and the performance of one, an audience unafraid of adventure. This the Metropolitan cannot claim to have. There are good audience members in it, but not nearly enough to leaven the lump.

The Metropolitan has not been behindhand in its attempts to educate the public. As long ago as 1931, when *Hänsel und Gretel* was broadcast from the stage on Christmas Day, the works performed at the Metropolitan were no longer heard only by New York residents or visitors to that city. A new and immense audience was offered opportunities for experiences it had never before had, with the one disadvantage that many of them sought listening pleasure only, and when subsequently visiting large cities made no attempt to enter theatres where operas were being performed. Some opera-going converts were undoubtedly made. Others, upon inquiry, found the admission prices too high for them, and quickly lost interest.

In the very first season Henry Abbey, after closing the first half of the New York season on January 13, took productions to eight other opera houses before reopening in New York on March 10, and later managers continued the practice, though costs were considerable and not many cities had theatres large enough to accommodate a Metropolitan production. Opportunities were provided, however, for actually seeing opera on stage, although in many instances the emphasis was more upon celebrated performers than upon the work performed or its musical and dramatic presentation.

In 1935, the establishment of the Metropolitan Opera Guild by Mrs. August Belmont provided radio listeners with an identity, and performed a further educational function by publishing an informative magazine, *Opera News*, arranging lectures and exhibitions, and making direct contact with high schools by organizing special performances for them at reduced prices. If the public is slow to take advantage of the educational opportunities, the blame cannot be placed upon the tireless staff of the guild. The public must accept its share of the blame but not quite all. The enormous size of the country, the great distance between cities, and the pioneer preoccupations during the country's formative years have all had their effect, while the development of other entertainment media have contributed to the problem.

Yet, even if distances are reduced to the point where the plane fare from Wichita to New York is no greater than the train fare from Warwick to London or the bus fare from Eisenstadt to Vienna, the sense of possession is lacking. There are many Austrians who have never seen the Vienna Staatsoper. There are many Viennese who have never been inside it, but they feel it is theirs. In one sense it is theirs because they help to support it out of their taxes. It is, however, theirs for less tangible reasons; this is one of the few advantages a small country has over a large one. When the Vienna Staatsoper was bombed and burned to a ruin many Austrians who had never attended an opera there wept, and their weeping was not an affectation. When it was reopened with *Fidelio*, many people who could not get inside for the opening stood outside in the rain and heard the music over a loudspeaker system though they could not see the stage. That is what possession means.

Covent Garden was not always an opera house, although it was built by money made from the enormous success of John Gay's *The Beggar's Opera* at Lincoln's Inn Fields, and in its second season two of Handel's operas were performed there. *Alcina*, which has been staged in our own time by Franco Zeffirelli, received its first performance at Covent Garden in 1735. The theatre was burned down in 1808 but rebuilt by Sir Robert Smirke, the architect who also designed the British Museum and the Mint. Not only was the portico one of the largest in Europe but the stage had a proscenium opening of 42½ feet and depth of 68 feet. It was at this theatre that Carl Maria von Weber succeeded Henry Bishop as musical director. In 1847, Covent Garden became London's second Italian Opera House, the King's Theatre in the Haymarket having been the first. Michael Costa, the musical director who had left the King's Theatre, became the musical director of the new theatre. He was strongly supported by the music critic of the *Morning Chronicle*, Charles Lewis Grüneisen, whose idea of an opera house was to have all great works, whatever the country they had originated in, performed in the Italian language, since he accepted without question that language as the only one proper for singing.

Royal Italian opera seasons continued under a variety of managements until 1891, with several English opera seasons in the autumn and winter.

A Royal Opera season opened in 1892, prefaced by an announcement that Sir Augustus Harris was planning to include performances of German opera in German. This had been done in the 1880's under Gye, and the enduring popularity of *Der Freischütz* and the newer successes of *The Flying Dutchman* and *Tannhäuser* were no doubt an encouragement. Harris was a manager of varied tastes. In the same season, 1895, in which he brought Adelina Patti to sing *La Traviata* at Covent Garden in a diamond-studded dress valued at £211,000 (at that time about a million dollars) he invited a German court company to Drury Lane to play a typical German repertory, consisting of *Der Vogelhändler*, *Die Fledermaus*, *Der Wildschütz*, *Fidelio*, and *The Bartered Bride*. A visitor to Germany today, over seventy years later, may easily encounter all five operas several times over, since they are among the most popular offerings of the state-subsidized theatres. In the same year, Harris brought nine operas in English to an autumn season. When he found too much tradition opposing his encouragement of opera in English he saw to it that the Carl Rosa company flourished.

Under the Grand Opera Syndicate management which followed Harris's, the first production of the entire *Ring* in English was given under Hans Richter in 1908. Opera in English has always been more acceptable in London than in New York. Lilian Baylis established opera in English at the Old Vic with *The Bohemian Girl* in 1900.

There had been attempts at opera in English in the 1850s, and the Carl Rosa company, giving its first London season at the Princess's Theatre in 1875, was to bring understandable opera to millions in London and the provinces, but the Old Vic was a permanent London theatre and Miss Baylis was a determined woman with two consuming interests, opera and Shakespeare. The English appreciation of ensemble may in part be attributed to the unflagging efforts of Lilian Baylis. Until 1931 the Old Vic was the home of opera and Shakespeare, three or four of each in a week. In 1931 Sadler's Wells was opened, so that North London could have equal cultural opportunities with South London. It proved impractical to exchange productions, which had been the original plan when the money was being collected, and London theatregoers of the period will remember the money boxes which passed along the rows at Old Vic productions. The plans were promptly changed, and Sadler's Wells developed into the opera and ballet theatre, while the Old Vic inherited the entire week in which to play Shakespeare and a few other playwrights. Many Londoners who never went to the international seasons at Covent Garden went to the Old Vic or to the Carl Rosa productions to hear opera in English at prices well within their modest means. Fashionable and unfashionable opera prospered side by side in London, and that is obviously the way it should always be. That is how faithful and well-informed audiences are built.

England is nothing if not a country of extremes. While it has been possible for several decades to attend opera at low prices and at Covent Garden for moderate prices, it is also possible to attend opera at high prices in a theatre so difficult of access that it costs even more to get there. Situated in the South Downs and attached to a country house of charm and distinction seven hundred years old, Glyndebourne (Plate 8) is a festival theatre operating only in the summertime. It was founded in 1934 by John Christie and his wife, the former Audrey Mildmay, a soprano who had sung with the Carl Rosa company. The idea behind the venture was to produce opera extremely well, with first-rate casts, a first-rate orchestra under a first-rate conductor, with plenty of rehearsals in order to ensure perfection of ensemble, in a small theatre suited to the size of the works to be done there, and in the relaxing atmosphere of the most beautiful countryside in the south of England.

The little theatre seated 310 but has since been more than doubled. In the first season only two operas were staged, *Figaro* and *Così fan Tutte*. *The Seraglio* and *The Magic Flute* were added for the 1935 season, and in 1939 the repertoire went beyond Mozart and added Donizetti's *Don Pasquale* and Verdi's *Macbeth*. It was in the 1951 season that Birgit Nilsson, now famous for easily filling the largest theatres with her ample voice, sang Electra in Mozart's *Idomeneo.*

The productions conducted by Fritz Busch for the first six seasons and a return in 1950 set a standard very difficult to match, and some of the later seasons have been uneven in quality. Works in the *opera buffa* style of Mozart, Donizetti, and Rossini seem thoroughly at home in the theatre, but apart from Italian *verismo*, the French "grand" opera, Moussorgsky, and much of Wagner, the well-equipped stage and the intimate auditorium lend themselves to an unexpected variety of works from the early seventeenth century to the twentieth.*

There are few theatres so compellingly atmospheric. The English love of quiet countryside and well-tended gardens, the English respect for formality and good breeding, are blended with the English devotion to taste, whether for the wines served in the restaurants during the long dinner interval or for the piquancy of the operas chosen to be performed. Glyndebourne is intended for opera lovers who are also ladies and gentlemen, or for ladies and gentlemen who are also opera lovers. One may spread picnics on the grass but one wears evening dress, and only a boor would allow a table napkin to blow into a hedge or throw a cigarette carton upon the walks. Glyndebourne does not welcome boors.

Its audiences now consist of those whose social, educational, and financial position gives them the absolute right to attend regularly, those who save up to attend occasionally, either because they

* For an account of *Der Rosenkavalier* with reduced orchestration and of John Christie's wish to have *Tristan* and *Parsifal* staged at Glyndebourne, see Wilfrid Blunt, *John Christie of Glyndebourne*, New York, 1968.

are interested in the opera and the way it is produced there or because they are eager for the novel experience of which they have heard and read, and, regrettably, a third group who attend because it is fashionable to do so. The small theatre is all too easily filled for the short summer season. Ticket prices are high but not unreasonably so, and it is often very difficult or impossible to obtain admission.

Particular care was taken when the theatre was built, and later enlarged, to arrange the seating so that each member of the audience looks at the stage between the two people seated immediately before him. The seats are staggered in the center of the auditorium but, for obvious reasons, not staggered at the sides. A seating capacity of 750 is almost the ideal size for a theatre, in that it provides ample space for the musical-dramatic work to be projected as a whole, but places no member of the audience in a position from which hearing and seeing are at all difficult. Anything much smaller requires the work to be self-consciously reduced in projection. Anything much larger offers problems of direct communication for those at the furthest distance from the stage.

If the cost of attending Glyndebourne seems high, it should be remembered that for the participants the cost is even higher. The requirements for rehearsing are much more stringent than in most opera houses. A single performance in a major opera house with one general rehearsal is, financially speaking only, more rewarding than the devotion of several summer weeks to the Glyndebourne enterprise. For singers who are also artists there are unusual but less tangible rewards at Glyndebourne, and many of them have said so. (There is, interestingly, a significant link between Glyndebourne and the Metropolitan lying in the fact that Rudolf Bing was general manager of Glyndebourne from 1936 to 1949 and began his opening season at the Metropolitan on November 6, 1950.)

American opera festivals attempting goals similar to Glyndebourne's are those at Sante Fe, New Mexico, and Central City, Colorado. Only a few years ago the first rose, phoenix-like, from the ashes of the conflagration which had destroyed its original building. Its standards are admirable and its approach adventurous. Central City, once a booming gold-mining town and for years a deserted ghost town, was astutely chosen as a festival center in 1932, opening with the play *Camille*. The place is now a tourist attraction, and operas and operettas form the bulk of the entertainment, for audiences somewhat more general than those of Santa Fe.

The stone theatre was dedicated in 1878, two years after Bayreuth, and it is interesting that instrumental and vocal music by Wagner, among others, was performed at the ceremony and that the drop curtain represented the Rhine, with an ancient castle in perspective. Although ambitious operas have been staged there and Douglas Moore's *The Ballad of Baby Doe* received its premiere there in 1956, lighter works seem especially suited to both theatre and summer holiday audiences. In 1932 Robert Edmond Jones staged *The Merry Widow* there, and in 1967 it was revived with settings and costumes by Donald Oenslager, who had also designed *The Ballad of Baby Doe*. (See Plates 7 and 19.)

The opera house is quaintly devoid of toilet facilities, and the intermissions are enlivened by processions along the street to the Teller House hostelry.

There are several continental theatres which have some affinities with Glyndebourne. Few are as superbly or as inconveniently placed, but most of them as theatre buildings are much older. A few of them are summer theatres only, while others have a summer festival season and also present the more intimate works during the regular season while the larger local house takes care of the heavier works. Some of the baroque or rococo theatres are exquisite examples of eighteenth-century architecture and interior decoration: the restored Cuvilliés Residenztheater in Munich is especially flamboyant and the open air festival theatre in Aix en Provence unusually atmospheric.

One of the most engaging is the palace theatre at Drottningholm (Figure 1 and Plate 3), a short distance outside Stockholm. It was built in 1766 by the mother of King Gustav III and designed by the architect Carl Fredrik Adelcrantz. First associated with plays by the French playwrights Beaumarchais and Voltaire, it betrayed the characteristic northern European sense of inferiority with its attendant devotion to French culture and manners. The first musical pieces played there were examples of French *opéra comique*, but when Gustav bought the palace and stated his intention of develop-

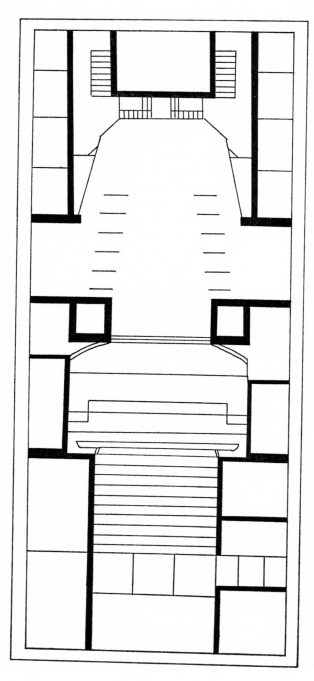

FIGURE 1
Ground plan of
Drottningholm
Palace Theatre,
showing the
great depth of
the stage, the
sets of wings,
and the space
at the rear.
Drawn by
Deborah Dryden.
(See also
Plate 3).

ing native Swedish culture, Drottningholm became an unusually progressive theatre for its day. It is noteworthy chiefly for its technical equipment and the extraordinary stock of eighteenth-century scenery discovered there in 1921, after the building had been used as a storage warehouse. The restoration was done with taste, and since 1947 there has been a summer festival annually. Not all the musical works use the technical facilities to the full, but one work usually displays the thunder machine, which consists of a long wooden trough in which round stones are rolled when a rope at the side of the stage is pulled. A work like Mozart's *Idomeneo* with a seashore scene also displays the gouged wooden "rolling pins" which, when revolved, give the impression of breakers on the shore. A museum attached to the theatre is of considerable interest.

Audiences at festivals, especially those in such glamorous surroundings, are heavily intermixed with tourists, most of them not regular opera-goers and most of them in a mood to enjoy their novel experiences whatever is put before them. While they are usually appreciative they are for the most part uncritical, and a somewhat bland audience spirit is the result. Summer festival productions often reach a high standard, but when the standard lapses the response is much the same, and there have been notable instances of poor productions being enthusiastically received, to the credit of no one.

A mixture of social self-consciousness, genuine devotion, and tourist curiosity may be detected at such theatres as the Cuvilliés or Residenz in Munich and at the festival in the Baroque theatre at Schwetzingen, just south of Mannheim. Both are very small and rather expensive. The Munich theatre (ground plan in Figure 2) dated originally from 1750 to 1753 and was built by the dwarf François Cuvilliés, architectural supervisor to the electoral court from 1730 to 1753. It was severely bombed during the war of 1939–1945 but fortunately, in defiance of Adolf Hitler's orders, the interior decorations had been removed, carefully marked for replacement, and hidden below ground. When in 1954 this theatre was rebuilt of concrete, its interior retained not only the charm of the original rococo decoration but, restored with cleaning and regilding, the brilliance of the eighteenth-century original intended, of course, to be seen by candlelight. With the patina of time removed,

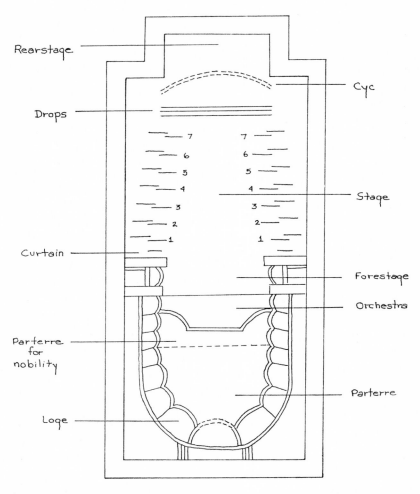

FIGURE 2   Ground plan of Munich Residenz

and seen by electric light, albeit muted, it presents an almost garish appearance. It seats only 462 for operas (525 for plays) and is suited to Mozart, Molière, and Congreve. Strauss's *Capriccio*, although a work of the twentieth century, is set at the time of the Gluck reforms and seems perfectly at home in this jewel-case theatre, where it is often and very successfully produced.

Schwetzingen's festival coincides with the asparagus season in the middle Rhine valley. The Schlosstheater has thirteen rows of about twelve seats each on the main floor, loges immediately above, and two galleries, also surrounding the main floor. A chandelier hangs from the painted ceiling and there are lights affixed to the front of the galleries. The dull pink and off-white décor, with some gold and silver to provide highlights, makes this a quieter-looking, less dazzling, and even more aristocratic theatre than the Munich Residenz.

Both theatres, as is usual with buildings of a period subscribing to class distinctions, have excellent vision for two-thirds of the audience and execrable vision for the remainder. The prestige value of obtaining a good seat is therefore very high. While the fortunate possessors of good seats are usually the best dressed, it is possible to observe a lucky tourist who has managed at the last moment to obtain a returned ticket sitting in ordinary travelling clothes with an unobstructed view of the stage, while several patrons in full evening dress, stationed behind pillars, are forced to stand and lean if they are to see anything of the stage at all, a state of affairs which would certainly have astonished the eighteenth century.

Small and expensive theatres are inclined toward formality. The Drottningholm Theatre, which has excellent sightlines, is far less formal than most, even though the central chairs for the king and queen are a permanent part of the seating and the evidences of former social demarcation and decorum are clear enough. There is even a discernible archness about the orchestra, the members of which are dressed in eighteenth-century costume. Many visitors are delighted by this touch of period flavor. Others, including probably the clarinettist taking his ease between acts with a cigarette and wearing modern horn-rimmed glasses under his white peruke, regard it as somewhat provincial.

Not all Baroque theatres are festival theatres nor expensive and fashionable. The Bavarian city of Regensburg operates its regular repertory in such a theatre, which is of the simpler sort. A plain white interior touched with gold against a wine-red background gives it an unselfconscious quality. There is a simple royal box dating from former times in the center of the lowest gallery. Above, there are two further galleries. At each side of the proscenium, below each gallery, are three side boxes.

It is the city theatre. Plays may be seen there, and opera from Gluck to Křenek. The always popular operettas figure regularly in the season's program. The stage is small, the scenery not always distinguished and sometimes even shabby. The singing varies from surprisingly good to average provincial. The prices are low, however, and the audience is an admirably attentive and well-behaved one. It is for the most part middle class and somewhat stolid. It is neatly dressed and not in the least pretentious. It chatters busily during the intervals, not always about the piece being performed. It is one of a large number of German theatres in which theatregoing is a habit, and although there are dangers of complacency and phlegmatism there is once again the reassuring sense of possession. It is *their* Stadttheater, and one senses both affection and concern and not a little pride. Many of the ordinary citizens of Regensburg, which is about the size of Chattanooga, Tennessee, have by the age of thirty-five attended more than three hundred operas and operettas and more than two hundred plays, all professionally performed, without leaving their native city. For the ambitious, Munich is sixty-five miles to the southwest. Quite without pretentiousness, a bank clerk or a shop assistant with never any dreams of a university education can be conversant in the literature of the theatre.

A small opera house of a different type in the Ruhr industrial area is that situated in Wuppertal. A large percentage of the audience are connected with the local textile, leather, furniture, carpet, machinery, and firearms factories, and the productions are more sophisticated than those in Regensburg. Wuppertal has access to vast audiences, since the city was formed in 1929 by an amalgamation of several small industrial cities in the valley of the Wupper. The population is now around half a million. The theatre is comparatively new, with a large stage and a rather small auditorium seating 839. There are only two balconies. The interior (Plate 5) is of dark brown wood with a white ceiling, and the foyer is colorful and attractive. A refreshment room with mosaic tables and colored chairs is cheerfully inviting. Intertwisting spiral staircases give the entrance and ascent an airy look. Prices are most reasonable. As a place of entertainment it is flashy enough to compete with an elegant cinema, and one has the impression of a loyal audience of astute regulars, proud of Wuppertal's high reputation and willing to encourage the Intendant in progressive experiments. There is less complacency here, and less danger that the theatregoing habit will decline from an active into a passive one.

The Salzburg Festival seems worlds removed from this everyday, unglamorous approach to musical theatre, but it should be observed that Salzburg, too, has its Landestheater, a modest theatre leaning heavily to a diet of operetta, but often playing standard Italian works of a more ambitious nature, and even occasionally venturing into contemporary operas. It is an old-fashioned theatre, and the spotlights caressing the bosoms of the statuary near the proscenium arch produce an entertaining effect. It is very much a theatre of the people, attending to the needs of the people at a price the people can afford, at a time of the year when there is no festival and comparatively few tourists. It has operated as part of the summer festival, but its main function is that of a district theatre. It is not uncommon to see the balcony half-filled with small-town and country people in the national costume of the area. The audience is vastly different in appearance from the international set and the tourists at the gleaming new Festspielhaus and the Felsenreitschule. Many of the townsfolk who attend the Landestheater are on the opposite side of the street during the festival, gazing across and beyond the policemen's backs at the rich and the travelled holding their expensive festival tickets at the lobby doors. From the first half of the *Ring* in the Festspielhaus at Easter, to Millöcker's *Gasparone* at the Landestheater, and back to the summer festival for *Don Giovanni* and *La Rappresentazione di anima e di corpo* covers a splendid range of interests. There is not much overlapping. The Landestheater patrons cannot afford the festival prices, and most of the festival audiences would be inclined to regard the Landestheater productions as provincial. If the festival productions were half as expensive and the local productions twice as good as they generally are, there might be more overlapping and a healthy climate for wider experience. There is as much inbreeding in the popular atmosphere of a district theatre audience as in the rarefied atmosphere of a fashionable festival.

To do proper justice to the festivals, Easter and summer, one must say that many visitors are eager for the musical and dramatic experiences and there is a wealth of opportunity. The stage works are the major part of many summer festivals, but there are concerts and recitals for five weeks at Salzburg, in addition to operas and plays, and an atmosphere of festivity and spending which pervades and profits the whole area.

Salzburg is a small Austrian city and its size and situation contribute to its suitability for a festival site, the prime reason naturally being that it is the birthplace of Mozart. The fact that he was unhappy there and detested the place is not permitted to depress the festive spirit.

The city has a distinguished operatic history and in 1618 performed the first opera to be staged north of the Italian border. There have been outdoor performances in the gardens of Schloss Mirabell since the early eighteenth century. There were intermittent attempts at establishing a festival there during the nineteenth century, the most interesting being Hans Richter's attempt, a decade or two after the foundation of the Bayreuth Wagner festival, to found a Mozart festival.

If it had not been for the war of 1914–1918, the summer festival might have started a decade earlier than the 1927 *Fidelio* which opened the Festspielhaus (now called the Old Festspielhaus). Although Mozart logically became the favored composer, a wider appeal was made by the inclusion of other composers, notably Gluck and Strauss and even, for Toscanini, Wagner (*Die Meistersinger*). The festival faltered during the war years, to be revived in 1946. The new Festspielhaus, cut into the great rock which skirts the city, was finished by 1960, and there was much talk of the extravagance of spending eight and one-half million dollars on a theatre which would be used for less than six weeks out of the year. In 1967, its summer use was increased by Herbert von Karajan's *Osterfestspiele* (Easter Festival), at which he began his *Ring* cycle with the popular *Die Walküre*, the second of the four parts. *Das Rheingold* followed in 1968, *Siegfried* in 1969, and *Götterdämmerung* in 1970. The disadvantage of spreading the gigantic work over four years was made evident when cast changes and cancellations played havoc with the originally intended continuity.

Mozart in the summertime provides a sharp contrast, especially when the courtyard of the Salzburg Residenz supplies the setting for his operas by candlelight. In case of rain, however, which in Salzburg is almost nightly, the productions are moved into the nearby Carabinierisaal. In front of the cathedral, in fine weather, a pedestrian production of Hugo von Hofmannsthal's *Jedermann* (*Everyman*) is given annually.

Vienna, the largest Austrian city, was in the eighteenth century the center of baroque *opera seria* north of the Alps. For more than a century, the Burnacini and the Galli-Bibiena families were in residence as designers and architects of international fame, and the great poet-dramatist of the era, Pietro Metastasio, was court poet there from 1730 to 1782.

From its opening with *Don Giovanni* in 1869 until 1918, the main opera house in Vienna was called the Hofoper (Court Opera); since then it has been the Staatsoper (State Opera) and as much a symbol and an institution as an opera house, although it is very much that, too. Joseph Wechsberg has written so affectionately, nostalgically, knowingly, and it might be added profitably, of it that it seems an impertinence to offer any further comment. Description, in any case, is useless. Whether the productions are superb or shoddy (and they can be either) it is impossible not to be conscious that one is in Vienna. Foreigners may be heard during the intervals at every performance in any season, and yet the prevailing spirit is so Viennese that one feels that if by some remarkable coincidence a performance took place without a single Viennese present, even in the *Stehplatz* (standing room), there would be no shred of difference in the familiar and pervasive atmosphere. The state opera is richly subsidized and is always in a state of managerial and critical turmoil. Without a doubt it is the most newsworthy opera house in the world.

An interesting key to the central European tastes of 1869 is displayed by the composers honored in the foyer. Along one wall are Beethoven, Haydn, Mozart, Gluck, and Schubert, with Weber,

Rossini, Cherubini, Boieldieu, and Marschner opposite. At one end
are Dittersdorf and Meyerbeer, and at the other Spontini and Spohr.
Donizetti and Wagner are represented on the outer walls, and inside
on the mantels are busts of Hofoperndirektor Gustav Mahler and
Staatsoperndirektor Richard Strauss. Perhaps Verdi and Puccini
will one day be added.

Many cognoscenti, as opposed to devotees of celebrity singers
and conductors, will pick productions of special interest at the
Staatsoper and go rather more frequently to the Volksoper, which
in addition to staging the predictable operettas and American musical comedies plays a number of standard Italian operas, and sometimes quite unusual works, like Verdi's *I Masnadieri*. The Volksoper
stands in somewhat the same relation to the Staatsoper as the Paris
Opéra Comique to the Opéra in the Palais Garnier.

With the reopening in 1962 of the Theater an der Wien, yet
another opera house was made available to the Viennese public, an
opera house founded in 1801 by Emanuel Schikaneder, the first
Papageno in *The Magic Flute*, and a house which adapts itself gracefully to Beethoven's *Fidelio*, first performed there.

Occasional performances take place in the Redoutensaal, a
former palace ballroom lined with Gobelin tapestries, but these are
operas of a chamber sort—*Figaro*, *Così*, and others. Even smaller
chamber operas are staged by the Wiener Kammeroper in the Baroque theatre in Schloss Schönbrunn, built between 1744 and 1749.
The Empress Maria Theresa played the piano and sang there, and
her son Joseph II sang bass, played the 'cello, and more than once
conducted. In recent years the productions there have included rarities difficult to encounter anywhere else, and for this one must be
grateful. The performances have varied from acceptable to amateurish.

There is nothing amateurish about the Komische Oper in
Berlin, which will go down in history as the base of Walter Felsenstein's Musiktheater productions. Beginning his career in the spoken
play and in operetta, Felsenstein has carried his theories of dramatic
realism into the stiffly formal tradition of opera; rehearsing patiently
with an almost fanatical goal of perfection, he has done his best to
oust the perfunctory *stagione* approach to production, or avoidance

of it in its concentration upon voice and personality. He works only with singers who are already actors or willing to work tirelessly to become actors.

He has opposed not only the vanity and distorted emphasis of the star system but the debilitating overwork of the conventional repertory system. Felsenstein works his actors harder than most companies, but with generous subsidies he is able to stage as few operas as he wishes, and to stage these astonishingly well. Beginning in 1947 he had in his first dozen years produced only nineteen works. Of these, four were popular Viennese operettas directed with a loving hand, but with discipline and wit replacing the routine and the unfunny clichés of the conventional production of typical Austrian *Schlamperei. Fledermaus, Gypsy Baron, Der Vogelhändler,* and *A Night in Venice* are four of the most frequent productions on the German lyric stage today. Felsenstein staged all four, but with a marked difference. Offenbach's *Orpheus in Hell* and *La Vie Parisienne (Pariser Leben)* demonstrated his flair for *opéra bouffe,* and during the twelve-year period he included the fantastic opera *Tales of Hoffmann.* The Lortzing favorite *Zar und Zimmermann* was done, and the Smetana *Bartered Bride,* both ranking among the favorites in Germany today. Orff's *The Wise Woman* was the first production of Felsenstein's second year.

The musically more ambitious *Carmen, Figaro, Freischütz, The Magic Flute, The Silent Woman, The Sly Vixen,* and *Otello* almost complete the nineteen, the remaining opera being a musical version of *Twelfth Night* by Arthur Küsterer.

More recently, Felsenstein has added Paisiello's *The Barber of Seville,* Verdi's *La Traviata,* a fourth Shakespearean opera, Britten's *A Midsummer Night's Dream* and his *Albert Herring,* yet another Offenbach, *Bluebeard,* Kurka's *Good Soldier Schweik,* and Mohaupt's *Innkeeper of Pinsk.*

Many of the works use speech between musical numbers. Under Felsenstein's direction even dry recitative is made to sound closer to natural speech, since he uses the technique of an occasional pause for stage business, excellently timed and giving a naturalness to what so often sounds, especially in rapid Italian, like a sprinting gabble to the next orchestrally supported number. The three Verdi works had

their respective origins in workable plays, two of them Shakespeare's. Meilhac and Halévy, represented several times, were the
wittiest librettists of the mid-nineteenth century, and only W. S.
Gilbert was able to match them. Petrosellini, the librettist for the
Paisiello *Barber,* stayed closer to the Beaumarchais play than did
Sterbini for Rossini's *Barber.* Felsenstein's interests emerge as clearly
from his choice of repertory as from his published conversations
with Siegfried Melchinger.* Texts with enough dramatic energy
not to be drowned in the music, pungent satire and bizarre or forth-
right fantasy (*Hoffmann* and *Vixen*), fall naturally as grist to
Felsenstein's slowly grinding mill, but his keen perception discovers
dramatic energy long hidden beneath the incrustations of tradition,
and there is a remarkable freshness in his attitude to operetta and his
understanding of the colorful variations (visually and aurally)
played upon age-old story and situation material which in less appreciative and refining hands emerges as something merely trite and
passé. When operetta is appreciated for what it sets out to do and
accepted as a challenge, what emerges is totally unlike the tired old
stereotype.

The interior of the Komische Oper is almost a symbol of
Felsenstein's approach. Instead of an aggressive modern theatre
with a ruthless lack of ornament defying the possibility of cobwebs
and outmoded tradition, it is a gold-and-white wedding cake, en-
crusted with prancing putti and improbable torsos but with one
notable exception. Instead of the soft light which is kind to cupids,
evocative of rococo grace, and lenient to layers of dust, there is a
most cheerful and cleansing brilliance which pours out of the chandeliers and tunes the spirits before the work performed begins to
play upon them. To astonish with honesty is Felsenstein's artistic
purpose.

If the temple of the progressives is in East Berlin, the temple of
the traditionalists is in Milan. The beauty of Milan's Teatro alla
Scala is world famous. After the ducal theatre in Milan was burned
down in 1776 a new opera house was built in 1778 on the site of the
church of Santa Maria della Scala. Christoph Willibald Gluck was
invited to compose the opera to open the new theatre, but he de-

---

* Walter Felsenstein and Siegfried Melchinger, *Musiktheater,* Bremen,
1961.

clined the offer. The stately new theatre, originally holding 3600, borrowed from its ecclesiastical site the Baroque symbolism of body and soul, of things earthly and things heavenly. Many secular buildings imitated churches in this respect, and in many instances the practical consideration of expense was a factor; but the dynamic contrast of a plain exterior and a glory within was often intentional, and to this day its theatrical effectiveness can at once be appreciated. The exterior of La Scala is surprisingly modest. Inside, the six half-hoops of red damask loges are an ineradicable sight as they blaze in full light, glow with a magical softness in the half-light of the dimming process and, with artful timing, sink gently into near darkness for the performance, while the faces of the audience are turned into reflecting surfaces from the light now pouring from the stage. It is a tiny drama in light, played before the sung drama on every night between December 7, the traditional opening, and early summer when the season closes.

The house now seats 2800, in addition to 400 standees, and therefore ranks with the world's largest opera houses, but its acoustics are astonishingly fine. Considering itself the major opera house in Italy, in Europe, and, in the opinion of many, in the world, it has been for generations the focal point of Italian opera. Arturo Toscanini was responsible for broadening its interests to include more German, French, and Slavic works, so that today La Scala stands as one of the greatest of international opera houses, welcoming, although with a few reservations, foreign singers, foreign conductors, and operas of foreign origin. Its deeply ingrained Italianism, however, has given some of its performances the unpredictable atmosphere of football games. The vast expenditures, the high fees for the world's celebrity performers, the quality of these performers, and the management policies are heatedly discussed in the street, in the restaurants, in the homes, and in the buses of Milan, and the vibrancy is communicated to the interior of the theatre itself, where factions are aroused to overt expression and intrigue is rife. A stately and fashionable opera house of distinguished tradition runs no danger of ossification when its management is not adverse to experiment and half its audience is as addicted to passion and intrigue as the characters in the nineteenth-century operas on its stage.

From the luxurious *poltrone* (easy chairs) of La Scala to the cane-bottomed seats of the Bayreuth Festspielhaus represents a greater journey than the mere crossing of the Alps. The one opera house was built on the site of a church. The other *is* a church, or rather a temple, the high priest of which is Richard Wagner and the divinity worshipped *Gesamtkunstwerk,* a concept of total theatre antedating by a number of years the most recent associations with that expression.

As famous as La Scala for its splendid acoustics, the Bayreuth Festspielhaus has a wooden interior and a canvas ceiling. Since the auditorium rises sharply, there is no low place at the rear to make the "dead pocket" so common beneath the balconies of many conventional theatres. The continental seating plan with widely spaced rows and no aisles has since been imitated in the most modern theatres.

The Festspielhaus was Wagner's personal dedication to his own concept of music drama, which returned to the classical ideal missed, in Wagner's opinion, by Gluck. Intended at the time as a temporary building built for the premiere of the entire *Ring,* it was solidly constructed of red brick on the "green hill" outside the humdrum Franconian town of Bayreuth in the years 1872–1875, and opened in 1876. Its huge stage was suitably framed by classical pillars decreasing in size as they ascended the sides of the cane-bottomed hill of the interior.

The theatre's most noteworthy feature, visually, is the creation by Wagner of "the mystic gulf" by lowering the orchestral space out of sight, so that a separation exists between performers and audience. With the seats rising as steeply as they do, the sight lines are extraordinarily good, and there are no side boxes to turn the attention on the audience instead of on the stage. The only boxes are twenty-one compartments on two levels at the rear of the auditorium, and they bear little resemblance to eighteenth-century boxes. The cool austerity of the six massive blocks on each side, surmounted with double classical pillars and dotted with Victorian glass globes, three apiece halfway up and six affixed just below the ceiling, is relieved by the spirit of worshipful excitement which at performances here is almost invariable.

Doors are firmly closed before a music drama begins, and latecomers must wait until the end of a Wagnerian act. The orchestra, invisible behind its curving shield, begins to play in the mystic gulf, and when the curtains part the stage may be flat or built up with constructions, the most famous of which was Wieland Wagner's tilted disc for the *Ring* (Plate 17).

Performances have varied, as performances do, over the years since the 1951 reopening, but the dedication and the imagination of the management, together with the prestige accorded Bayreuth singers, have set a high standard. The orchestra and the chorus have contributed the most steadily to this standard; the changing production approaches, the conductors, and the individual singers of the key roles have received the keenest criticism.

The audience at a festival of this eminence is likely to be sharply divided. The genuine devotees of Wagner are a group distinct from the eminent Germans belonging to the cult or to the high fashion which prescribe appearance at the nearly century-old festival, and this group, vaguely confused in many minds with National Socialism, differs sharply from that of the eminent foreigners, the less eminent foreigners, the members of the press, the former singers, the active singers, the students and artists, and, last of all, but contributing generously with the purchase of highly priced tickets, the curious tourists. The most powerful group is the German cult, and the admirable silence, grave respect, and dogged enthusiasm combine to produce a somewhat oppressive atmosphere at its worst, and at its best, an exhilarating one. If the performance is exciting, as it can be, it manages to turn the self-hypnotized puppets into the human beings who constitute a genuinely responsive audience. A less than exciting performance makes the final orgy of enthusiasm sound as hollow as the classical wooden pylons.

The journey from the Bayreuth temple to the Mecca Temple in New York is even greater than from Milan to Upper Franconia. One of the most remarkable opera companies in the world is one of the youngest, the slightly more than twenty-five-year-old New York City Opera Company. It began in 1943 in the unlikely pseudo-oriental décor of the 55th Street Mecca Temple, which the city had reclaimed from the pseudo-oriental Shriners, who were having tax payment difficulties. Fiorello LaGuardia, mayor of New York, and

Newbold Morris, president of the City Council, summoned a group of interested and qualified people to consider a proposal that the decrepit old building might be turned into a popular theatre at low prices. The City Center of Music and Drama, Inc., began its operation with plays originally produced on Broadway, and by 1944 Leopold Stokowski was conducting the New York City Symphony, a new orchestra playing for working people in the early evening hours and for children on weekends. The St. Louis summer opera company had recently closed, and a double stroke of good fortune descended upon the proletarian theatre: the conductor Laszlo Halasz and the settings and costumes no longer needed in Missouri. They were old-fashioned enough to remain in key with the Mecca Temple, and a beginning was made. Works of the popular appeal of *Carmen, Martha,* and *Tosca* were staged, and the Center, offering opera at prices the working classes could afford, rapidly became a resounding success. Not content to repeat the old-fashioned repertory nor to wear its old-fashioned settings and costumes longer than was necessary, the company pushed ambitiously forward, increasing its audiences' operatic experience while at the same time raising their tastes and its own standards. Many conductors of distinction led the orchestra and singers there, and there were American premieres and New York premieres of works of quality and unusual interest.

In 1957 Julius Rudel, a thirty-six-year-old member of the musical staff, took over from the departing Erich Leinsdorf, and in addition to continuing the policy of unusual operas and American operas with American singers, welded the company into an even more tightly devoted ensemble. Several singers of international reputation now were young members of the company during the years of struggle in the late 1940s and into the 1950s. What is more significant is that several singers have stayed with the company and achieved high reputations, some of them international, the best-known being Beverly Sills. The New York City Opera Company in this way bears some resemblance to a first-class German ensemble of the kind that may be heard and seen in Cologne, Stuttgart, or Frankfurt.

Their concern with the American composer has given the New

York Opera Company an enviable reputation, and the willingness to try out new works which run the risk of total failure is evidence of their adventurousness. Douglas Moore's *Wings of the Dove* and *The Ballad of Baby Doe*, Floyd's *Susannah*, and Ward's *The Crucible*, while not competing in popular taste with *Carmen* and *Figaro*, have nevertheless made themselves widely known, and opera workshops in particular have helped to win audiences for them. The opera workshops, however, would scarcely have been able to do so without the initial encouragement of a New York City Opera production.

With the European breadth of approach to musical theatre (*My Fair Lady* and *Die Meistersinger* at the same theatre), the New York Opera Company has spread into what in Europe would be the operetta wing of the theatre's activities. In 1961 the City Center Gilbert and Sullivan Company was inaugurated, with most of the participants members of the opera company, to the great benefit of the musical aspects of the performances and the dramatic experience of the singers. Seven years earlier a Light Opera Company was formed to stage American musicals like *Show Boat, Pal Joey, Guys and Dolls*, and *Porgy and Bess*.

When, in 1966, the move to the New York State Theatre at Lincoln Center was planned, Julius Rudel opened the theatre with Alberto Ginastera's *Don Rodrigo*, a new work which was astoundingly successful and encouraged a later production of the same composer's *Bomarzo*. Hugo Weisgall's *Six Characters in Search of an Author* similarly led to the new *Nine Rivers from Jordan*, staged in 1968.

Good judgment, good casting, good designing, and good directing contributed to the great success of the first fully staged professional production of a Handel opera in New York, probably one of the company's most ambitious undertakings. It is no discredit to Julius Rudel, Ming Cho Lee, and Tito Capobianco, three of the many who were responsible for the success of *Julius Caesar*, to urge that all this would have been impossible without the audience, a loyal audience trained over the years to take an interest in new works, in old works, in foreign works, and in native American works. It is a circular or parabolic matter, this training of an audience. First of all there have to be the productions which generate loyalty and confidence. The New York City Opera Company has been described as an enterprise more interested in the work performed than in the people performing it. This is the kind of company which encourages an audience more interested in the work performed than in the people performing it, a most healthy climate in which musical theatre can prosper. If it seems unappreciative to place the emphasis on a scarcely known ancient work or on a completely unknown modern work instead of on the talented and already much-admired participants backstage, on stage, and in the orchestra pit, it is an illusion only. The greatest respect and affection that can be bestowed upon a theatre company is to look and listen with open eyes, open ears, and an open mind to what it has considered worth its attention in time, expense, and energy. Good performances and good audiences depend upon each other. Neither can exist for long without the other. Any theatre which has a high degree of both is fortunate, and in whatever country it exists there is hope for the musical theatre.

2

Systems and Subsidies

Theatrical performances are produced according to various systems: the short run, the long run, the modified repertory, the festival, the full repertory, and the *stagione*, named from the Italian word for season and referring almost exclusively to opera.

The short run may be a single performance or as many as a dozen. Renaissance entertainments costing vast sums of money and celebrating weddings or birthdays were short runs for invited audiences. Tate's and Purcell's *Dido and Aeneas*, written for a fashionable school in Chelsea, had only a single performance at the time, although it has had many more since. Amateur productions of plays and musicals are short-run productions. For a short run the number of performances is generally decided in advance, but extra performances may be added if the production is a success.

The long run is invariably professional, and only a spectacular failure has fewer than a dozen performances. It is hoped that the run will not only defray the original costs but provide a living for the participants for months or years and reward the investors handsomely for their perspicacity. An occasional limited run may be advertised. The limited availability of a leading actor or a theatre building is generally the reason for this. Plays, musical plays, operettas, and musical comedies planned for a long run may run poorly for a short period or successfully for years. *The Governor's Son*, with the four Cohans, ran 32 performances. *Show Boat* ran over 500 performances, *Annie Get Your Gun* over 1000, and *Oklahoma* over 2000.

Modified repertory, which may or may not be called a festival, may consist of plays or of operas or of a mixture of both. In some festivals there may also be concerts and recitals. The stage pieces, which may be as few as three or four or as many as a dozen, are played in alternation, each a few times in a short festival, each many times in a longer one.

The Stratford Festival in Ontario has played four of Shakespeare's plays while a separate music company contributed two operas. The Tyrone Guthrie Theatre in Minneapolis has played four plays under the title of a classical repertory. The Bayreuth Festival has usually staged two cycles of the *Ring* and a selection of other Wagner music dramas during its summer festivals. The Salzburg Festival has in five weeks programmed ten stage works and a number of concerts and recitals. Other festivals may consist largely of performances by several companies invited to play one or two works from their own repertories. This happened at Expo 1967 in Montreal, and has happened for many years at the Edinburgh Festival.

What is called a summer theatre season, a play a week for ten weeks, is not modified repertory but a series of short runs. Only if the plays were alternated could it properly be described as repertory.

Full repertory alternates productions throughout an entire season, often from early September to late June. From thirty to sixty different works may be performed, but fewer if the theatre is devoted exclusively to one form of drama, such as the spoken play or operetta. The Comédie Française in Paris and the Abbey Theatre in Dublin have become famous for their operation of true repertory. The dozen opera houses of Czechoslovakia and the ten times that number of theatres in West Germany producing operas, operettas, and plays for ten months of the year are characteristic of the repertory system.

In opera south of the Alps, the Italian *stagione* system prevails, and was imported from there into the Latin American countries. In Italy there is an autumn season corresponding to the first third of the repertory season, but the fashionable season is the second, extending from Christmas to Easter. This is followed by a spring season, ending, like repertory, in June. There are occasional summer festivals aiming for tourist money, the best known being the open air spectacles at the Baths of Caracalla in Rome and in the Verona amphitheatre.

The difference between repertory and *stagione* is far more than a mere arrangement of seasons. It lies in strongly contrasting attitudes toward the art, the business, and the practice of musicodramatic production.

For repertory, as it is pursued in France, Germany, Austria, Scandinavia, Czechoslovakia, Hungary, the Soviet Union, and elsewhere, performers live in the city in which the theatre is located and they appear in a variety of roles from September until June, at which time they are free for vacation, study, or appearances in summer festivals. For *stagione*, artists are hired from other cities and often from other countries. These "outsiders" sing the leading roles and often the smaller roles as well, and if any local performers are connected with the enterprise they are singing very small roles indeed, or in the chorus. On the national level, as in Italy, artists may be hired to sing three or four roles during the *stagione*. This may also happen on the international level, or an artist may be hired for a single role and after appearing five or six times in it depart, often to another country, to sing the same role elsewhere.

The *stagione* system, even at its best, tends to offer a concert in costume, and the emphasis is on individual voice, reputation, and personality more than upon integrated performance of music drama. When the conductor and stage director are as capable in their own fields as the singers in theirs, and when the same "stellar" cast can be retained for several performances, *stagione* has all the advantages of repertory, with the added advantage of exceptional voices. When, however, the cast is changed or the performers sing elsewhere between the performances or the performances are weeks apart, the disadvantages are in the ascendant.

The world's most celebrated singers subscribe to the *stagione* system. It provides enviable publicity and generous financial reward. For the operagoer who can afford the high-priced ticket, it offers the prestige of being able to attend, and sometimes a sensational performance by gifted singers electrifying each other as well as the audience, and such occasions are memorable.

While some *stagione* performances are memorable indeed, there are more that will not electrify anyone, and most of them are totally lacking in dramatic cohesiveness. There may be individual acting performances of merit, but seldom anything resembling effective ensemble. Many *stagione* productions are underrehearsed, since celebrated singers who have performed their roles many times on many stages with many conductors are personally responsible for their conduct on stage, and often arrive only a day or two before the first performance.

There is an enthusiastic public for such productions. They are costly. They may be handsomely mounted. They generate publicity. They are fashionable. One may hear the outstanding singers of our generation nowhere else.

Repertory, even at first-class theatres, is not likely to be quite so dazzling, but apart from the dozen most exceptional voices in the world, the musical standards will be as high and the works often better rehearsed, while the dramatic standards will invariably be higher. There is a solid public for repertory, the costs on both sides of the proscenium are less, and the scenery will be quite as handsome, with the additional advantage of being meaningful because it has been rehearsed in. Of far smaller impact will be the publicity for the performers and the prestige for those who attend.

There is no reason why both systems should not coexist, if only for the enlightenment of adherents of the one when they attend the other. Repertory enthusiasts tend to condemn *stagione* far too readily as ostentatious, dramatically inept, and personality ridden. *Stagione*, however, can sometimes succeed in sustaining interest in opera where every other method would fail. Carol Fox has given Chicago a *stagione* with her Lyric Opera. Many of the productions have been expensive concerts in costume with the emphasis on stars (and this is reflected in the publicity) rather than on the music, and with more emphasis on the music than on the drama which inspired it. Yet in one season Carol Fox provided an opportunity for Midwesterners, and anyone else who cared to come, to see and hear Monteverdi's *L'Incoronazione di Poppea* and Prokofieff's *The Flaming Angel*.

There is coexistence of repertory and *stagione* in New York's

Metropolitan Opera House. The San Francisco autumn season is pure *stagione*, but its recently added spring season offers less-celebrated singers, many of them American, in better-integrated performances at less cost.

London's Covent Garden, before the turn of the century, of-fered an autumn opera season (Moody Manners) in English, while the Royal Opera, playing at that time only from the middle of May to the end of July, produced opera on an international scale. Italian autumn seasons followed a few years later and a midwinter German season in 1907, several Carl Rosa opera seasons, several Beecham opera seasons, and before the crisis of 1924 four British National Opera Company seasons. In this way the nationalists and the inter-nationalists, the repertory enthusiasts and the *stagione* enthusiasts, the opera-in-English devotees and the opera-in-the-original-language devotees, were given what they wanted. This is how it should al-ways be.

Stagione frequently enters the regions of repertory, and on a smaller scale the most modest provincial German theatres will invite guest singers from Berlin or Hamburg or Munich to perform with the home company. For these performances the prices are raised. Sometimes the guests are successful singers who were originally members of the home company, and older audience members have a pleasing sense of having helped them, by their regular patronage, to reach the more exalted level. In the German programs the *a.G.* notation (*als Gast*) is a familiar one.

Hamburg itself, one of the best German repertory houses (Plate 4), staged a few *stagione* performances in April 1965. Seats for *Tosca* with the leading roles sung by Régine Crespin, Franco Corelli, and Tito Gobbi cost, twenty minutes before the curtain, DM 75 ($18.75) each. This was the box office price, not a scalper's price. Ten minutes earlier there had been seats available at DM 55 ($13.75).

Regular prices in Hamburg's Staatsoper that season, as dis-played outside the box office, ranged from DM 2 to DM 20 ($.50 to $5.00) with a separate price scale for special events, DM 3 to DM 24 ($.75 to $6.00). There are still cheaper seats, with no cheapening of the production. During the same week as the costly *Tosca*, *Così fan Tutte* was performed. The top price was DM 7 ($1.75) and the singers were Arlene Saunders, Kerstin Meyer, Erna-Maria Duske, Horst Wilhelm, Tom Krause, and Theo Adam, a cast which would not be out of place at the Metropolitan. Some of them have already sung there. The conductor was Leopold Ludwig and the costumes were by Leni Bauer-Ecsy. It was a so-called closed production (*geschlossene Vorstellung*) for the Hamburg *Volksbühne*, but for closed productions at special rates there are often tickets to be purchased shortly before the curtain. Not only was this work excellently sung but it was spiritedly acted, and under the stage direction of Dieter Wagner given as a sophisticated *opera buffa*, not as a crude farce.

The most distinguished repertory opera company in America is the New York City Opera. Under General Manager Julius Rudel, with Ford Foundation assistance, with low fees for singers and correspondingly low ticket prices, it has offset the more expensive, more traditional, and more fashionable Metropolitan by staging modern works, largely modern American works, and older works (Handel's *Julius Caesar* with set designs by Ming Cho Lee, costume designs by José Varona, and stage direction by Tito Capobianco), and comes closest to the repertory as practised in Germany. Both the Metropolitan and the N.Y.C.O.C. are necessary to New York. America needs more of each kind to enjoy nationwide operatic health.

Opera in the United States is not subsidized by the state. In the nineteenth century it managed very comfortably on rich patronage, and the box holders, as private sponsors, were satisfied with what they paid for. It looked and sounded splendid and it was fashionable. To be involved was a mark of prestige.

The twentieth century has brought a shattering change. Costs have risen, but the patronage is now far wider and includes the lower income, even the lowest income, classes. The Metropolitan Opera Guild at its founding invited the radio public to tax itself voluntarily, and thousands of them were delighted to do so, feeling more than repaid by the Saturday afternoon broadcasts of full-length opera to which they listened. Others went on listening free of charge, and still do so in large numbers. Far more funds than the general public could offer were supplied by fund-raising organizations, and large private gifts and business corporation gifts have made revivals and new productions possible where before they could not have been attempted. Ticket prices at the Metropolitan may be thought high, but they do not nearly cover the costs per audience member. There is municipal assistance to opera in several American cities. Even providing a rent-free auditorium is one way of keeping production going and ticket prices down. The help from foundations, notably Ford and Rockefeller, is not on a continuing or operational basis, but it is provided for special works or projects like the ten American operas at New York City Opera in 1958, or for Lincoln Center itself, which could not otherwise have been built.

In Germany when the monarchy disappeared at the end of the first world war, the opera houses which had been supported by the courts of the various states were accepted as the responsibility of the newly organized states, and the practice has continued to the present time. The theatres for spoken drama were not as fortunate. They achieved state support, and state control, after Hitler became Chancellor in 1933.

The regional ministries and the town councils contribute the subsidies, respectively, to the *Staatstheater* (state theatre) and the *Stadttheater* (municipal theatre). The *Landestheater* is a form of *Staatstheater*, and *Städtische Bühnen* (municipal stages) is a form of *Stadtheater*. The opera houses of Hamburg, Munich, and Wiesbaden belong to states. Frankfurt, Mainz, and Kiel have municipal theatres. The sale of tickets in these theatres usually brings in between 25 and 35 percent of total expenditure, which means that a ticket purchaser is getting his ticket for about a third of what it costs, and if he buys a season ticket he gets reduced rates. The *Volksbühne* system, a club providing low-cost theatre tickets with less choice than a general subscription, is most valuable in exposing working class people to good theatre. They may miss some of the more successful productions and they may help to fill the auditorium for more of the unpopular ones than they would have chosen, but they are assured of a specific number of productions by their membership, and the membership generally covers the three categories, plays, operas, and operettas, at low prices. It is the equivalent of the cut-rate prices and "twofers" for Broadway productions, but at a cost that Broadway could never match.

Opera subsidy on an annual basis in Great Britain began, rather modestly, at the close of the second world war. The chief recipients were the Covent Garden Opera Trust and the Sadler's Wells Foundation. Britain followed the continent in this way, and it may be that the United States will follow Britain and that some form of government subsidy will share the responsibility with foundations, private donors, and the general public for the support of opera.

Two questions are naturally asked. Will government subsidy bring with it the much-dreaded government control? If by that time censorship is already wholeheartedly accepted by the American people, an unlikely event, it may. If not, there is a chance that America may one day possess a theatre as vigorous and dignified as that of Germany, a country that suffered total defeat in 1945, to restore its theatre within five years. In the Germany of the post-Nazi period there has been no more than the merest hint of censorship.

The second question is this. If musical comedy and popular plays can pay for themselves in the open market, why should classical plays and opera, representing the taste of the minority, be subsidized? While a single day's contemplation of entertainment supposedly catering to the tastes of the majority is something of an answer, it is not enough. Many aspects of education are in the realm of minority taste. The standard repertory of the theatre, musical and nonmusical, is as necessary to the fullest appraisal of modern works as past history to today's politics. A public interested only in contemporary works of art denies its heritage, neglects the opportunities offered by comparison, and misses the enjoyment of works too good to be soon forgotten. Only a fraction of the output of the past is represented in the twentieth-century repertory. Only a fraction of the successes of today will find a secure foothold in tomorrow's repertory. Things of lasting value deserve recognition and support.

It has already been noted that classical plays and modern opera are in greater need of subsidy than modern plays and a handful of popular operas, most of them at least fifty years old. It might be added that the risk of opera production is greater than that of the spoken play. However small the singing cast of an opera, the participants, needing to be paid, are numerous. Only the most modest production can be staged with an orchestra of fewer than twenty players. In addition to the stage director, the musical production requires a conductor, a rehearsal accompanist, and several other experts, in addition to the designers and technicians necessary for any stage production. If ticket prices kept pace with the staggering production costs, only a small minority of the public could afford to attend the opera. When opera was a court luxury only a small minority did so, and since they were guests of the court it cost them nothing. Since 1637 the public has attended, but for many years composers and librettists were not rewarded as they deserved, and while leading singers were often overpaid, their humbler colleagues on stage, in the orchestra, and backstage were underpaid and, lacking pensions, sometimes died in poverty.

If we welcome the improvements which the present century has brought, we find ourselves in the dilemma of either recommending government subsidy or of abandoning the production of great operatic works of the past and promising operatic works of the present, on the ground that without subsidy they cost altogether too much and that only the very rich can afford them. A vociferous minority, mostly not rich, is determined not to let this happen. On the other hand, the present times are difficult for the advocates of government subsidy on as general a scale as some European countries provide. Without subsidy on a generous scale, however, opera in America is doomed, not so much to die as to linger in half a dozen cities as a status symbol. Extinction is preferable.

3

Singers and Actors

Although the composer, the dramatist, the conductor, the orchestra, the director, the designers, and the technicians are largely responsible for the success of a musical theatre production, the average audience is generally more aware of the singer, actor, or stage personality who appears before them than of any of the other contributors. The three terms are used intentionally, since anyone who appears and sings upon the opera, operetta, or musical comedy stage invites an estimation of his singing voice, his acting ability, and, somewhat less tangibly, his personal magnetism.

Much has been spoken and written about singers to characterize them as excessively stupid, vain, jealous, and uncooperative, and operatic singers have generally been regarded as the worst of the breed. Like all generalizations it distorts the facts. Singers are much like other people, but the nature of their equipment and the hazards of their profession tend to bring qualities which would otherwise lie dormant very much to life. Since singers are public performers, their idiosyncrasies are more in the public eye than the idiosyncrasies of plumbers and insurance agents. What is surprising is that, considering their problems, singers are as normal and agreeable as many of them are. From the moment a singer is discovered to have a voice worth training, the tensions begin. His instrument, like an actor's, is his whole body, with special emphasis on his breathing apparatus and a more special emphasis on his tiny larynx and the vocal folds situated there. The colds and the allergies which are minor annoyances to ordinary people are serious to a singer. Other physical disabilities affect the tonus of the whole body, and what affects the body indirectly affects the voice. Singers are for the most part extremely hardy. If they were not, they could scarcely hope to succeed in a strenuous and competitive profession. When a singer has to cancel a performance the publicity is considerable. When a singer meets every engagement, only those in the profession are interested.

A singer's active professional life is not as brief as a dancer's, but it is brief enough to cause anxiety. He may be amply rewarded in his twenties. On the other hand he may have to wait until his thirties or even his forties for wide recognition. To some it must seem as if they have only reached the summit when the critics detect a decline in vocal ability. While a singer can profit from genuine criticism by a writer who has studied both music and drama and contributes an objective but understanding point of view impossible for the singer himself, he must endure discourtesies and cruelties from many who have made no attempt beyond the most superficial to understand either. It is tempting to laugh off the blame and gratefully savor the praise, but the intelligent singer is torn between the suspicion that he may be at fault and the need to maintain his self-confidence. Audiences contribute to the confusion with a loyal stupidity, invariably taking far too long to recognize talent on the way up and then encouraging an aging singer to continue when it would be wiser to retire. Loyally applauding the memory of the singer's earlier performances, unlikely to be repeated, they do the worst disservice to the performer they admire, showing themselves as unwilling as he to admit that his powers have faded. The singers who are also good actors are tempted to sing longer because of the "authority" of their interpretations. Some roles are vocally less exacting than others, and an astute singing actor can legitimately extend his career four or five years by avoiding the taxing roles with which he made his reputation in his late thirties and early forties.

Reviewing of the less responsible kind follows fashion, and the singer finds it difficult to decide whether a sharp change in view is prompted by the mere removal of novelty or by a serious decline in vocal quality or technique. This is especially true in America, where the public is likely to find a reasoned review very dull reading. A "rave" is far more exciting and a "pan" far more titillating. In the first season of a singer's discovery the adulation is heady, even though the kind that declares "he did not *sing* Tristan—he *was* Tristan" may instantly be dismissed as fatuous. In the second season, unable to go farther and unwilling to repeat, reviewers begin to detect the faults, and a baritone who last year was a model of interpretative sensibility now worries meanings out of every word, a soprano whose virtuosity astounded everyone now displays intonation weaknesses or lapses in diction, while a tenor praised for singing all the notes as written and causing a sensation thereby is discovered to be mechanical and dramatically uncommitted. To the outsider these may seem petty matters, but to one appearing constantly before the public, most of them not critical enough and a minority of them hypercritical, they are important. Not only are these tensions detrimental to vocal assurance and physical relaxation, but added to them are the tensions induced by well-publicized rivalries and jealousies, aided and abetted by organized factions and a paid claque and further abetted by a sheeplike public who will applaud upon stimulation, without realizing that the paid claque is urging them to it.

Side by side with the stories of nailed-down chairs, sopranos kicking tenors, tenors holding high notes longer and louder than sopranos, basses and tenors upstaging each other to the point of fisticuffs, and singers malingering until a young rival shows signs of success are stories quite as true but only a tenth as popular: of singers who meet their commitments in spite of vocal indisposition, taking the risk of revealing themselves at less than their best rather than let down a performance, who help a sudden replacement through the stage blocking of an opera, and who reduce the plenitude of their own healthy voices when a colleague is having vocal difficulty. The stories of malice are more entertaining, but the others deserve a fair share of attention, too.

Contrary to an often expressed and thoughtless opinion, many singers are extremely capable actors. Somewhat fewer actors possess serviceable singing voices. The more fortunate performers possess both talents. The most fortunate are in addition physically well favored, the possessors of a handsome face and an engaging personality.

There is no denying the existence of imbalance. Among first-class singers are those with minimal acting ability. Many actors, realizing that they are indifferent singers, sensibly confine themselves to the musically less-demanding roles in musical comedy. In addition, there are strong stage personalities with pronounced singing or acting deficiencies. In them the single talent is extraordinary enough to make up for the lack of the others.

Where the emphasis is upon the singer and the vocal requirements are of paramount importance, the tradition has been to forgive much in the singer's personal appearance, physique, and acting, and the possessor of a unique voice was for generations not expected to offer much else. Singers for Mozart, Verdi, Wagner, Puccini, Strauss, and many other composers must still first of all be singers, fortunate in their vocal equipment, wise in their schooling, and assiduous in their study; but the theatre public, especially since the 1920s, has been grateful for more and demanding of more, even for works of musical theatre urgently requiring sumptuous voices. At the beginning of that decade the slender figure of Amelita Galli-Curci was an unusual sight on the operatic stage. By the 1940s the concern for something resembling realism in the nonrealistic medium of opera and the face and body worship induced by the motion pictures began to exert pressure, and the public expected other sopranos and mezzo sopranos to look like Jarmila Novotna and Risë Stevens.

In musical comedy the emphasis is more often on personality and comedy acting, and a well-trained voice is not a requirement, although the voice must not be so misused as to affect its durability. Some very well trained voices have been heard in musical comedy, and some singers who later sang more taxing roles in opera acquired valuable experience in musical comedy or operetta. In these less exacting works a voice of unusual timbre and a highly personal style of singing are of greater importance than vocal quality and a high degree of technical facility. The music is for the most part easier to sing, but the voice and the personality that goes with the voice must be immediately identifiable. Some leading roles require good looks and good physique, but the comedian, male or female, is usually equipped with physical peculiarity or exaggeration which further establishes identification. A wide mouth, a large nose, projecting ears, shortness, corpulence, or excessively long arms are by no means disadvantages. A readily recognizable feature supplies an interest lacking in the average person of average dimensions and average features. Most important is the intangible personality, a characteristic which quickly secures the straight line response necessary for strongly personal performance.

Operetta, which, with some forms of comic opera, falls between opera and musical comedy, requires the well-trained voice, the good looks for the romantic leads, and the ability to act in comedy and with comedians without necessarily being a comedian.

Where the divison between the forms is strictly maintained, as in America—the Broadway long-run system dominates the lighter form, while the Metropolitan Opera, the New York City Opera, and other companies operate repertory, *stagione*, or a mixture of the two —the ambitious singer may enter the operatic field with little stage experience of any other kind, or he may tour in operetta or sing in Broadway musicals for some years before he is accepted by a major opera company, at which point he often abandons the lighter form altogether. Some, beginning in opera and finding the competition considerable and the financial gain slight, move into the lighter field for the remainder of their careers.

In Europe, the repertory system encourages a diversity of interest, at least in the early and middle stages of a career. In larger cities there may be an opera house for more ambitious music drama and a smaller house for comic opera, operetta, and musical comedy. Smaller cities have a single theatre at which the spoken play, opera, and operetta are performed in something like rotation. In such theatres some singers perform in both opera and operetta, though there is usually a nucleus of specialists for each and it is not unusual to find comedians of the spoken-play division appearing in operetta. The adaptability of these performers is admirable, and when such comedies as *Figaro, The Barber of Seville, Albert Herring,* and *The Young Lord* are performed by experienced comedy singers, there is a welcome absence of the heavy-handed treatment accorded such works by singers of international reputation who have forgotten how to play deft comedy, if indeed they ever knew. Not all singers of international reputation are deficient in comedy. Sylvia Fisher, Sir Geraint Evans, Erich Kunz, and Sesto Bruscantini are only four of a number of singers with a comedy technique nonsinging actors might envy.

Several distinguished Wagnerian singers cope successfuly with the staggering difficulties of acting in the slow-motion epic, and would put to shame many equally distinguished actors of the spoken stage if those actors ever ventured into the territory of the *Oedipus Tyrannus* of Sophocles or the *Iphigenie* of Goethe.

The singer is likely to be a more versatile actor than a speaking actor of the commercial stage, where repertory experience is lacking and he is apt to be typecast and play mainly the roles for which he is physically and stylistically suited. Every singer submits to vocal typecasting, but within his kind and weight of voice there can be a startlingly wide variety in the acting demanded. Furthermore, the repertory system demands rapid adjustment from character to character and from style to style. A mezzo soprano in a single season may find herself performing the widely differing trouser roles of Cherubino in *Figaro*, Siébel in *Faust*, and Octavian in *Der Rosenkavalier*, in addition to the strongly feminine and just as widely differing roles of Mignon, Carmen, and the *Rheingold* Fricka. There can be no typecasting here. Incidentally, all these roles have also been sung by sopranos.

Typecasting is customary in musical comedy and to some extent in operetta. There is some typecasting blended with vocal casting in the careers of a *basso buffo* like Salvatore Baccaloni or Fernando Corena. Their successor Ezio Flagello, on the other hand, has been careful to sing roles requiring a full *basso cantante legato* in addition to the *basso buffo* roles, thereby opposing any tendency to narrow his casting.

Hero and heroine roles, traditionally tenor and soprano, may extend vocally from the light voices of Nemorino and Adina in *L'Elisir D'Amore*, through the heavier Cavaradossi and Tosca, to the strenuous Tristan and Isolde, and the vocal casting not overlap. Enrico Caruso, on the other hand, sang Nemorino and Cavaradossi in the same season. He never sang Tristan, although toward the end of his career his voice had darkened to the point where he was singing heavy tenor roles and was considering Wagnerian roles. He was also at this time singing Nemorino, but Caruso was something of an exception. Many singers who go on to heavier roles abandon the lighter ones.

Fashion, both temporal and national, plays a considerable part in casting. In America today we are accustomed to a heavier soprano voice in the *Trovatore* role of Leonora and in the *Rosenkavalier* Marschallin, and it would be a shock to hear once again Adelina Patti in the former and Frieda Hempel in the latter. The basses with the necessary high notes who now sing the baritone role of Don Giovanni have almost cleared the field of the high baritones who can easily manage the high A natural in the final scene (not in the score but too tempting not to interject), instead of lunging at it with a dramatically permissible yowl.

Intelligent acting singers can find plenty of variety of character in the heroes and heroines of romantic opera, but there is a regrettable tendency among many first-class singers to portray all characters alike, so that a soprano's Norma, Leonora (*Trovatore*), Gioconda, and Tosca are almost indistinguishable except for costume. They are all women in love, their lives are turbulent, and their deaths sensational (fire, poison, knife, and a fall from a height, respectively), making it possible to imbue their music with a generalized sweet-voiced anguish. This antitheatrical concert approach is encouraged by audience members who neither expect nor demand anything more than voice and personality. Both are absolutely essential to these demanding and exciting roles, but a great deal else is missing if the dramatic content remains unexplored. The simple question of how each of them earns her living is a good beginning. Two of them are professional singers of widely contrasting social position. One of them is not a Roman Catholic. There is much in the text to provide assistance.

While the tenor romantic hero is often just as colorless, he need not be, as a careful reading of text and music will generally show. The character, or buffo, tenor, often listed as a *comprimario* (supporting singer), cannot be colorless, and the opportunities for real acting are generous. He may sing Pedrillo in *Seraglio*, a more rewarding tenor role than many leads, he can delineate an oily Don Basilio in *Figaro*, play three bravura roles in *The Tales of Hoffmann*, the fearsome and sinister police agent Spoletta in *Tosca*, the marriage broker Goro in *Butterfly*, the apoplectic Captain in *Wozzeck*, and the grotesque Auctioneer in *The Rake's Progress*. This should be enough to correct the mistaken impression that to play secondary roles one need only be a secondary singer. Solid and long-lasting careers are built on such roles, and more than one tenor who could have joined the throng of lyric tenors in strong competition with each other has won security and high regard in the more challenging domain of the character *comprimario*. Angelo Bada, Giuseppe Nessi, Alessio de Paolis, Piero de Palma, and Paul Franke are names of distinction.

The opportunities for singers who take their acting seriously are considerable. The fact that a number do not contributed to the sensation caused by Maria Callas, who rapidly became famous for her scrupulous attention to the sense and dramatic content of the role she was singing. One can be a successful and popular operatic singer on voice alone, provided that the voice is a really exceptional one in the first place and deployed with skill in the second. One cannot be a successful operatic singer on acting alone and a poor voice poorly managed.

It has been a vulgar custom, from time to time, to deride the operatic singer for his slackness in acting, or in some instances his total inability to act. It is only fair to make the proper distinctions between those who act and act well, and those who make no effort. It is only reasonable, too, to inquire into the nature of operatic acting and to appreciate the wide range of it.

For those who are not acquainted with the problems of a singing actor, let it first be stated that it requires a good deal more energy to sing than to speak. It requires accuracy of pitch, whereas speech does not use exact pitches, and it requires accuracy of time. Unless the composer has indicated that a passage may be sung freely, it must be sung exactly as written, with whole notes and half notes and dotted notes and grace notes fully respected. In acting a spoken part, timing is a personal matter. An experienced actor senses from the audience and from his fellow players the correct timing and makes his points accordingly, knowing very well from audience reactions or the lack of them whether he is timing successfully or unsuccessfully and whether the tempo of the scene is right. Experienced players quicken, retard, and employ timed silences almost instinctively. A singing actor has to take his timing from the composer who has dictated the notes and the rests and from the conductor who is dictating the tempo. Obeying all this, he still has to give the illusion of expressing himself naturally and making his points, whether serious or comic, as if they were spontaneous and a part of his total expression. Furthermore he has to sing across an orchestra, which may or may not be difficult, depending upon the concern of the composer and upon the composer's skill in orchestration and the skill of the conductor and the orchestral players. While he is engaged in this, often in a language which is not his native tongue, he is expected to project the dramatist's character, respect the director's interpretation, and present at least a reasonably convincing job of acting.

If the singing actor were permitted to indulge himself, as well as be indulged, with typecasting, and to confine himself to one species of drama, his job would still be a superhuman one; but in addition, the singer is expected to be convincing in several styles, often two or three different ones in a week. In European repertory he is expected to essay a dozen different roles in a single season. American professional theatre adheres largely to the long run system, and even our spoken-play repertory companies are a modification of the repertory system. The Stratford Festival Theatre (Ontario) or the Guthrie Theatre in Minneapolis will alternate four or five plays throughout a season. A European repertory actor may find himself playing Shakespeare, Sheridan, Schiller, Ibsen, Shaw, O'Neill, and Albee in a single season. A leading bass baritone may have to adapt himself to the demands of Mozart, Rossini, Verdi, Moussorgsky, Wagner, Tchaikowsky, and Strauss in the same season.

Ignoring for the moment the vocal adjustment, which is considerable, it is something of a histrionic feat to do justice to the varying styles demanded by Don Giovanni, Don Basilio (Rossini's), Amonasro, Boris, Vanderdecken, Eugen Onegin, and Mandryka. They all *look* different. They all *move* differently. They must all even *feel* different.

The mezzo soprano who already ranges from Cherubino to Fricka may occasionally be required to sing the contralto roles of Orfeo and Dalila and to rise beyond the soprano of Cherubino to the soprano of Adalgisa. Once a reputation is acquired she is more likely to stay with her most successful roles, and many mature singers specialize in a few roles to the close of their careers, dropping the more taxing of them one by one. A heroic tenor may have sung forty roles on his way up but climax his career with Tristan, Siegmund, Florestan, and Otello. A soprano admired for her coloratura will drop the lyrical roles and settle for a series of Gildas, Lakmés, and Rosinas, transposing Rosina's role upward in strategic sections.

Those who learned to act on their way to singing success will continue to grow in the interpretation of their roles. Those who did not will rely upon concert techniques and audience affection. This is not to imply that audiences withhold affection from singers who are deeply concerned with interpretation. Lotte Lehmann, an accomplished actress, intuitively gifted but not content to rely upon her gifts, worked at her roles and throughout a long career inspired an unusual amount of affection.

More public appreciation of good acting and more public disapproval of laziness and personal vanity would set new standards for behavior on the operatic stage, but as long as the public accepts whatever is put before it without complaint, and sometimes without seeming to notice the most obvious defects and the most outrageous lapses in taste, improvement will be long in coming.

In a Paris production of Bizet's *The Pearl Fishers*, the tenor singing the role of Nadir sings an aria and falls asleep with his head on a rock. Hearing the audience applaud he raises his head, acknowledges the applause with a grateful smile, and falls sleep again. In a Vienna Staatsoper *Fidelio*, Anton Dermota in the role of Florestan rises to his knees after a collapse induced by starvation, in order not to offend the ticket purchasers. To do Paris justice, Guy Chauvet in the same role remains unconscious throughout the enthusiastic applause. In a poorly rehearsed production of Janáček's *Jenůfa,* half the cast members are, as characters, completely uninvolved between phrases and showing no reactions, but revealing tension in the eyes as they watch for the conductor to give them their musical entrances. Chorus members in *Otello*, after singing excitedly, place their hands casually on a railing as they descend a stairway to go offstage. A German Violetta in *La Traviata* sits or stands when she is not occupied in singing, and displays no interest whatever in the proceedings. She could scarcely do more damage to the drama if she took out her knitting between arias.

A Wotan sings his entire *Rheingold* role facing front, and never personally addresses Fricka, Loge, Erda, Alberich, or anyone else, although there is no hint that this is an experimental-oratorio production of Wagner. A bass of international reputation in an Italian festival production stands eight feet from the prompt box and, unsure of his cues, engages in a duet with the prompter. He assumes this position in every scene, wherever the other characters are placed, and in order to be informed of his words, cannot risk facing any direction but front. A German mezzo soprano playing a breeches role in Handel's *Xerxes* walks from spot to spot on stage and enters and exits without the slightest assumption of a young man's walk, all her movements and her attitude toward the female characters being as feminine as if she herself were in a skirt. Recollecting the attention Risë Stevens paid to differentiating between the physical movements of her Cherubino and her Octavian, one wonders why the German singer chose a profession calling for appearances on stage before a public. Another German singer, Judith Beckmann, by way of contrast, appeared most convincingly in the breeches role in Lortzing's *Der Wildschütz*, and two nights later was a most alluring Eurydice in Offenbach's parody of the Orpheus story.

Operatic acting is seldom realistic, but it must frequently give enough illusion of near-realism to enable us to accept the characters in the milieu in which they appear. The comparatively realistic first half of the first act of *La Bohème* gains by a believable informality not usually associated with romantic opera, and loses the moment there is any hint of posturing. Romantic opera loses by posturing, also, but not as obviously, since the larger movements required by the costumes and the more picturesque movements and groupings are more difficult to distinguish from the movements recollected from a class in deportment and used in every role regardless of the differences of station, character, and position in the story development. Edward D. Easty's recent book *On Method Acting* (New York, 1966) severely deplores the work of teachers of movement and diction, accusing them of substituting for the natural beauty of appropriate bodily action and the native color of unaffected speech a set of stereotyped graceful movements lacking individuality and a standardized and utterly unconvincing stage diction. The poorest actors in the hands of the poorest teachers may very well achieve no more than this brittle mask of stage competence, but intelligent actors cannot leave everything to nature. Most of them are obliged to go through a learning and improvement stage during which they lose some naturalness as they increase their physical flexibility, and whether they are singers or not, acquire clarity of enunciation which they did not before possess, making them subject to accusations of pretentiousness. One must take the risk of remaining in this apprentice stage forever. If one remains in it, the training was a total waste of time. The successful artist is the one who, having learned his craft, recaptures the spontaneity of movement and the genuine quality of speech or song. One's mature acting must have nothing of the classroom in it, and one is obliged to make the careful enunciation of words seem both effortless and natural.

Singers have for the most part more to learn than actors in spoken plays. They can scarcely hope, in the repertory system, to avoid a number of periods and styles which actors seldom have an opportunity of experiencing. Many American actors are ill at ease in period plays and bring an ambiance of the corner drugstore to the classics. Singers are more likely to find themselves in seventeenth-, eighteenth-, and nineteenth-century costume than in contemporary, and when, rarely, they are in contemporary costume they have the additional problem of making their movements seem natural while their vocal emission is far more stylized than elevated speech.

In addition to clarifying his diction in his native language, the serious singer must be able to sing in other languages, often in the countries where those languages are spoken daily by the members of the audience. What often passes in America for foreign languages is simply not adequate. With some seven hundred American singers on the stages of Germany cast alongside a preponderance of natives, the German has to be good. French, Italian, and German operas are generally sung, in the few major opera houses in America, in the language of the original text: *Faust* in French, *Aida* in Italian, and *Lulu* in German. In smaller companies or for special performances the singer may have to relearn the role in an English translation. If he travels to England and is engaged for a role he already knows in the original language and in English, he may find a different translation in use. Foreign singers have taken the trouble to learn an entire role in English, only to have the opera accorded one or two performances. It is therefore small wonder that a singer should be unwilling to learn a role in a second or third language unless he is sure of using that version profitably. An American tenor who has sung *Albert Herring* on several stages in Germany must still be refused when he wants to sing the role in German in America, either with all the other singers singing English or requiring all of them to learn their roles in the German version, but at least his point of view can be understood, since the invitation is for two performances only.

A Hungarian, Finnish, Czech, or Jugoslav singer is expected to sing all roles in his native country in his native language. If extending his career takes him to Germany, he must learn his Verdi and Puccini roles in German. In Italy he must relearn them all in Italian, and if he also learned his Mozart and Wagner in German he must, if they are including Mozart and Wagner in Italian seasons, relearn them in Italian.

The operetta and musical comedy singer seldom has to face these language problems, except in rare instances when international celebrities like Richard Tauber and Jan Kiepura repeat their continental operetta successes in English-speaking countries. This, however, is invariably for a long and extremely profitable run.

The long run is convenient for musical comedy, operetta, and the musical play, but it frequently demands a durable leading singer or, in strenuous works, an alternation of leading singers. *The Medium, The Consul,* and *The Most Happy Fella* can be done in this way, but anything heavier must subscribe to the repertory or *stagione* systems.

The advantages of the long run system are mostly financial. Singers are marking time, as it were, and although there is much they can learn from the varying audience reactions, they are much more likely to suffer from the lack of stimulating experience and, except in leading roles, from sheer boredom. In New York, most musical comedy singers think themselves lucky to be in a job for two or three years, since they may well be out of a job for the next four.

The European repertory system guarantees employment from September to June and the advantages are considerable. Many young American singers have put themselves heavily in debt in order to gain the repertory experience denied them in their native country. In Germany especially, where the theatres are numerous, the singer can acquire a breadth of experience in different styles and periods in roles often varying from small to large. What is perhaps just as important, he can make a psychological adjustment to the spirit of ensemble, that is to say, an awareness of the necessity for teamwork and the suppression of ego in actual performance. Such performances must, of course, be firmly directed by a *régisseur* who condemns stepping out of character to acknowledge applause, except in works which call for it and provide "spaces" in the music for it, and by a musical conductor who will not permit a distortion of the vocal line or of vocal dynamics for the same purpose. In the best companies, where there is good discipline, the audience can usually be controlled and there is plenty of opportunity for adulation at the curtain calls. The frequent changes of role provide the singer with a freshness of approach and outlook. Two successive performances of the same role are comparatively rare, and there is consequently little danger of staleness.

The disadvantages of the repertory system to the singing actor are considerable. He must learn quickly and remember accurately. While he is given ample opportunity to reveal his versatility, he is given little to grow in a role, to profit in performance from a series of productions without the disrupting necessity of performing other roles in between. While there is little danger of long run perfunctoriness of performance, a routine slickness may often be observed, as if the overworked participants are regarding memory work as the prime requisite and are finding to their pride and pleasure everything going with tolerable accuracy and smoothness. It is this tolerable accuracy and smoothness which can dull and deaden what should be living excitement. Perhaps what is worse, it encourages the average, well-schooled *routinier* to think he is better than he is, and discour-

ages the more talented but perhaps somewhat less reliable performer.
Later in his career, this talented performer may concentrate on five
or six roles and the pressures are of a different sort. In the early and
middle stages of his career he must adapt himself to the repertory system or withdraw from the competition.

An American singer with the operatic stage in mind often de-
cides to join the hundreds in Europe who are learning their craft in
the theatres there for the simple reason that the theatres in America
are too few for the vast numbers needing the experience. If he goes,
he must decide whether to make a career there, most likely in Germany, or whether to return to America and establish himself full
time or part time in his native country, maintaining a regularity of
income by teaching.

American singers, excellently trained at home, provide stiff competition for European singers and have acquired the reputation of being aggressive, which makes some of them unpopular with their colleagues, and of being hardworking and reliable, which makes most of
them popular with managers. Many have displayed their musicianship
and disciplined memories by accepting and learning roles in the contemporary operas which managers stage for prestige reasons or, in
some instances, for a genuine missionary purpose. A Berlin cast of
about fifteen for a modern opera may easily have four or five American names on the list. While *Wozzeck* and *Lulu* may receive enough
performances to make the effort worthwhile, many a contemporary
work, laboriously learned, may be forgotten after a few token performances.

Not all singers are prepared to study the technique of *Sprechstimme* of the kind used in *Wozzeck*. *Sprechstimme* is rhythmic declamation, the notation of which suggests pitches but does not require
the singer to be true to the exact pitches attached to each syllable.
The intonation pattern of speech is required in these sections, and a
special kind of easily recognized notation distinguishes them from
the music to be sung, like most music, with exact pitches respected.
The effect is something between singing and speaking, less songlike
than song and more declamatory than realistic speech. While
Sprechstimme is given the freedom of not adhering to the exact
pitches on each syllable, the direction of the intonation pattern, up

or down, is clearly indicated, and so is the approximate interval. The time values must be strictly respected. *Sprechstimme* is a disciplined technique, intended to be powerfully expressive. Berg heard it as "a welcome and attractive sonorous contrast to straight *bel canto* singing" (H. F. Redlich, *Alban Berg, The Man and His Music*, p. 271).

The more songlike *Sprechgesang*, similar to the Wagnerian and Straussian method, with fixed pitches, leans toward pure cantabile, while a short scene in plain speech across an orchestral background (Act 1 scene 3 of *Wozzeck* between Marie and Margret) uses the eighteenth- and early-nineteenth-century technique of *mélodrame*, to be heard in Mozart's *Zaide* (twice), Beethoven's *Fidelio* (the dungeon scene), and Weber's *Der Freischütz* (Wolfsschlucht scene) and to be heard also in film, radio, and television, though with somewhat different application.

Some singers can adapt themselves readily to a convincing *Sprechstimme*. Others may be detected using snatches of something like it when they project the drama of a line or a word over the music in Italian opera, for example on such flaming words as *assassino*, *infame*, and *perfido*, with exciting departures from a strict observance of pitch. Similarly, some singers adapt themselves from song to speech and back again in operetta and *Singspiel*, while others carry a peculiar singer's vocal production into their speech, with oddly academic and unconvincing results. When there are enough works in the international repertory using *Sprechstimme* and they are all frequently performed, audiences and singers will be accustomed to the technique, and the disadvantages, and advantages, of novelty will no longer obtain. We shall then be better equipped to judge it and to distinguish the merit, or otherwise, of its choice for certain passages in place of speech, *parlando* recitative, or *arioso*.

The methods of approach to a role are as varied in singing-acting as in speaking-acting. The approaches may also range from the most profoundly considered to the most superficial. The differences are not so much between actors and singers as between the requirements of long run performance and repertory. Preparing for a single role in a play or a musical comedy which may run for a year or more would seem to encourage long and careful study, while the necessity for performing ten to fifteen roles between September and June would seem doomed to haste and superficiality.

Serious actors, whether admittedly of the so-called Method school or not, make considerable demands upon themselves and others and will spend a great deal of time in study and preparation, at the same time keeping themselves flexible and improvisatory for rehearsals so that they perform as part of a whole instead of by and for themselves.

It must be admitted at once, however, that side by side with this approach is an approach of personality and technique, requiring no less work but of a totally different kind and for a somewhat different purpose. The actual purpose of both is to entertain (in the more dignified sense of the word), to hold an audience for a variety of purposes but to hold them together and to control their reactions. A successful production by Method actors will hold an audience by virtue of the illusion of reality and identification with the compelling characters they are able to create. A successful production by Brechtian actors will attempt no illusion of reality but will hold an audience by virtue of the didactic subject matter, and the reasoning audience will leave the production determined upon positive action. A successful production of a musical comedy or a light comedy containing no music will hold an audience by force of personality, and by the dexterity with which variations are played upon and by the personality or personalities.

Singers with a genuine desire to act as well as sing have many difficulties placed in their way. The theatres in which they sing are often ill-suited to the roles they are playing. Some theatres have an intimate auditorium, a *piccolo teatro* or *kleine Bühne* seating from 400 to 600, in which works of a nonheroic nature do not need to be "blown up" in any way. In larger theatres, a singer trained to sense the size and acoustical nature of the auditorium in which he is singing can rarely make a physical adjustment without destroying something valuable. He lacks a dancer's immediate assessment of distance and cubic space and often, in an attempt to compensate for what he feels but cannot measure, produces what registers only as exaggeration and distortion.

The acting fashion of naturalism or a strong degree of realism could scarcely be transferred in its entirety to musical theatre. With many singers not caring to learn much about acting or to change their style of performance to suit the widely differing works in which they appear, several generations of audiences have been treated to the grotesque spectacle of meticulously realistic scenery and properties, while actors wearing realistic costumes perform in a strongly conventional style, limited in its range and unskilled in the movements of that range.

In a frankly conventional production of an eighteenth-century or early-nineteenth-century opera it is quite inoffensive for a singer to look openly at the conductor. Like enthusiastic Brechtians, we want in this kind of work to be reminded constantly that we are in a theatre. With the turn-of-the-century fashion in realism, it now becomes necessary for the singers to pretend, in works which seem to call for it, that there is no conductor. We in the audience can see him, unless we are in the Bayreuth Festspielhaus, but we must not be made aware of him by the singers who have now become characters instead of performers. The composers, however, of operas asking for some realism in order to be fashionable in the world of theatre did not always help the singers by making all vocal entrances easy. Puccini's Butterfly must not break the pathetic illusion by watching the conductor, Charpentier's Louise destroys the fragile atmosphere of the opera if she is caught following the beat, and Janáček's Jenůfa, in spite of some entrances that are far from easy, has to seem totally concerned with her personal troubles and must therefore as far as is possible conceal her musical ones.

Singers for the stage have learned the trick of catching the conductor's beat and the entrance warnings out of the corners of their eyes, and some of them are remarkably skilful at deceiving the audience. The necessity for being where one can see the conductor is not conducive to realistic relationships and effective grouping of characters, so that the stage director is often hard put to vary the stage positions as much as he would like. Singers prefer, for vocal reasons, to be closer front than stage directors wish, and a somewhat planar effect is achieved by default. Young singers profit by having a good resonating surface behind them, but not all designers want to close off their visual effects in this manner. Compromises are made, but it is the singer who is before the audience on the stage, and it is he who is blamed for inaudibility and clumsiness of effect.

Boris Goldovsky, a champion of opera as drama as opposed to opera as concert, has encouraged devices to free the singer of dependence upon the centrally located and visible conductor (*Accents on Opera,* p. 267). The orchestral sound when piped into the stage area, for instance, is far more easily heard by the singers than when it merely floats back in from the auditorium. Singers long accustomed to conductor focus, however, adapt themselves somewhat unwillingly to such experiments, and many opera singers find themselves at a loss when not only the conductor is gone but even the prompter's box with the helpful prompter inside it.

Many members of the opera-house audience can see the prompter's box quite clearly but remain unaware that the prompter assists the singers on their musical entrances by supplying the words and, upon occasion, the correct pitch. For many years good productions of spoken plays have dispensed with the prompter, relying upon memory, experience, and an ability to improvise if it becomes necessary to do so. Musical productions are understandably far more complex. With a composer's score which the orchestra is following from the parts, singers can scarcely hope to recover by improvising. A full repertory, calling for a dozen or more works, each played six or eight times over a period of months with an occasional single production repeated from a previous season, makes it difficult to abandon the tradition of having a prompter. Even if it is possible to arrange a season's program with all the time necessary to enable each member of the company to be absolutely confident in his role, the appearance of a guest actor or a sudden substitution may upset the plan. The prompter's box is there and it is generally occupied.

Actors in spoken plays have difficulties enough in repertory, but singers' difficulties can be prodigious. They may have thirty roles at their command, and this means words, notes, note lengths together with phrasings, and effects called for by the conductor, who may himself not be the company's regular conductor. In a lengthy work there may be traditional cuts, but the traditions are not consistent and a new conductor may want to open up some of the cuts. Stage action changes from director to director and designer to designer.

Ideally, the director and the designer are in agreement, but in many instances business planned in rehearsal cannot be executed as planned, once the singers are on stage. A guest singer or a substituting singer may be accustomed to a different staging. One of the singers may even be singing the role in a different language from the one in which he last sang it. A repetition from a previous season may take place in April. The work may not have been done since February of the last season. Good musicianship and a quick and accurate memory are of inestimable value, but much can slip away in fourteen months of a busy career.

The repertory of a German opera house for a single month will often list from twenty-five to thirty performances of a dozen or more operas or operettas, with six or seven of the works performed only once during this month and no single work performed more than three times. Not every singer in the company is in every production, but many are needed for half the performances, and the chorus for most of them.

While substitutions are common enough in the spoken play, they seem almost endemic to the musical form. There is a hilarious account in the Mapleson memoirs of his cancellation at four o'clock in the afternoon of that evening's performance of *William Tell*, the prima donna having contracted diphtheria. Mapleson changed the opera to *Lucia di Lammermoor*, only to discover that this prima donna had never sung the role. The opera was changed to *Aida*, but when the orders for music, scenery, and costumes had been issued, the third prima donna was discovered to be ill in bed. The opera was now changed to *Rigoletto*, but the second prima donna, who was still healthy, declared herself unable to sing Gilda at such short notice, whereupon the resourceful Mapleson changed to the most difficult opera in the repertoire, *Les Huguenots*. One of the sopranos for this had taken medicine which made it impossible for her to come to the opera house. Mapleson changed the opera to *La Favorita*, but the tenor was exhausted from a *Carmen* rehearsal and would not sing. Another tenor was secured, but the costumes had to be altered to fit him. The soprano for the leading role was meanwhile suffering from boils. These were promptly lanced, she put on her costume during Act 1 and made her first appearance in Act 2, and thereby helped to save the evening.* Even allowing for the Mapleson exaggerations and inaccuracies, this operatic experience of four hours throws a considerable amount of light upon the problems not only for the manager, but for the technical staff and for the singers of all the other roles in the six operas involved. None of this is conducive to anything resembling a dramatic realization; the most one is entitled to expect is a hasty assumption of the required role with the maximum accuracy in musical matters. Experienced singers who have an instinct for acting, however, very quickly overcome the tensions and are propelled by the music into a recollection of how they felt on previous occasions in the role. This can very easily be superseded by a fresh enactment in place of the imitation of an imitation to which we in the audience are so often subjected.

The reference to a fresh enactment brings us close to the affective memory applied to the actor's art by Constantin Stanislavsky and his followers. Mrs. Siddons in the eighteenth century undoubtedly employed it in some measure. The recapturing of emotions from one's past is a standard procedure of actors who base their approach upon Stanislavsky's teaching, and exercises are designed to make it easier to tap the sources of various emotions at will. On the basis of reasoning that the actor must feel real emotion himself in order to make the character he is playing seem real to the audience, he must find in his own past, preferably not the most recent past, the only real ways to express the emotions of the character. To accomplish this he uses the bodily equipment he possesses; this is the instrument upon which he plays. Achieving this, he avoids the artificial assumption of the emotions required by the script and avoids the sham theatricals we immediately recognize as an insincere substitute for sincere acting.

The singer, presumably responsive to music, can profitably use the emotional readiness which music can so rapidly supply to recapture emotions of his own from the past which are essential to his recreation of the character's emotions. Good singing actors do this consistently, whether they have experienced the Method or not. Poor ones are content to employ gestures and attitudes learned in

* Harold Rosenthal, ed., *The Mapleson Memoirs: The Career of an Operatic Impresario, 1858–1888*, New York, 1966, pp. 158, 159.

classes, with vocal approaches imitated from other singers. Productions of opera which often display excellent singing betray their routine quality in this way, and although we are inured to the acceptance of unsatisfactory drama side by side with much more acceptable music, the feeling of dissatisfaction remains.

The press has performed considerable service in recent years by acknowledging the presence of genuine acting when it senses it, and thereby encouraging the singers who want to act to continue to do so. This was not always so, and although exceptional personalities who were also actors, like Mary Garden and Feodor Chaliapin, were assured of the publicity on which they throve, the fashion was for expert voices, and acting, when it occurred, was mainly confined to the larynx. Mary Garden, accused of not having a voice, responded tartly that one voice was inadequate for her purposes. She had two dozen, one for every role she sang and acted, and she was justifiably proud of the fact. She seized upon the accusation that she was no singer to claim that she was a great deal more.

Acting with the entire body in a literary play is a comparatively recent practice, not long antedating the Russian director Vsevolod Meyerhold, who was especially concerned with the athletic training of actors. The actors of the eighteenth century, an age of great acting, were mostly overweight, and on candlelit and oil-lit stages their strength lay largely in their voices and in their line readings. In the Georgian era of small theatres, facial expressions were of considerable value, though a facial expression which is clearly visible in soft light would look like mugging if it were to be illuminated by the much stronger electric light of the present day. Facial expressions would be difficult to appreciate unless the wearers were comparatively still while they held them. One has the impression of a somewhat stately set of motions, a good deal of facing front, and most careful delivery of lines, with slower pacing than that to which we are accustomed today. While David Garrick was described as "quicksilver" and "darting" through a play, these terms are picturesque and relative. Garrick must have seemed startlingly vital after the senatorial Quin, and Garrick, in his turn, was succeeded by the dignified Kemble.

Many of the characteristics of old acting may be discerned in operatic acting much closer to our own time. Indeed, some operatic acting and some operatic staging may be accepted in all seriousness as valuable museums of former practices, long discarded elsewhere. While plays and musical comedies have kept pace with technical advances and in America have for the most part abandoned the repertory system, opera has had to cling to it. And opera, in spite of some technical advances, has clung to a number of old-fashioned acting techniques, some of them occasioned by the musical nature of the pieces performed, some of them purely traditional. It is more difficult to move swiftly in a sung play than in a spoken play, but it is possible to move more swiftly than most opera singers are accustomed to move. It is helpful to be facing more or less front in order to see the conductor's beat, but most opera singers look to the front far too frequently and far too long, even in works calling for an inclination toward realism. The fact that the operatic repertoire is an old one, strongly dominated by romantic melodrama written between 1850 and 1910, encourages statuesqueness of stance and stateliness of movement. At its worst, operatic acting is a bundle of clichés learned in deportment classes, the haughty head swivelling on the columnar neck, the grand stride, the sweeping arm, and the careful, cushioned fall to the floor in moments of violence. Watching it in a large opera house, lighted by electricity but romantically dim, it is not difficult to recreate a picture of the movement from attitude to attitude which must have constituted the choreography of much of the seventeenth-century and eighteenth-century stage.

Plays of that era were first of all performances before audiences and only secondarily performances of plays, and the operatic parallel is immediately discerned. Only after the onset of realism did performers in spoken plays ignore the audience as if there were a fourth wall along the proscenium line.

Madame Vestris, in the nineteenth century, gave an encore to a favorite speech in the play *London Assurance,* a testimony to the essential theatricality of the piece. Encores in opera are diminishing, but they are taking a long time to do so. In some opera houses they are forbidden, but they may be heard now and then and they are common in operetta. In the nineteenth century they were an established part of a performance. Even so, a realization of a certain inappropriateness made itself felt toward the end of the century. A curiously arch juxtaposition of convention and lifelikeness was evident when Marcella Sembrich, singing Susanna in *Figaro* and participating in the duet of the dictated letter, after smilingly acknowledging the applause, picked up the letter she had written and showed the audience that she had smudged it and that it would have to be done over and therefore sung over. By the 1920s, singers, at least in certain works, were being sharply criticized for tastelessly breaking dramatic continuity with concert hall encores. Henry Pleasants in *The Great Singers* quotes Richard Aldrich's 1922 *New York Times* account of Chaliapin's stepping forward to acknowledge applause and to supply an encore for King Philip's monologue in *Don Carlos* (pp. 325–26).

Even the special carpet upon which actresses of the early eighteenth century could die without spoiling their costumes was evident as late as the 1940s in a Metropolitan Opera production of *Manon* at the Chicago Opera House. On the bleak road to Le Havre in the final scene there was a log upon which to sit, and quite handy to it the rectangle of carpet upon which to die. Bidu Sayao used it as it was intended, and preserved her costume for the next performance.

It is little wonder that with this fondness for tradition much operatic acting in the 1960s, in Europe and in America, still recalls the older approach to acting, and the staging that is dependent upon acting. When seen against scenery as progressive and original as any on the stage of the spoken play, the difference is disturbing. To watch behavior more suited to the flapping backdrops of yesteryear against settings by Teo Otto, Günther Schneider-Siemssen, Josef Svoboda, or Leni Bauer-Ecsy prompts us to wish for the tired old scenery or for a totally new concept of operatic acting.

A new concept would have the responsibility of effecting a compromise between the musical and the dramatic demands, a compromise demonstrated in our own time most successfully by the singer Maria Callas and the stage director Walter Felsenstein, separately. There will always be extremists on both sides, drama enthusiasts who insist that an opera be as much like a play as possible, and vocal music enthusiasts who demand golden syrup from all the participants whether it is appropriate to the dramatic action or not. Maria Callas has been widely appreciated for her dramatic commitment, and at the same time her vocal method has been as widely criticized. Walter Felsenstein's realization of dramatic energy in works of which most productions had been limp and perfunctory has commanded the greatest respect, but there has been no lack of fault-finding based upon the director's preference for intelligent singers who are eager to be meticulously directed over the possessors of great voices whose eagerness is confined to displaying those voices. The singing of Irmgard Arnold, Anny Schlemm, Hermin Esser, Werner Missner, and Rudolf Asmus does not bring excited purchasers to the record shops of America, but wherever they are singing and acting, which they do simultaneously, they are, as workers who have learned from Walter Felsenstein, bringing an astonishing amount of sense and vitality to an art form which for far too long had seemed to lose both.

There remains one compromise to be appreciated, a compromise that can be paralleled with the best spoken acting of the seventeenth, eighteenth, and nineteenth centuries and extending into our own century, especially in the acting of Shakespeare.

Between the singers who display beautiful voices beautifully and those who throw themselves bodily and emotionally into the acting of their sung roles are a number who, moving about in the stately manner of seventeenth-century actors and applying a set of acquired gestures in the old style to their unresilient bodies, nevertheless change their vocal color in accordance with the requirements of the situations they are in and the words they are singing. They do not move dramatically but they sing dramatically, and in a drama their singing is to be prized above singing which is undramatic. Dramatic singing is not a matter of lunges, gulps, sobs, shouts, and excessive vibrato, and it might be argued that all intelligent singing, singing which takes full account of the meaning and expressiveness of the words supplied, is dramatic singing.

The singing of art songs, German *Lieder* and French *chansons*, bears the same relationship to dramatic singing as the reading of poetry bears to stage acting. It is interpretation rather than impersonation. Interpretation and impersonation meet as they cannot fail to do to some extent in the singing of a Brecht ballad in a stage production, but they meet only rarely. Interpretation is largely subjective or narrative and involves no interchange between characters. The communication is directly between the interpreter and his audience, and he uses only a suggestion of physical action, or often none at all.

An actor or actor-singer is frequently called upon to alternate between a comparatively realistic interchange with other characters and direct address to the audience in the form of soliloquies or arias or, to use a term appropriate to sung as well as spoken plays, monologues. The impersonator, however, retains his character in the drama unless specifically instructed to step outside his character, and usually he does not, immediately upon addressing the audience, begin to interpret. He is still an actor. He is still impersonating, even though he is using direct address. The Shakespearean actor is accustomed to this adjustment and the singer-actor should be, so that in arias and monologues the character is consistently maintained.

Unfortunately, not all singers are singer-actors and the solo reveals them. Instead of continuing to be the character they are supposed to be portraying, they become concert singers, self-conscious performers smiling at the audience as themselves, with the drama in pieces about them. Any attempt to reassume the character and resume the drama after this interruption is almost certainly doomed to failure, and even if it is not, the next aria or monologue will promptly destroy what has freshly been recreated.

It is one thing, and perfectly acceptable, to write an entertainment for bravura performers, linking their show pieces with transitional passages of sung dialogue and providing the entertainment with a decorative background and suitable costumes. This is what those responsible for the Baroque *opera seria* concocted.

It is another thing to write a music drama or opera and have it performed as a consistently dramatic piece, but it can be done and it is done with encouraging frequency, especially in theatres with a respected stage director and operating with an ensemble.

It is a third thing to have a music drama or opera performed partly as a dramatic piece and partly as a concert, although this seems to be generally accepted as opera production by audiences for much of the *stagione* type of production, for many festival productions, and for a large number of productions in theatres possessing a well-trained but perhaps somewhat undisciplined ensemble.

The nature of the works usually determines the approach. Wagner, Debussy, Strauss, Berg, and Britten seldom invite even a fleeting concert approach. The Donizetti, Rossini, and early Verdi operas, while not as concert oriented as the *opera seria* of the Baroque era, are close enough in libretto organization to make it difficult for a stage director to maintain the dramatic continuum and easy for singers to drop out of character. When all action stops for a reflective or descriptive or informative aria and that aria is supplied with melting *cantilena* and a *cadenza* at its close to exhibit the singer's skill, only a disciplinarian stage director and singers of unusual dramatic integrity can resist the temptation of lapsing into concert techniques.

Later Verdi, with its more dramatically written texts, presents challenges so generally accepted that even an untutored audience would be disturbed if not downright offended by concert lapses. The Puccini works are problems. Eager to serve two masters at once, the public's fondness for vocal display and the public's acceptance of the new century's *verismo* that was far more subtle than that of Leoncavallo and Mascagni, Puccini composed works with one foot in each camp. Ostensible music dramas suddenly give the actors the opportunity of turning into concert singers with numbers which are not vocal displays of Handelian or even early Verdian character. They are, instead, vocal-dramatic numbers, but for all their dramatic pretensions they are quite as detached from the dramatic continuum as the honest exhibitors of Baroque *opera seria,* and all the more disturbing and disrupting. This accounts in part for the strong feeling of dissatisfaction with Puccini felt by many theatregoers, who have difficulty reconciling Puccini's artful vulgarity with his unquestioned melodic, instrumental, and dramatic gifts. When Verdi lapses we are less dismayed, feeling that the great man at that particular time in that particular place in the score could do no better. With Puccini there is the uneasy feeling that he could very easily have done better but chose not to do so.

A certain consistency is possible, even in a work of an ambivalent nature, and by this means displays of vocal skill may be rendered as inoffensive as possible. Some theatre managements, however, have demonstrated an irresponsibility in this respect, and a willingness to condone what can only be described as chaotic, undisciplined performance in which some of the performers clearly regard the work as music drama while others as clearly do no such thing.

In a 1968 Frankfurt production of *La Traviata* the soprano and the baritone gave total performances, the Violetta, the intelligent Sylvia Stahlman, making no attempt to win applause after "Ah, fors' è lui" but going on promptly to the cabaletta, keeping the "Amami, Alfredo" passage a part of the whole instead of a bravura effort, and handling "Addio del passato" with imagination and taste. Ernst Gutstein's entrance as the elder Germont immediately set the scene's meaning. Instead of entering with the confident stride of the company's principal baritone, he communicated shame and embarrassment and for some time did not look directly at Violetta. His attitude not only depicted quietly and unfussily the paramount importance of respectability to a gentleman of Provence and for once made believable the necessity to extricate his son from a courtesan's wiles, but it also made it possible for the audience to watch the impression which Violetta made upon him as the scene progressed and her true character made itself evident against all prejudice. Its final touching moment was built up to from this entrance, and a long passage which all too often is only musically beautiful became dramatically beautiful as well. The Alfredo made no attempt to act, dropped out of character on his second-act aria, and the moment he heard the applause bowed his gratification. It is only fair to add that this production came in an awkward period for the Frankfurt Opera House, following Harry Buckwitz's departure as Intendant of that institution. One can take the concert approach or leave it, and many *stagione* productions have accustomed us to it, but to find it intruding itself into a production otherwise handled with the greatest dramatic care by Otto Schenk is somewhat upsetting. In another German *La Traviata* production, the only attempt to sustain a character was made by the singer playing the role of Flora Bervoix. With the three leading singers in no mood to cooperate with her,

Flora's efforts were wasted and the production lapsed into the traditional and routine.

Not all singers can be accomplished actors, but a modicum of acting energy in two or three can generate enough power to change a scene from dull competence to exciting spontaneity. It takes, however, at least two to give the audience the triangular response. There is the straight-line response (often called circular, though parabolic would perhaps describe it best) between a single actor and his audience, upstairs and down, but the most satisfying is the feeling generated between actors which in turn acts upon the audience and is acted upon by the audience.

The title of Charles J. McGaw's well-known book on acting is *Acting Is Believing*. Acting is sharing, too, and the presence of a nonsharer in a production lowers the temperature of the whole to a depressing chilliness. The Wotan in *Das Rheingold* who did not look at or turn toward any of the other characters at any time, but sang the words to the audience, did not even begin to realize the dramatic values of the piece. Wotan is acted upon by Fricka, by Loge, and by Erda. Since several of the other singers made an attempt to communicate with each other, the effect was disturbing. Totally different was a Bielefeld *Lohengrin* directed by Friedelind Wagner. There, in a rather small theatre, the remoteness peculiar to the drama and most beautifully realized in the music was further projected by an intentional distance placed by the director between the characters, who did not employ or display the normal relationships but sang forward much of the time. The first time Elsa looked at Lohengrin was as a reaction to "Elsa, ich liebe dich," and the effect was extraordinary. In a larger house the Lohengrin remoteness is too often the result of small voices and poor acoustics.

In a Vienna Volksoper *Magic Flute* a lively Papageno easily achieved a straight-line response, but the triangular one was made impossible because Tamino was unusually wooden and concerned only about his singing, with the result that Papageno's acting was less effective in his numerous scenes with Tamino and he was tempted to force his comedy instead of letting it work naturally.

Singers in a *stagione* production are likely, even with the best will, to carry to the production the acting approach and the influence of a strong director. Anja Silja, a compelling actress who sang Senta in *The Flying Dutchman* at Bayreuth under Wieland Wagner's direction, took much of her feeling and action in the role to Zürich where she sang under a different stage director. On this occasion the Dutchman, who has a great deal of acting to perform with her, was sensible enough not to violate the style, but since he was not an accomplished actor he merely looked static. She, in spite of using very few movements, did not. The tenor playing Erik simply looked uncomfortable, and it was obvious that he could not readily adapt his set of learned gestures to the few but intensely motivated ones too near for his comfort. On the other hand, the bass playing Daland, a less complex character, was perfectly able to operate in his own sphere without disturbing the prevailing style.

In *South Pacific,* a long run production having the advantage of enabling actors to work together over a long period of time, Ezio Pinza and Mary Martin were very successful in their blending of two different approaches to both singing and acting, so that the effect was something of a pleasing unity. A similar adjustment, with different talents and for different reasons, was made in a Vienna *The Merry Widow.* Danilo was a personality comedian with almost no voice, but he was clearly a great favorite with the Viennese and had been so for a number of years. The soprano, Mimi Coertse, an accomplished singer, made up for her modest acting equipment by the display of a warm personality and an inclination to reduce her own resources whenever they sang together. A union of purpose was revealed which did much to offset the contrasting nature of their respective abilities. The tenor had a far less agreeable personality, glanced frequently at the conductor, communicating a lack of confidence or of preparation, and either stood complacently or moved uneasily and seemed not in accord with the otherwise quite beguiling proceedings.

Lest it seem as if tenors are mentioned only to be defamed, it should be stressed that a number of tenors, British, American, and German, have successfully played David in *Die Meistersinger,* a difficult role requiring not only plenty of voice but energy, liveliness, and subtle comedy without clowning. In quite small German theatres the tenor comedian is often the best actor in the company. England's

Peter Pears has an astonishing acting range, and there are German heroic tenors and Italian lyric tenors who bring dignity, sincerity, pathos, and masculine vigor to the roles they essay. The irresponsible gibe of "the higher the voice the smaller the brain" is not applicable. It is likely, however, that stupidity is more readily tolerated among the higher voices because of their rarity. The more individual or spectacular the voice, the fewer the competitors. With greater security of employment and financial reward some may be tempted to let acting take care of itself. The competition among baritones is very strenuous and a wise one will put himself ahead by acquiring more than simply a pleasing, well-schooled voice.

Some able actors in musical theatre, for lack of time or encouraged by an easily pleased audience, will use clichés which spoil the freshness of their otherwise original characterizations, or intoxicated by the laughter they hear will clown a role which is only distorted by clowning. The Dame Quickly in *Falstaff* who employs the hoary device of curtseying, getting stuck and having to be raised to a standing position degrades the characterization, especially when she rises thereafter with perfect ease, knowing better than to repeat the gag ad nauseam. The Nick in *The Girl of the Golden West* who limps in order to resemble a celebrated television "western" character is injecting foreign material into an opera which is foreign enough already. The singing actors of real ability who clown such roles as Rossini's Dr. Bartolo, Nicolai's Slender in *The Merry Wives*, or Verdi's Fra Melitone in *Forza* are winning ready laughter from the unthinking with short memories, and losing the respect of the thinking, who generally have longer ones. At the same time they are lowering the quality of the production in which they are appearing, and putting difficulties in the way of more conscientious actors.

In a poorly directed or wilfully acted production of *Don Giovanni*, the young peasant Masetto is frequently played as a rustic lout, sometimes attempting to outclown an undisciplined Leporello. He is certainly rustic, with a country boy's naiveté, but he is sharp enough to see what the Don is after and courageous enough to defy him as far as he prudently can. In a production in which Masetto looks eighteen and Zerlina sixteen and in which the eighteenth-century worlds of palace and village green are clearly demarcated, the relationships are suddenly believable, and while the comedy is not lost, it has acquired a touching quality of far greater depth.

Similarly, when Beckmesser in *Die Meistersinger* can really sing with every academic flourish known to formal art, the comedy and to some extent the seriousness of his public defeat are richer, and a further richness is added to the humanist monologue of Hans Sachs, the culmination of the opera. The easy defeat of a total incompetent is not much glory for the Franconian knight and speaks without eloquence for a more generous approach to art.

The leading character in the popular German comic opera *Zar und Zimmermann* is the pompous Mayor of a Dutch seaport. The key to this character is the fact that he takes himself with the utmost seriousness. That is what pomposity is. In some German theatres he is played in this way and his embarrassments are a delight. In others (of a Hans Wurst persuasion) Van Bett enters wearing a putty nose, crimson cheeks, and comic whiskers, and immediately proceeds to demonstrate that he is the company comedian.

A firm director can apply some of the necessary control, but singers on the stage in an actual performance may revert to a former conception and lose everything they gained in what in all probability were hasty and inadequate rehearsals. In a first-rate production it is impossible to distinguish between the acting and the directing. The wise director with good actors does not plaster his ideas over the production, but encourages it to grow out of the actors and their sensitive and intelligent interaction. The director of a cast of inexperienced actors may be forced to let his ideas show, since the actors obviously have none of their own. There are, however, competitive and exhibitionistic directors who are not satisfied unless their ideas are the most visible element of the production. On the other hand, a first-rate actor will be readily discernible in a production which is otherwise undistinguished, and it is not his fault if he seems to be operating independently.

The unfailing sign of an exceptional company is a chorus whose members are acting just as thoroughly as the leading singers. By acting is meant not the employment of distracting business poorly timed

nor efforts to compete with the leading singers, but feeling and thinking with the situation and seeming to belong to the surroundings.

In recent years musical comedy choruses have been more skilled
in dancing than in singing, and apart from the dancer's predisposition
to an "at ease" attitude when not actually dancing, his lapses are generally less offensive than the singer's, who sometimes neither moves
nor stands convincingly.

Stylized productions of such works as the Gilbert and Sullivan
comic operas present the chorus dressed identically or almost identically for the purpose of pointing up the work's inherent satire of
chorus behavior. Since they are so obediently responsive, with apparently only a single mind for twenty-four bodies, they are treated
as a single unit, sometimes wittily, sometimes mechanically. The contrasting approach which treats members of the chorus as individuals,
dressed differently except when in uniform demanded by the text,
has become a recent vogue even in Gilbert and Sullivan. When
wittily done, the unanimity can be even more sharply delineated in
this way. For any works attempting the illusion of realism, differen-
tiation is essential but with control. Only chaos can result from
everyone doing his original best with no objective and controlling
point of view, and a chorus can only be dramatically effective with
skilled and patient directing and a great deal of time spent in rehearsal.

Felsenstein's company at the Komische Oper in East Berlin affords
the time for this, and the dedicated workers really act in a controlled
and organized way, with astonishingly persuasive results. Many
opera choruses in Italy might as well be singing in an oratorio. Considering that their job is only to sing the choruses lustily or gently
to the conductor's beat, they line up and sing. A certain impatience
is evoked if an eager stage director wishes them to behave otherwise.
Some even adopt their positions of seniority on stage, regardless of
the opera in which they are appearing or the characters they are portraying. Between these extremes are a number of variations, the most
offensive being the apparently undirected chorus with several members adopting the oratorio approach while the conscientious ones are
busily overacting. Each group is calling the most unflattering attention to the other.

A chorus seldom has an adequate amount of stage rehearsal time. If its members are regarded as an inferior branch of the profession and merely told to move back when the *corps de ballet* rushes in, it is not surprising that they are dispirited and disinclined to offer more than the token behavior expected of them. Placed on the dignified level of important members of the company and in the hands of an energetic and imaginative director, the chorus can be as memorable as any of the soloists. The consistently good work of choruses under the direction of Walter Felsenstein, Günther Rennert, Friedrich Petzold, Karlheinz Haberland, Kurt Pscherer, Jean Gascon, and others is especially heartening when one considers the difficulties—especially, for all except Felsenstein, the lack of time.

One chorus, in a major opera house production of *Fidelio*, acted in spurts, the stage director clearly having had no opportunity to enliven more than a few key moments. After each spurt the members returned to their oratorio positions, faced front, and sang. One woman, in the scene of the freeing of the prisoners, found her husband, embraced him warmly, and then lost him in the crowd. Nothing daunted, she picked the man whom she happened to find standing next to her and accepted him with equal affection until, a few moments later, she lost him too. It could have been an ingenious attempt to draw attention to the main theme of conjugal fidelity by displaying an instance of brazen infidelity, but it was more likely carelessness and the desperation that comes from not having nearly enough time to reason out relationships and attitudes, and scarcely any time at all to walk through the planned movements. Rehearsals are expensive and crowds and choruses difficult enough to direct without pressure. Under pressure, it is virtually impossible. Only a well-subsidized company with a tireless stage director, a patient conductor, and a dedicated chorus is likely to break out of the routine into the rewarding territory of a real acting experience for all concerned.

The vexing problem of applause—when it is appropriate, when it is inappropriate, and in what way to handle it—is a problem equally of singers and actors, producers and audiences. There are management regulations at many institutions but these regulations are not always respected. Audiences can be trained, but audiences differ from theatre to theatre and from country to country. Since, however, the kind of applause which does most injury to musical and dramatic continuity is the kind condoned and even encouraged by many singers, an immediate consideration of the problem is pertinent.

The most sensible and the least invidious curtain call is the company call at the end of a production. It provides an opportunity for the audience to show its appreciation of the company's work and its pleasure at their success, or, in some instance, its gratification at their avoidance of total disaster. Since there is usually someone who deserves applause, it is unusual for a performance to be received, at its close, by absolute silence (although in Cologne, in 1968, a production of Donizetti's *L'Elisir d'amore* received almost no applause at all). A tradition of no applause has been established in the case of *Parsifal*, and there are concerts of sacred music after which one is not quite sure whether the applause is going to be welcome or greeted by impatient gestures from a shocked conductor. In most theatres, however, the applause is more than welcome.

Tradition in opera, operetta, and musical comedy has decreed a hierarchy and a pattern of behavior in which solo curtain calls and curtain calls with conductors, and even on some occasions stage directors, designers, and choreographers, are arranged in order. Some are deftly managed with swiftly moving curtains and a care not to "milk" the applause too obviously. Some are slow, awkward, and heavy-footed and soon become tedious to the fast-disappearing audience. Solo calls are invidious, but singers are pleased to see and hear themselves marked as favorites and the exhibition of poor sportsmanship is rare. There have been historic occasions upon which a new young singer suddenly became the audience darling, to the astonishment and disappointment of an established favorite, but most singers are fully aware that they are in a highly competitive profession, and for the duration of the curtain calls at least, gracious smiles are the rule. Most singers behave with admirable dignity during these curtain calls; some of the most dignified are the ones who earlier in the evening have done their best to disrupt the performance.

Some operas and most operettas and musical comedies are written with applause after specific numbers in mind. The composer has thoughtfully inserted a *fermata* if what follows is more music, and if what follows is spoken dialogue or dry recitative there is a natural break in the texture. With that, if the audience wishes to applaud no great harm is done unless it goes on too long, in which case the rhythm of the piece is injured and the actors speaking the following dialogue are hard put to draw the audience back into the dramatic action. A long evening in the theatre, with everyone anxious to leave, can often be attributed to too many pauses for applause, and therefore too many separate scenes and too little surge and build. This damage, however, is slight compared with the damage inflicted upon through-composed or continuous music. In such work the applause covers the orchestral music which follows, sometimes ruining a beautiful effect meant to be heard. If the composer had realized that there might be applause at this point he would have written it differently and saved his effect for later.

Applause on Desdemona's Ave Maria in *Otello* can extend into and across the sinister E natural which signals Otello's entrance, an intentionally shattering effect. Applause on Ford's monologue in *Falstaff* can drown out completely the delicate texture of sound which accompanies the appearance of Falstaff dressed for his amorous visit, and the charming postlude to Zerlina's second aria in *Don Giovanni* is sometimes not heard at all. The baritone's high A flat near the end of the *Pagliacci* prologue, if applauded, takes all the dramatic value out of the one remaining word, *Incominciate*. Needless to say, the A flat is not in the score. The intended climax is on the word *Incominciate*. This, as originally written, sounds anticlimactic after the high note. Baritones, realizing this, have for years interpolated another high note, this time a high G on the penultimate syllable. Few baritones would now dare to sing Leoncavallo's original modest line, for fear the audience might think their voices lacked these notes.

In many instances the singer is less to blame than the audience. The behavior of the public bears a relationship to the behavior of singers, and if applause is too readily given it becomes increasingly difficult to control. Some singers, however, are very much to blame, and the tricks are obvious enough, the sudden pacing to the front, the arms extended, even on some desperate occasions the fingers fluttering, the vocal increase of pressure or the dragged-out high note, often a note not written in the score.

Anything resembling continuity of character is destroyed when there is acknowledgment to the audience in the middle of a dramatic sequence. Although musical theatre does not attempt the illusion of realistic drama, there is a musical and dramatic continuum which can readily be broken if only one of the participants withdraws from the character he is portraying, to become the grateful and gracious concert singer.

Many singers, respecting the house rules or at the conductor's request, do their best to reduce the audience interruption and proceed, an almost sure method of cutting off the applause and saving the work which is being performed. There is little consistency, however, and the inconsistency is more distracting than wholesale license.

An operetta production in which all the performers are eagerly looking forward to the moments of acknowledgment may lose what little dramatic continuity and character consistency it may have possessed, but it acquires, instead, a naive but not displeasing quality of a series of parades, and we are invited to adapt our interests accordingly.

A Handelian *opera seria*, with its neat arrangements of exit arias, includes the applause as a part of its structure, and one would have to be very pedantic to insist upon a respectful silence for fear of interrupting the dramatic or musical continuity. There is scarcely a hint of continuity. Each little parade ends with a climax of its own, and the whole piece is a linear display of one jewel after another, each intended to delight us in a different way.

Some astute directors have treated these acknowledgments in a picturesque way, almost ridiculing the tradition while maintaining it. For example, a series of elaborate approaches toward the audience has been used, with all the Baroque flourishes imaginable in an *opera seria*, or a device in harmony with the theme of an operetta, such as salutes in character for half a dozen different characters in *The Grand Duchess of Gerolstein*.

An arrangement or an agreement of some kind is usually satisfactory, especially if handled with taste. What is not at all satisfactory is a combination of vagueness and personal vanity. After a rousing duet between tenor and baritone followed by exits on opposite sides of the stage, it is not effective to see the tenor bound back to acknowledge the audience applause while the baritone remains in the wings. To see one member of a cast slyly or openly inclining his head and smiling while the others ignore the applause by holding their positions, remaining in character, and then moving abruptly to continue the action is to be reminded unpleasantly of the weakness and vanity of the human species, the tensions and jealousies of a competitive profession, and a host of considerations having no connection with the work being performed.

Only a total traitor to the art form in which he is appearing will acknowledge the applause on his first entrance, but it has been done, with character establishment wrecked from the start and an entire passage of meaningful orchestral music rendered inaudible. The audience is often willing to ruin ten bars in order to demonstrate its attachment to a particular singer. The singer, with a little cunning and great lack of wisdom, can easily extend the ruination to thirty bars if he chooses.

While understanding the singer's need for encouragement and appreciation and the audience's pleasure in responding with enthusiasm, it might be asked how frequently and damagingly to the music and the drama one must respond. At the close of the first act of *Die Walküre* at the Salzburg Easter Festival under Herbert von Karajan, the applause for all concerned, including Gundula Janowitz, Jon Vickers, and Martti Talvela, was tremendously exhilarating, and the three singers did not seem displeased by the demonstration. One felt, indeed, that the torrential sound owed a part of its abundance to the attentive silence which had gripped the audience from the first notes to the last of an act slightly over an hour in duration.

Thomas Betterton, one of the greatest of English actors, declared, according to Colley Cibber, that he never thought any kind of applause was equal to an attentive silence, "that there were many ways of deceiving an audience into a loud one; but to keep them hushed and quiet was an applause which only truth and merit could arrive at."*

When a baritone Ford elicits no applause after a splendid rendition of his monologue and a soprano Cio Cio San after a moving "Un bel dì vedremo" is permitted to continue uninterrupted, one feels the spirit of Betterton applauding, but silently, the audience, the conductor, the stage director, and most of all the singer.

* *An Apology for the Life of Mr. Colley Cibber, Comedian*, London, 1740, p. 92.

4

Staging

Staging, Good and Poor

Staging in opera is designed to add visual meaning to the already meaningful words and music of a work of lyric drama. The intention is usually to harmonize what one sees with what one hears, so that there is no feeling of distraction or perplexity. The scenery, if there is any, and there usually is, may be mainly decorative, or it may quite literally depict the specific locality in which the action takes place. The setting, which includes the space as well as the scenery about or above or beneath that space, surrounds the participants as a group, and it is now possible to control our awareness of it with the most subtle devices of modern stage lighting. At one time we may be made strongly aware of one part of the visual surroundings. At another we may be only partly aware of it. Much of the scenery we think we are seeing we are merely recollecting.

The costumes which surround the participants on stage individually are also intended to harmonize in totality, and to be decorative or appropriate or both. Harmony in totality implies the inclusion of dissonance when dissonance is appropriate, so that in the most pleasing stage pictures we may expect to see clash as well as serenity, imbalance in groupings in order to give meaning to the balance to come, just as we take pleasure in aural dissonance and prefer it to the dreary blandness of a Victorian hymn.

Since stage lighting usually attempts to light the actor most of the time, we are inclined to look at the costume for longer than we look at the scenic surroundings. The actor's movement attracts attention in a way that scenery employs only seldom, and the close proximity of a part of the costume to the actor's face makes it difficult to fade it out. The actor's movements also display the costume, and even individual parts of the costume, in a way that scenery is not displayed. Scenery is immobile for long stretches of time and sometimes altogether so. Furthermore it can be dimmed by removing the light. Costumes accompanying the lighted actor may change their "expressions" more frequently than some actors. Costumes, too, are sometimes more logically changed than scenery; if not more logically, then more simply.

The purpose of performing is to bring to life the work which its creators, dramatist and composer, imagined. Instead of a list of names, a simple series of words, and a more complex series of notes, we are given real people to assume the characters, real people wearing real costumes and moving about in the space provided, singing and sometimes speaking words, and generally entering into the spirit of the work for the purpose of projecting it clearly in the manner in which the creators intended.

Good staging clarifies meanings and projects emotions without interruption or distortion. Poor staging neglects the work of the dramatist and the composer, and permits interruptions or distractions or both, destroying the work instead of supporting it.

Good staging is the result of fidelity to the drama and the music, coupled with imagination and secured by the authority to demand and obtain the cooperation of technicians and performers. Poor staging results from misunderstanding or ignorance, laziness, lack of imagination, and inability to inspire the participants, or it may result from a deliberate but pitiful ambition to draw attention to one or more aspects of the production, while distorting the total concept.

Designers for the stage are concerned with the surface upon which the performer treads, the depth against which he is visible, and the space above, where there is usually no motion. They may work in cooperation with the stage director or they may work independently, but the first method produces the better results. Since cooperation is a two-way procedure, it is possible for a designer to provide the director with a setting of which that director makes too little use, and conversely, a designer may hamper the director's

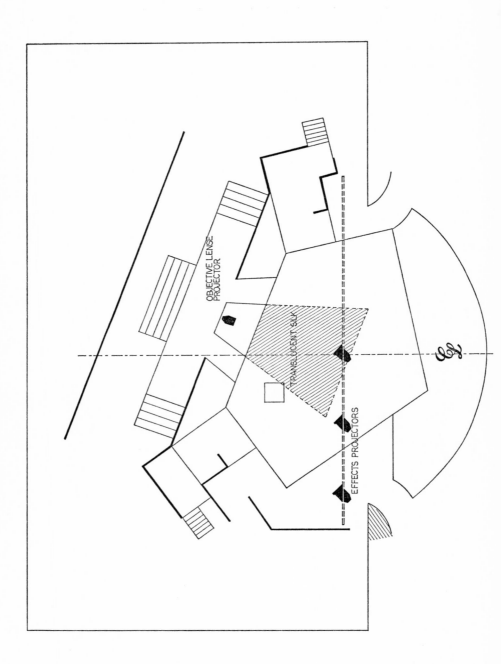

FIGURE 3   Ground plan for stage design for Verdi's *Macbeth*, by John
Ezell. A scrim or gauze is frequently used, especially in works of the
romantic period. Lighted only from the front it will give the appearance
of solidity. The addition of light at the rear produces a misty,
transparent effect. As light from the front is reduced to nothing
the scrim seems to vanish.
Images may be projected on a scrim from the rear as well as from the
front. In the apparition scene in *Macbeth*, the images of the three
spirits were thrown, one after the other, from a projector placed
on the floor behind the scrim.
From the first pipe, above the stage, hung three separate projectors
with revolving film of moving smoke. Since the rotation of each
was set at a different speed, the pattern of the smoke was irregular
and therefore looked more natural. (See also Plates 1 and 2).

achievement of attractive composition and make it difficult for the
actors to move with grace and comfort. Discussion during the planning period, long before casting, is obviously mandatory. The two
must agree on the aims and the style of the production, and they
must understand each other's problems.

The designer's task is to vitalize the space in which the performers are to operate, the methods he adopts varying as the works
themselves vary. A work demanding a large flat space for dancers
will curb his understandable desire to break up the even surface of
the stage floor with steps or ramps. But just as he can vary the flat
surface with levels and provide the director with opportunities for
interesting composition, so can he vary the depth with flat surfaces
and three-dimensional objects. By using scrim he can actually vary
the depth from moment to moment, and with the use of projected
images make effective use of the space above, even to the extent of
having movement in that part of the stage not usually associated
with it. (See Figure 3 and Plates 1 and 2.)

A thoughtful designer, aware of the stage director's and the
musical director's concern for continuous performance, will provide
the necessary changes of scene with the minimum of fuss and without ruinous pauses punctuated by thumping, hammering, and audible
cursing. When it is appropriate to the work being performed, a
revolving stage will satisfy the director and the performers, at the

same time giving the designer the visual variety of which a single, motionless setting robs him.

Audience members with no stage experience find it difficult to distinguish the work of the stage director from that of the individual actors and singers. In a well-directed production, if the actors have any ability at all they have brought thought and hard work to the creation of their roles, and good actors are largely responsible for the individual effect they achieve. The total effect, however, is the director's responsibility. He controls the totality and makes unified what would otherwise be chaotic. Movement must be planned, distances adjusted, and relationships established. This is the director's job, this and a great deal more. Ideally, he and the actors agree upon a total interpretation and exert every effort to achieve it. The wise director does not impose interpretations upon puppet actors. He may have imposed an overall point of view or style of production, but within this framework he uses thinking actors, encourages individual enterprise, and shapes the results into an entity. He has the advantage over the actors of seeing the production as a whole, from the outside.

The director's work is made difficult by talented but wilful actors who wish to be noticed as performers rather than to contribute to the perfecting of the whole, respectful of the work being performed. In such circumstances, firmness and tact in the director are absolute requirements.

The director's work is made even more difficult by actors of negligible ability. In a spoken play or a musical comedy, professionally produced, this is a less likely problem than in opera, where vocal ability is indispensable, and where much of the director's time can be wasted on elementary matters.

A stage director of opera frequently has to deal with singers of considerable vocal ability who move poorly, and who find it difficult to execute comparatively simple motions in character or with an easy grace. Patient directors, given time and a willing pupil, can arrange the movement, placing, and business to favor whatever physical advantages the singer may possess, and to conceal the disadvantages.

Shortening a stage cross may involve other characters or lead to blocking difficulties later, but altering such a single requirement can remove tension, increase the singer's confidence, and do away with the awkwardness of an entire scene. It is possible to find a singer who has acted capably under congenial direction and with cooperative associates acting clumsily in a production under a different stage director and with different colleagues.

In a *stagione* production of the worst sort, each singer comes on stage and performs his or her role independently, and there seems to be no stage direction at all beyond the most primitive control of traffic. Stage directors, in fact, are often given only enough time for this. In a *stagione* production of the better sort, however, with gifted and experienced artists in the major roles, an extraordinarily electric and persuasive performance may take place. *Tosca* is especially receptive to this treatment, possibly because of its three-way competition. No soprano, tenor, or baritone of standing can afford to be the tamest third of a tame *Tosca*.

The examples that follow, drawn from specific productions, will illustrate more specifically the complexity of the problem and the delicacy of the director-actor-singer relationship.

A stage director is most needed for a work requiring dramatic discrimination. The transitional *opera buffa* works of Donizetti are especially delicate and all too frequently spoiled, often by the same competitive enthusiasm which may save a performance of *Tosca*.

L'Elisir d'Amore is more than a simple story of a young Italian, Nemorino, who buys ordinary red wine at a high price from a travelling quack, believing it to be a love potion, but at the close, winning his Adina just the same.

Doctor Dulcamara, the quack, is a lovable rascal who has probably been overplayed far oftener than played intelligently. The repulsive old picture of Luigi Lablache clowning it with Henriette Sontag implies that this overplaying is not a product of recent generations. The words and music call for nothing of the sort. Indeed, the graciousness of some of Dulcamara's music bespeaks a persuasiveness of the greatest dramatic importance; otherwise one would have to conclude that the entire village is composed of idiots. Italian villagers are mostly a shrewd lot, and it requires someone even shrewder to outwit or impose upon them.

Similarly, Nemorino's drinking of chianti, supposing it to be a magic potion, releases his inhibitions to some degree but it does not make him tipsy. Caruso, and others after him, have clowned the drinking scene so that it stands out from the opera, and fashionable audiences have laughed at celebrated tenors simulating inebriation. This has nothing to do with the story or the character. It must be pointed out, too, that the girls meet Nemorino more than halfway because they have just discovered that he is, although he does not yet know it, a rich young man.

Nemorino is a good-looking young peasant having difficulties with a spirited girl who seems far out of his reach because she can read. The fact that Nemorino, in the Italian countryside at this period, cannot read does not mean that he is a dolt. His simple faith in a potion can be matched by the simple faith of vast numbers of twentieth-century Americans in the potions of the drugstore. An oafish Nemorino makes a hash of a good story. He cannot read. Adina can. Drawn as she clearly is toward the handsome illiterate she very sensibly, as a better-educated woman and a landowner, tries to overcome the attraction. Most of us are realistic enough to appreciate the position from which her apparent heartlessness derives, and yet most of us are romantic enough to be touched and delighted when "the furtive tear" gives her away.

The fact that the subject matter of Adina's reading at the opening of the opera is the story of Tristan and Isolde (a pre-Wagnerian version) only serves to add to Nemorino's respect for education and love potions. It is significant, too, that Sergeant Belcore can also read (his first remark is a classical allusion) and is therefore in Adina's eyes, if only temporarily, a more suitable match than Nemorino. True love triumphs, and after the curtain falls, for all we know, Adina settles down to teaching Nemorino to read. It should be noted that the placing of the lovely and justly famous aria "Una furtiva lagrima" is most skilful, coming like a refreshing shower after an afternoon of heat.

Mozart's *The Seraglio* packs into its small compass the most prodigious difficulties for a stage director, not to mention appalling vocal difficulties. Many productions laboriously filling in the sixty bars of orchestral introduction to the heroine Constanze's aria "Martern aller Arten" ("Torture me and flay me") instead of deleting them and letting her begin at once, still treat the opera as a series of show pieces (which it admittedly is) allowing Osmin, the bass, the steward of the Pasha's house, to indulge himself as a clown and treating the only speaking character, the Pasha, as a disagreeable necessity between vocal numbers, but without taking him seriously as a character.

A 1968 Wuppertal production of *The Seraglio*, without flinching from any of the comedy, gave added depth to a total concept by harshening Osmin out of his *buffo* extravagances, and even going so far as to have him, under the influence of unaccustomed liquor, overaffectionate with Pedrillo, the second tenor, his rival in love. This placed his revenge aria in the last act in an entirely more convincing light.

Balancing this, the Pasha was for the major part of the work implacable, yet sympathetic. Accustomed to authority, his tyrannical position justified historically and geographically, he seemed trapped by his country's traditions, and for once both his cruelty and the fact that he refrains from rape were convincing. Indeed, in this production rape quite clearly occurred to him, since he was shown once almost at the point of committing it.

Supporting this ambivalence and lending credibility to the final sudden act of magnanimity (he gives the woman he wants to her young lover, who has just been revealed as the son of his lifelong enemy) was a production device of the greatest significance, adding a comic and wry touch to the concept of this extravagant "noble savage" opera. A circular harem stood upon the stage. Welcoming the Pasha's first appearance, a row of little shutters opened and wan faces stared out of their prison to sing. Then the windows were closed. Throughout the bungling attempts on the part of the lovers to escape, we did not see these caged faces, but we remembered them. At the end of the opera, when the Pasha sent the westerners back to freedom and happiness, the harem opened to reveal ten impassive women, prisoners in actuality and victims of the country's traditions. The Pasha stood alone, equally trapped. He was not a tragic figure, but he was a curiously moving one.

This is not the only way to stage *The Seraglio* and it may be thought a rather extreme one, but Imo Moszkowicz, the director, instead of accepting clichés from the ragbag of former productions, had chosen a point of view, and this point of view he projected with clarity and consistency throughout the production. He also avoided the temptation to make his production like nothing ever seen before anywhere (a German tendency). He had the good fortune to be working with capable singers who were intelligent actors, and they had the good fortune to be working with him. The result was memorable.

Good staging may be seen in a wide variety of productions, from the humblest repertory (if a good director is in charge) to the expensive festival, and even, though rarely, in a *stagione* performance. Poor staging may also be seen in all three, and poor staging in a really inadequate provincial repertory company is seldom offset by good singing or good scenery. Only enthusiasm and the strongest personalities can in some measure save such a performance.

The most frustrating experience of all is to attend a festival or *stagione* production with first-rate voices, excellent scenery, and well-designed costumes side by side with no evidence whatever of a controlling, unifying hand, musical or dramatic, and no attempt on the part of the participants to unite their efforts for the sake of the work they are performing.

For those audience members interested exclusively in the superb voices of "star" singers, why trouble these performers with the necessity of moving, why discommode them with heavy costumes, and why distract audience attention with a scenic background? Why not, instead, present a concert? Concerts are an admirable institution.

Interruptions

Interruptions, unless they are a part of the play's conception, can destroy the dramatic and musical structure of a work. A Baroque *opera seria*, since it is constructed specifically for the display of bravura numbers, is not in the least marred by the interruptions for applause. The interruptions are as welcome as in the concert hall, and we readily accept the convention of beginning another sequence with dry recitative, which in turn will lead to a rewarding number for singer and audience. Operetta and musical comedy follow a similar pattern, and each number is followed by dialogue which drops the emotional temperature and which in turn leads to yet another number.

Where there is no dramatic or musical continuity such interruptions are inoffensive, even when accompanied by concert-hall acknowledgment of applause. There is virtually no drama to ruin.

It is when such interruptions intrude in through-composed works that offensiveness begins. When genuine dramatic or musical material follows the interruption, an adjustment has to be made, emotions sound false, and the actual time lapse of the interruption slackens the tempo and is rhythmically disturbing. Tosca's "See my hands outstretched before you" at the end of the applause often following "Vissi d'arte, vissi d'amore" strikes a note of mockery, and destroys the effectiveness of Spoletta's entrance with the news of Angelotti's suicide. Without the applause, the scene retains its dramatic drive. Some are of the opinion that without the aria it would retain still more. Perhaps it could be sung in the theatre restaurant during the intermission.

A notorious miscalculation occurs in *La Traviata* after the elder Germont has sung his famous aria "Di Provenza il mar il suol." In the original text, the second stanza is followed by a short passage in recitative dialogue, seven phrases, and by Germont's cabaletta reiteration of his plea for his son to give up his mistress and return to Provence. Alfredo, however, seeing the open letter inviting Violetta to a dance at Flora's home in Paris, starts up and in a single brief line informs us of his intention to follow her. Germont's response is even briefer, and the curtain falls for a change of scene.

In modern productions Germont's reiteration, less likely to receive applause than the two stanzas of the aria, is invariably cut, together with the preceding recitative, with the result that there is a storm of applause for Germont's aria followed belatedly by two unconvincing lines and almost immediately by the applause invited by the falling curtain.

More damage is done by interruptions for scene changes. Pauses in concerts and pauses between the movements of a symphony or a concerto are rhythmically related, though loosely, to the structure of the performance. We are consciously disturbed if these pauses are too brief or too long. In a dramatic performance such waits are not merely annoying but destructive.

A *Don Giovanni* in Berlin (the East Berlin Deutsche Staatsoper) began poorly by allowing latecomers to enter after the overture. Although it is an overture rather than a prelude, and ends with a *fermata,* the D minor–D major tonality slides into a final C major triad on its way to the key of F, for the opening solo of Leporello, Don Giovanni's servant. In this particular production the curtain puller had been prepared to raise the curtain immediately upon the assumption of the key of F. It must obviously not be raised on the final bars of the overture and it takes a few moments for an opening curtain to render a large stage space entirely visible. There are ten preparatory bars before Leporello begins to sing. Even at *molto allegro* there is plenty of time so that the curtain has ceased to move when Leporello sings his first words. The conductor's decision to pause for latecomers surprised the curtain puller, and when the conductor started the ten orchestral bars the curtain puller responded too late. The conductor, realizing that the curtain would now not be completely drawn for Leporello's first line, stopped the orchestra, repeated a phrase, and the opera began, but so lamely that the exciting trio which follows very shortly lost a great deal of its effect.

If this had been the only interruption the opera might have recovered, but heavy and literal scenery was used. Since Act 1 contains six scenes and Act 2 five, pauses for the scene changes were necessary. All musical and dramatic continuity was lost. The waits between scenes were long, and in order to relieve the audience's uneasiness at waiting in the dark the house lights were partly raised, making the nine waits seem even longer. The intermission, because it was planned by dramatist and composer, did not destroy continuity.

A firm hand could have prevented the stage designer from breaking *Don Giovanni* into disconnected pieces, especially since many of the scenic devices were out of proportion to their necessity and the time taken to place them. A huge portico appeared only once, and served to hide Masetto for thirty seconds. The enormity of the equestrian statue in the churchyard made the Don's "Isn't that the statue of the Commendatore?" sound ludicrous, and in the final scene it was impossible to have the statue enter on foot, attached as he was to his horse. The statue, therefore, appeared for this scene at the rear of the stage behind a scrim. The Don stood downstage, facing the audience, and anything resembling a handclasp between them, called for in the text and music to the accompaniment of a chilling E natural in the bass against B flat and D flat above, was impossible. When the drama and the music make demands which the production ignores, a considerable disservice is done to the work. A less pretentious production would have avoided the absurdities and the awkwardness of the long waits.

It is only fair to mention that in this disastrous production one scene, considered by itself, was excellent. The ballroom had been constructed with three circular balconies having no visible support (a Baroque conceit) to hold the three onstage orchestras asked for in the text. This was an admirable solution to a difficult stage problem, but unfortunately the three balconies took even longer to erect than the other unwieldy settings, so that the audience's admiration was tinged with exasperation.

A visual reminder that *Don Giovanni* was written for a much smaller stage was offered in this Berlin production. Several exiting characters were still visible and their walking still audible for several bars after the music had changed. Bars of music and tempo are related to visible entrances and exits, and a failure to synchronize produces an untidy effect. The Prague theatre in which *Don Giovanni* was first produced seats only 1100 now, and was smaller in 1787.

A Franco Zeffirelli production of the same work tried to solve the problem of many changes of literal scenery by having characters move forward on stage to continue the action and the music while the act drop descended behind them and the technical crews shifted the scenery as quietly as possible. Whatever illusion each scene succeeded in giving was spoiled by the awkward device of the descending drop.

Something of the sort was practised in a Metropolitan tour production at the Chicago Opera House during the 1940s, but only against the tenor. Don Ottavio, admittedly, has only a shred of character but his two arias are beautiful, and in this production it was disconcerting to have them both sung in front of a black curtain which was billowed throughout by currents of air while behind it the stage hands changed the scenery, their feet frequently visible against the strains of "Dalla sua pace" and "Il mio tesoro."

Musical comedy practice has for many years been so professional in its approach to scenic changes that the amateurish awkwardness to be seen in some the world's great opera houses is something of a shock. Many a missionary in the cause of opera has taken a friend to *Faust,* to be informed quite accurately that they manage matters far better in *Gypsy.*

Dance and Divertissement

Dance is the very life blood of American musical comedy. To opera it is more often the death blow. When in the second half of the nineteenth century the homegrown musical struggled against the European operetta, only to be defeated by it time and time again, the American characteristics of the vernacular, of country dance, of tap dance and soft-shoe routines, of broad native comedy and somewhat cruder spectacle were establishing themselves. In the twentieth century they came forward with confidence, seizing their big chance during the 1914–1918 war, with its cutting off of European models and with its isolationist forces and hysterically patriotic sentiments.

In its separation from opera, the American musical lost much of musical value but gained greatly in the freedom it won from the traditions of ballet. By the time such choreographers as Martha Graham, Agnes de Mille, José Limon, Doris Humphrey, Charles Weidman, Hanya Holm, Jerome Robbins, and Gower Champion had taken over in the twentieth century, American dancers were able to apply a new discipline to natural movement. An American musical generally has four or five major dance sequences in its two acts, and a dozen or fifteen songs. Since the songs are often much shorter than the dance sequences, the proportion in time is something like 40 percent of dance to 60 percent of song. Reprises add to the time taken by sung music, but short dances following songs add an equivalent amout of time to the danced music. The refreshing vigor of American dance has crossed the Atlantic, to the profit of the British musical. Many American musicals, recollected two decades later, place the dances uppermost in the recollection, and it is likely that the British *Half a Sixpence* will be more warmly remembered for its movement than for its tunes.

In most of the good American musicals dancing is almost synonymous with expression. Even in musicals in which the dances are awkwardly introduced, they take over triumphantly once the participants are in motion. With the increasing sensitivity to integration seeming to culminate in *West Side Story*, even the motivation for dancing was improved to satisfy those who felt the need of it in an otherwise nonrealistic form.

In its history opera has been plagued, almost since its inception, with the ballet *divertissement* or *divertimento*. Used with skill by some of the seventeenth- and eighteenth-century French composers, in particular, it nevertheless was too often an expected insertion rather than a logical part of the whole entertainment. When a ballet is inserted because it is expected rather than because it performs a dramatic function, the insertion will become either matter of fact and pointless, or will be managed with such self-conscious ingenuity that unnecessary attention is called to it. Since the company of dancers is usually quite distinct from the company of singers, something resembling technical equality is needed to maintain balance in the production. If this is not achieved, the audience finds the interruption of the singing by an inferior group of dancers an unwelcome intrusion, or if the ballet is excellent, becomes dissatisfied with the singers from that point on.

Even the position of the ballet in opera has to some extent been fixed, whether it is dramatically justified or not. The sensation caused by Wagner in Paris at the *Tannhäuser* opening is well known. The Jockey Club members arriving fashionably late and expecting the ballet to divert them were outraged to discover that Wagner had placed the ballet where it made the only sense in his opera—at the very beginning.

When the ballet is frankly a *divertimento,* and as good as but no better than the remainder of the production, including the singing, it can serve the double purpose of giving pleasure and of resting the other participants. John Cranko's brilliant entertainment, logically placed in *The Grand Duchess of Gerolstein* (a Stuttgart 1968 production), entertained the audience immensely while seeming to entertain the Duchess (Anny Schlemm), in whose honor it had been staged. This, however, is rare. Many German theatre groups, with a subsidized ballet attached to the company, will interrupt an opera once or twice, and an operetta four or five times, with ballet sequences which are wholly unconnected with the work being performed. They are costumed inappropriately and generally performed to the audience in the theatre with no regard for context, not even the customary trumped-up entertainment situation involving the principals and the chorus. Just as singing must be directed to the audience even though the illusion is given of making personal contact in a variety of directions, so dancing should include the situation in which it is placed instead of ignoring it.

The dances in *Aida* are essential, but they can be blended with the total production in a way which makes them a part of the whole rather than an interpolation. The dancers in the opera, however, are cast as professionals; their dances on this festive occasion must of necessity be expert, with moments of exciting bravura, all perfectly justified.

The same approach in Act 3 of *La Traviata,* when guests at Flora's mansion in Paris enter pretending to be gypsies, matadors and picadors, is not at all appropriate. They are amateurs and it makes far more sense if they look like amateurs. Since they are lively sophisticates accustomed to masquerade parties, they will naturally be accomplished amateurs. To seize upon this scene as a pretext for ballet display is to run counter to the style and spirit of Verdi's opera.

Worse yet is done when in *Otello,* during the scene in which flowers are presented to Desdemona, the static nature of the scene is enlivened by the performance of a short ballet before Desdemona or the theatre audience. While this could be justified on the grounds that the Cypriots might have welcomed the lady in this way, the text does not ask for it, but for a scene of simple directness in which the sailors offer necklaces and the women scatter flowers. The natural grace of the islanders, combined with a little shyness and pardonable curiosity, can contribute to the charm of this scene and avoid the arch exaggeration which dance so frequently brings to a moment of this sort. This scene in *Otello* has been much debated. Some critics regard it as a blemish, adding that it is a frankly operatic interpolation, with inferior music, and having no parallel in the Shakespeare play. Others defend it as a relief to the tension, as a device to separate two extended scenes betwen Otello and Iago, and as leading to a valuable moment of poise in which Otello confesses that the song has conquered him, and Iago, observing Otello wishfully thinking Desdemona innocent, redoubles his efforts to spur him to jealous rage. The scene can be effective only if a stage director emphasizes its sweetness and innocence, or better still allows these qualities, so clear in the music, to come across untouched. Fussing the delicate scene destroys its effect, and an exhibition of any sort at this point destroys not only it but a major sequence in the opera.

Skilled dancers are as essential to a production of Handel's *Alcina*, Gluck's *Orfeo*, or Borodin's *Prince Igor* as they are to *Brigadoon*. In the matter of proportion and appropriateness, every management and stage director is in the position of having to decide on the basis of taste, paying the proper respect to the style of the production and to the dramatic and musical continuity.

Singers in Costume

Musical comedies, operettas, and some operas invite colorful costuming. In the forms in which voices are of less account than personality and appearance, a designer can readily achieve the chic and bold effects expected. When vocal splendor is paramount, the costumer too often has a considerable amount of visual flattery to arrange, in spite of the fact that since the 1930s and 1940s operatic figures have made some anguished movement toward improvement. There are still ample sopranos and turtle-shaped tenors who somehow have to be draped and squeezed and lined into something resembling the romantic characters they are portraying.

One's sympathy is on the side of the costumer when the stirring voice pours from a larynx lodged in a body which refuses to do credit to any costume. On the other hand, one's sympathies are with the singer when a fifty-pound costume is presented to a lady who can barely carry her own weight. Insult is added to injury when the costume, in addition, is tight about the neck, constricting about the diaphragm, and overlong about the feet. Some costumes seem to have been designed by someone who has never walked upon a stage, much less embraced a fellow player while taking a musical cue from a conductor.

A Palermo production of Bellini's *Puritani,* in recent years, was sumptuously set and costumed by Franco Zeffirelli and Peter Hall respectively, but beauty came first and practicality a distant second. An effective looking flight of steps was made so steep (in order to get it on stage at all) that the tenor tripped and leaped to safety in one scene, and the baritone fell down them in the final scene, only to rise, somewhat injured but helped by his colleagues to limp to stage centre and make his musical entrance on cue.

The chorus ladies, looking superb in clusters of gold, orange, and two shades of green, spoiled the effect by tripping over their hemlines or standing on the trains of others. The resulting angry jerks and graceless stumbles distracted from the tenuous proceedings of *Puritani,* already handicapped by being one of the least dramatically compelling operas.

The costume department, taking its orders from the designer, was mainly responsible, but it must be remembered that an aroused Italian chorus (and Italian choruses are easily aroused when anything in the least progressive is afoot) is quite capable of communicating more sense of difficulty and discomfort than is really necessary. Before attaching the blame anywhere, facts about costume fittings and adequate dress rehearsals would have to be unearthed. The disastrous proceedings on stage were doubtless a fusion of ambition, inefficiency, vanity, hysteria, resentment, and malice, a combination not uncommon in the theatre.

Not all singers are uncooperative and not all costumers are

wilful. Some singers welcome what other singers would call dia-
phragmatic constriction, claiming that it gives them added support.
Some costumers are eager to find out what is required of the singer
in the costume before the costume is even designed. Other costumers
make no inquiries. Some singers will contrive to trip on a knee-
length skirt in order to blame the costumer. Other singers come to
costume fittings to time, stand patiently, and wear the finished costume without complaint and even with grace. Singers may want to
wear costumes in rehearsal before the costumer wants them to be
dragged around a stage, but there are costume protectors and sub-
stitutes, and if each side is reasonable, a compromise can be reached.

Elaborateness and Simplification

It is not always easy to distinguish between the stage director's plan
of production and the designer's original contributions to its execution. Ideally, each inspires the other to the point where a final
decision must be made. A director will often derive his best ideas
from a designer's inventiveness, and a good designer will seek to
help a director express his ideas in visual form, instead of hindering
him with suggestions that may be good for another sort of production but not for the one being prepared. Elaborateness for purely
decorative purposes is usually a hindrance to a production. Elaborateness for an agreed purpose may contribute enormously to the
production's effectiveness and clarity.

In a New York City Center production of *Don Giovanni* which
toured the country, Leopold Sachse capitalized on the fact that
simplicity was mandatory by staging the opera in what was virtually a single setting, with a few necessary changes. Into this he even
managed to get Donna Anna's bed. The dramatic and musical continuity made it far more memorable than many more elaborate and
far more expensive ones.

Meaningful elaborateness is just as necessary to some works as
simplicity is to others. Simplified productions of *The Magic Flute*
and *Die Frau ohne Schatten* may give us the music and the required
action, but they are works of which spectacle is an integral part. In

tawdry budget productions we are uncomfortably reminded of Robert Edmond Jones's attack, in *The Dramatic Imagination,* upon economy masquerading as art (New York, 1941, pp. 24, 25).

Janáček's *The Sly Vixen* demands the closest attention to its scenic and costume requirements, and any attempt to simplify them reduces the effectiveness of the work. *The Tales of Hoffmann* cannot be done simply or cheaply. A gemütlich *Rathskeller,* a fantastic laboratory, a sumptuous Venice, and a ghostly parlor are absolutely necessary.

A Budapest State Opera production of the native classic by Béla Balázs and Béla Bartók, *Duke Bluebeard's Castle,* neglected to follow the directions in the text which require that the seven doors be dramatized by stage lighting (since what lies beyond the doors is of greater importance than the doors themselves). While realistic doors are a possible device in this opera, they are not necessary, and a variety of solutions can be found. The criss-crossing lights from the openings, however, and the pattern of Judith's movements to and from the doors and across and along the paths of light are an unavoidable part of the music drama. Stock stage movements are not appropriate to this remarkable work. While the music alone will carry the work in a recording or in radio, it should not be expected to do so in a stage production.

A Darmstadt production of *Così fan Tutte* used a small revolving stage. Ingeniously planned with much inventive and well-timed business, the staging required the actors to perform on one-fourth of the revolving stage and to use the doors from one section of this revolving stage to another. The stationary stage in front was used to a certain extent, but on the revolving stage the cramped quarters, the ill-fitting doors, and a wealth of muslin curtain inhibited the actors cruelly. It was a stylish, fast-moving production catching the spirit of *opera buffa,* but it lacked the freedom of movement in space with which this work can be wonderfully enriched.

The Secret Marriage, Cimarosa's *opera buffa,* can be staged in a single setting and is often presented in this way. A Hamburg production called for sixteen scenes, but the scenes were so dexterously changed by the simple method of lowering a decorative drop at the rear, while the bulk of the setting remained the same, that the joking approach to scenery seemed to become a part of Gustav Rudolf

Sellner's witty directing. From a literal point of view the unnecessary changes were excessive, but they made such merry comments on the action and on the opera that they became a necessary part of the production. The singers all acted not in competition with the scenery but complementing it. If they had not, the cleverness would have seemed fussy and mannered, and instead of delighting the audience would soon have bored them.

Rossini's *The Italian Girl in Algiers* is a lively *opera buffa* providing strong temptations to overstage and overact. A Frankfurt production of the early 1960s had the benefit of comedy acting, without overplaying, by Sylvia Stahlman and Georg Stern, but the tenor buffo overbalanced the role of Taddeo by clowning it, and the designer clowned the scenery with rocks and walls sliding in, occupied beds making swift appearances, circular sofas entering and exiting with characters at the pivot, and an unnecessary escape by balloon for the denouement. The 1960s was the decade for balloons, whenever true imagination failed the designer or the director.

A 1968 production of the same opera at Essen interpolated a bath scene, and a camel upon which a duet was sung. Apart from these extravagances, both productions caught the breathless *brio* of Rossini and could be forgiven their respective lapses. Tastes differ in different countries, and German audiences respond so readily to the cruder forms of farce that the temptation to overplay is always present. If it does not make itself evident, one may be sure that an unusually strong director is at the helm.

In a Frankfurt production of Nicolai's *The Merry Wives of Windsor* during the early 1960s, with an opening scene in a courtyard, Mistress Ford's house on one side and Mistress Page's on the other, it was difficult to appreciate the purpose of having the two ladies seated in movable bathtubs for the letter scene, scrubbing their backs with brushes and displaying frilly legs when they moved the tubs from place to place. When Ford, Slender, and others came rolling in on a trolley car, the director's hand was more evident than any other aspect of the production.

In spite of these excesses and those of having Ann Page and Fenton use a gondola with waves attached, and Caius and Ann play pantomine tennis at a picnic, the production was spirited and the final scene brilliant. German stage directors, eager to outdo their competitors at nearby theatres, often succumb to the temptation of staging an opera in a way in which it has never before been staged. Irritating as some of these desperate productions can be, they come as a breath of fresh air after a sequence of typical *stagione* productions in which everyone sings straight front from as close to the center as he can get, and no vestige of acting ability or directing inventiveness can be discerned.

Every stage device, from the most basic to the most superficial, can be used either effectively and with taste, or clumsily and with more emphasis on the device than the purpose for which it is used. A revolving stage, unless used with discretion, flaunts its mechanical nature with depressing crudity. Some theatres seem to use it because it is there and presumably must be regularly exercised. A Munich production of *A Night in Venice* twirled gondolas, emerging from under bridges, with a regularity which rapidly lost its novelty and became tedious. For a production of *Fra Diavolo* in Hagen, an effective simple setting of the Alpine inn had been arranged upon the turntable, with the exterior on one side and the interior on the other. All that needed to be done was to turn the stage half a revolution to satisfy all the setting requirements, with no waits and with the greatest decorative charm. Once, however, as if to justify the possession of the turntable by using it beyond this functional simplicity, the soprano ascended a little hill to one side of the stage and, unaccountably, in the middle of the action, the hill and the inn together swung ninety degrees, to bring her to stage center for her aria. After the applause it returned to its former position, and it was not clear whether the applause was entirely for the soprano or was meant to be shared with the turntable.

For Janáček's *The Sly Vixen,* in Munich's Gärtnerplatztheater, the opera, plentifully supplied by the composer with atmospheric and descriptive interludes for scene changes, employed a simple revolving arrangement of ramps blended with running, dancing, and stationary humans and animals in such a way as to connect the scenes and add meaningful visual touches to the evocative music.

Thoughtful composers with a practical knowledge of the theatre have usually provided enough music for a scene change, whether hidden or *a vista,* and a conscientious producer will respect the music written for an estimated long change even if he has new devices at his disposal which could reduce the time needed. To cut the music in order to display the marvels of newly acquired machinery or the efficiency of the stage crew displays insensitivity to the aural structure of the work.

A revolving stage, or a treadmill which operates quietly, is useful in handling the journey in Wagner's *Parsifal*. The use of one or more in the first scene of *Das Rheingold* might solve problems which in most productions, so far, have not satisfactorily been solved.

The present fashion for nonliteral scenery has coped successfully with the problem of changes by avoiding them. A reliance upon light changes and projections upon scrim either at the back of the stage or at the front has simplified the labor in one department, to increase it in another. In nonrealistic work or works calling for effects which realistically treated are ridiculous, the advantage is considerable. *Die Frau ohne Schatten* is fantastic enough to incorporate a nonrealistic dyer's hut which looks realistic enough by contrast to the rest. Even its open-to-the-sky nature is accounted for by its vague location in the South Eastern Islands. The old-fashioned and derisively hailed swan in *Lohengrin* has for the most part been banished in favor of a projected swan on the rear scrim, or better still, on the downstage scrim, to fade away on cue during the greeting. Even so, there is the uncomfortable feeling that so tenuous a swan could scarcely have brought so imposing a hero along the river, and the necessary lack of contact between the real man and the unreal swan draws embarrassing attention to the convenience of the device. The swan is probably most convincing when it is not seen at all but swims invisibly among the audience. This at least motivates the choral singing out front, necessary at this point not only so that the chorus can watch the conductor but so that it can project its full body of sound. There is always something rather ridiculous about a large chorus sighting the hero at the rear or at the upstage side and then turning their backs on him to comment to the theatre audience.

An especially awkward problem for director, leading singer, and chorus is posed in the final scene of Lortzing's *Zar und Zimmermann*. The Tsar has settled everything and is about to depart by ship for Russia. The curtains at the rear of the town hall are usually parted at this point, allowing us a full view of the harbor. On a ship stands the Tsar, and from it he sings his address to those who had been his companions. They sing back to him, and the opera ends.

For vocal reasons the ship out in the harbor generally resembles an anteroom to the town hall, ill according with the cannon shots we have just heard at some distance. If the ship is placed at the far end of a deep stage, the Tsar's last words are too faint to be effective. If he is placed at the rear at all, there follows the operatic absurdity of the chorus singing to the audience words intended for the Tsar. It is foolish enough to sing with one's back to the person one is addressing even when he seems to be a fellow carpenter. When he is the Tsar it is inexcusable.

It may be that a stage director has already used the obvious device of putting the harbor and the open sea, imaginatively, behind the audience. The cannon shot can also come advantageously from the rear. Apart from not seeing the Tsar on a lighted stage in his uniform, we lose nothing by having him appear at the back of the auditorium where some at least can see him, an agreeable compensation for sitting in what are the poorest seats for the rest of the performance. His voice would be clearly heard, and the townspeople could face the Tsar and the theatre audience for their final "Heil dem Zar und seinem Haus."

Even *Lucia di Lammermoor* has shed its old brown canvas baronialism to acquire a less literal touch with the vague lustre of projections, not always to its advantage. The mocking laughter of Robert Edmond Jones makes us feel a little uneasy, as we ponder, through the harp solo, upon how much the management saved by not having to provide the customary solidity. Expedient simplicity should perhaps be as strongly mistrusted as the literal clutter of unimaginative realism, or as the old-fashioned flapping backdrops which are neither one style nor the other but a distressing mixture of convention and literalism.

Realism and Detail

Strict realism, done with skill, taste, and affection, can be most persuasive, even in a period when realism is out of fashion. Nothing is out of fashion if it is well and honestly done, aiming to match the realism in the work itself. It is even something of a relief today to see an unashamedly realistic setting after an assortment of grills, scrims, sliding wagons, and vague structures which we suspect may be phallic symbols.

Janáček's *Jenůfa*, in a 1968 production in Wuppertal, showed a curving road with a steep pine-covered slope at the side, mud tracks in the road, and a whitewashed farmhouse. The light of the setting sun caught the edges of the pines, caressed an old farm cart which, wearing its years of use smoothly and relaxedly, would have delighted Bertolt Brecht, and this light painted the farmhouse with a soft, rosy glow. There was no lowing of cattle from a tape recorder nor had the smell of the barn, stronger in the evening damp, been projected artificially into the auditorium, but the affectionate setting evoked them, silently and odorlessly. In these surroundings the young man, whittling with the knife which plays such a prominent part in the action of *Jenůfa*, looked as if he belonged there. All too often we see merely a tenor seated, going through the stage business of using the knife as a stage property.

Attention to visual detail is most helpful in a work like *La Traviata* in which the gentle passion in the music seems to grow out of the drama instead of being superimposed upon it, and a naturalness and inevitability result. On the surface *La Traviata* is as laughable for its sweet, wan preoccupation with pulmonary decline as *Il Trovatore* is for its unrelenting frenzy. One laughs at neither in the theatre unless the production is poor.

Günther Schneider-Siemssen, designing settings for *La Traviata*, caught the feverish brilliance of the first-act salon, the cool coziness of the hunting-lodge retreat where one could feel the music combining with the reddish brown to warm the surrounding winter chill, more harsh brilliance for Flora's salon, and the bleakness of the attic in which Violetta dies on New Year's Day.

Some designers have taken liberties with the first scene of the second act, which is supposed to take place in January, by placing the action in an autumnal garden, probably to reduce the four interiors to three and provide greater variety.

However effectively stage designers and costume designers are able to capture the illusion of place and time and to give us the pleasurable feeling that we are actually there, all their trouble and skill are wasted if the participants are obviously not. A realistic setting demands something resembling realistic behavior, even though we all know that we are in a theatre.

Even the necessity for singing toward the front is carefully motivated by good directors, and capable singing actors use natural-seeming movements merely by relating to other characters and making shrewd capital out of a turn or a walk, thoughtfully planning their forward direction for when they most need it.

Through-composed works verging on realism are the most difficult, since the occasional need to face front becomes noticeable and the illusion of characters interacting is lost. Through-composed works in a conventional style are easier, since direct address is likely to be a part of the prevailing style. A work which consists of a series of solo "numbers" presents minimal difficulties in this regard, since the numbers are expected to be addressed to the house in the manner of soliloquies in plays, and much astonishment would be occasioned if they were addressed anywhere else. Duets and trios can give the illusion of interrelationship without the loss of forward direction and the vocal impressiveness dependent upon it, and a little naturally motivated movement will help. Anything a stage director can do to prevent an ensemble from resembling a field of turnips, from the first note to the last, is most welcome.

5

The Stage Director's Hand

A stage director's hand must be firm but unobtrusive. He must present complicated dramatic action with clarity, he must control the adjustment of illusion and symbol, he must match the composer's music to the visual setting (with the stage designer's help), and (with the lighting designer's help) make that visual setting as visible as it needs to be at any given moment. He must organize the singers and and actors into a meaningful unit, and he must be an arbiter of taste and an observer of proportion.

He must perform all these tasks every time he stages a production, and every production rearranges the order of importance of his responsibilities.

If he is staging Bartók's *Duke Bluebeard's Castle* he must plan a stage movement pattern with two characters only and perhaps discourage an enthusiastic choreographer from adding a dancer to explain the internal action. With Britten's *Albert Herring* his cast of ten may consist of four competing comedians and six bystanders. For Poulenc's *Dialogues des Carmélites* he must be a superb traffic controller, while for Moussorgsky's *Boris Godounov* he may in addition have to restrain a designer from putting all Russia on stage.

Figaro, an eighteenth-century comedy of intrigue, demands the greatest attention to clarity of motive and action. *The Ring*, a monumental retelling of ancient myth with nineteenth-century social and political crises in mind, cannot project its meaning and power unless illusion and symbol are in accord, and there is, perhaps, no work written for the lyric stage so dependent upon illumination. The twentieth-century nostalgic comedy *Der Rosenkavalier* raises problems of taste and proportion, and the stage director must not be found wanting.

Figaro: *A Matter of Clarity*

LE NOZZE DI FIGARO *Text by Lorenzo Da Ponte, after the play* Le Mariage de Figaro *by Beaumarchais. Music by Wolfgang Amadeus Mozart. Play first performed in Paris, 1784, opera in Vienna, 1786.*

Figaro is complex. The story holds no terrors for those who can cut a clear path through the intrigues of Congreve's *The Way of the World,* but many who claim the opera as their favorite would be hard put to relate or account for much of the action. For most listeners and theatregoers the music is so enchanting that only a sketchy idea of the plot convolutions is considered necessary.

Those who perform in it or stage it must be better acquainted with it, and the audiences who enjoy *Figaro* the most are those who have read the Beaumarchais play as well as the Da Ponte libretto and who have studied the Mozart score with some thoroughness.

Da Ponte's libretto damages the play only slightly by the necessary contraction, and even improves it by the excision of some sentimental elements no longer pertinent.

The story follows the attempts of the lustful Count Almaviva to obtain sexual possession of a young girl, Susanna, before her marriage to Figaro, the Count's servant. This is in accordance with the feudal principle of *jus primae noctis* or *le droit du seigneur,* a principle that has been publicly abjured by the enlightened Count. Being human, this Count wants the reputation of enlightenment, but he would also like Susanna.

Susanna sees through the Count (his methods are not subtle) and, warning Figaro, enlists the assistance of the neglected Countess, who would like to put an end to her husband's tomcat proclivities.

They plot to embarrass the Count by involving him in a nocturnal assignation with the young boy Cherubino, dressed as a girl.

They abandon this frivolous plot and substitute a sentimental one with just enough lightness of tone to save it from solemnity. This blend of frivolity and tenderness is a rococo characteristic. Instead of tricking the Count into making love to his youthful male rival, they trick him into making love to his own wife disguised as Susanna.

The headlong pace of the plots is checked by the Count's counterplot to prevent Figaro's marriage by forcing him to marry a woman old enough to be his mother. This is hilariously exploded when Marcellina discovers that she *is* his mother.

The sentimental plot succeeds, and the Count, in the very moment of trying to expose Figaro for making love to the Countess (Susanna in disguise), discovers that he himself has been caught making love to Susanna (the Countess in disguise).

The opera provides rewarding roles for three sopranos, a tenor, a baritone, and two basses, in addition to the singers of four small roles. There is plenty of acting opportunity for all. There are four separate settings for the scene designer, and the costumes are of a most attractive period. (See Plates 9 and 10.)

Figaro is difficult to stage well and yet, undoubtedly inspired by their material, singers and actors will frequently outdo themselves to produce a surprisingly sparkling performance where one had scarcely expected more than average competence.

The opera is a mixture of the traditional string of solos, thirteen of them, and ensemble numbers, from duets (six) to a sextet and three concerted finales, two of them with chorus.

The adjustment of the arias, several of which are soliloquies addressed to the audience, to the more realistic recitative and ensemble sections is a problem in itself. Cherubino and Marcellina present problems of a different sort. The complexities of the plot are seldom clearly enough treated, so that the audience sees a pretty but meaningless charade. There is more than that in *Figaro*.

As soon as the curtain rises we see a room "partly stripped of its furnishings." Susanna is sitting at a dressing table, trying on a hat in front of a mirror. Figaro is measuring the space for a bed, or in some productions the actual bed frame. In the text Figaro sings, "I am seeing if that bed which the Count intends for us will look well in this position." Figaro's odd units of measurement, from 5 to 43, have generally been ignored by commentators. Moberly suggests that the units are feet but implies that Figaro is not using a rod and adds that Da Ponte was more concerned about rhyme than exact measurement (*Three Mozart Operas*, p. 49). He could be measuring by "hands" (4 inches), reducing the 43 feet to a little over 14, which would be close to two sides of a rococo marriage bed. If the bed frame is used, amusing capital can be made out of it, with characters stepping in and out of the open rectangle.

A specific requirement in this first scene is an armchair intended for important business later in the act. In a naive production this armchair declares itself at once to be a stage property of considerable importance. A sophisticated production, for more than one reason, will blend it into the total picture, preferably turned with its back or its side toward the audience so that we are not immediately made conscious that it is waiting for its cue. Some productions add a stepladder, a logical piece of equipment for a partially furnished room, and some have added a pail and a broom, both of which can be deftly used to dance Cherubino off to the army at the end of the act.

It is unfortunate when the designer, pleased with his second-act chamber, his third-act salon, and his fourth-act garden, treats this half-furnished room as an unsatisfactory project and starts *Figaro* with a poor setting. The temptation is to use an inset against an already erected second-act setting. Unless the inset has been thoughtfully placed and skilfully lighted, we are unhappily aware of the more splendid setting behind, waiting for the first act to be finished before revealing its rococo beauty to us. A small inset is easier to light without spilling unwanted illumination on the set behind, but the parsimony is obvious. An East Berlin production used a scrim inset on its huge stage with the most unfortunate effect. Not only was the scenery behind visible through the scrim, but entering and exiting actors were visible also, frequently before or after the music attached to them.

At least one production has designed this room together with a section of passage at one side of the stage, so that we can see the approaching characters (but only occasionally and always with the proper time control) and even see the rococo door to the Countess's room across the passage. It is possible that the Count's room also opens off the passage, although it is sometimes assumed that the room designed for Figaro and his bride is between the Count's and the Countess's rooms, a less likely arrangement. Proximity, however, is essential, since it forms the matter for the second duet between Figaro and Susanna. This room is obviously not the one referred to in Act 2 as Susanna's room, which is apparently adjacent to that of the Countess. It is logical that Susanna would have a room of her own as long as she remained single.

Some productions call for an entrance into the garden at the rear. Unless this is at the top of an outside staircase it is a little difficult to account for the subsequent leap from a window of the Countess's room, unless her room is on the floor above, which is improbable. The stage direction "Entra Cherubino dalla finestra" (by the window) calls for this neat reversal of his famous leap, in the second act, into the carnations below. It would be in character for Cherubino to enter an upper-floor room by a window, especially if he expected to find a girl there.

It is not easy to explain why Marcellina and Dr. Bartolo come into this room set aside for Figaro, but a stage director can motivate it easily if the passage is clearly in view. These older characters would scarcely enter by the window, even if it were furnished with stairs. Although it is not clear from the recitative, Marcellina lives in the castle, and Dr. Bartolo has been summoned to attend the Countess. We are merely informed that Marcellina is eager to prevent Figaro from marrying Susanna, that she plans to claim the Count's assistance, and that Bartolo will assist her for personal motives of vengeance.

It is here, in an aside, that Bartolo refers to Marcellina as "la mia serva antica," a phrase which is usually translated as "my old servant" rather than the more correct "my former servant." Scores, libretti, and program notes often refer to Marcellina as Bartolo's housekeeper. In the Beaumarchais play she is nothing of the sort. She was once the young Rosina's governess in Bartolo's household, and is now apparently some sort of female companion at the castle. There is no need for Da Ponte to have changed all this, and Bartolo's first line implies that he did not. Bartolo has just arrived at the castle, and Marcellina is explaining matters to him. Marcellina, incidentally, is about forty-six or forty-seven. Seduced at fifteen or sixteen when she was in Bartolo's service, she gave birth to a son (Figaro) who is now thirty.

If it is understood that Marcellina lives at the castle and is walking with the newly arrived Dr. Bartolo along the passage, their entrance into the room is easily motivated. Susanna has departed. Figaro sings his little warning to the Count and also departs. He may not see Marcellina and Bartolo but they can see him, and Marcellina, always inquisitive, naturally looks through the open door and seeing that the room is empty, enters it. The harpsichord arpeggio covers the entrance, and the recitative dialogue begins with Marcellina looking about the room.

Bartolo's aria of vengeance is frequently a contest between bass and mezzo soprano. Marcellina is a soprano, but since her only aria calling for high G's, A's and B's is usually cut, mezzo sopranos are often cast in the role. Bartolo exults in the vengeance he plans to enjoy, and promises Marcellina that Figaro shall be hers.

It is in the handling of Bartolo's aria that the director who thinks all arias are an undramatic bore reveals his inadequacy. In a Vienna production the Marcellina, an enthusiastic scene-stealer, was permitted to wander over the stage during Bartolo's aria, reacting to various objects while Bartolo vainly addressed the audience and tried not to notice what was going on behind him. In a Munich production with the same Marcellina, director Rudolf Hartmann reduced the amount of business, with happier results, but it remained for a director in a much smaller theatre (Mainz) to solve the problem by letting Bartolo push Marcellina (obviously not the same one) into the chair with its back to the audience. He then sang to her *and* to the audience, with no distractions. If this method is used, it is at once incumbent upon Bartolo to make use of his opportunity and act as well as sing. In all fairness to the directors who allow Marcellina to distract, it must be conceded that in some instances distraction is advisable. The Bartolo who sings his entire aria to the audience from a central position above the footlights (without including Marcellina) deserves a wandering Marcellina. A Kiel production, directed by Wilhelm Petzold, allowed Marcellina to recline in the bed frame during Bartolo's aria. This had the virtue of connecting Bartolo's vengeance with Marcellina's delight in the prospect of consummating it, but imposed upon Marcellina the discipline of not being crudely obvious or tiresomely distracting.

The discovery of Cherubino hiding in the chair is comedy business of an engaging sort and difficult to spoil altogether, although it can be done, chiefly by mistiming and mugging. Cherubino himself is something of a problem. Delicately drawn, he is a boy on the brink of manhood, and it would be interesting to see and hear the role performed by a well-built boy of thirteen whose voice is still a clear soprano, preferably in one of the tiny and expensive festival theatres seating no more than three hundred. Needless to say, such boys are rare and must be caught in the few months or so during which they are ideally poised between boyhood and manhood. It is unlikely that we shall see many, so we must accept the female soprano or mezzo soprano, unsuitable as many of them are. The first Cherubino was Dorotea Bussani, who later sang Despina in *Così fan Tutte*, and the Beaumarchais Cherubino was a girl, though a boy had originally been intended.

Cherubino is twice dressed in girl's clothing, but he spends most of his time being a boy and an aggressively masculine one. His newly awakened interests are at war with his voice, but he must on no account possess a luxuriantly feminine shape. He must walk like a boy, and on the occasions upon which he runs he must lead with his shoulders and not with his pelvis. A soprano or mezzo soprano physically suited to the role is fortunate. Much credit must be accorded those who, perhaps not quite so naturally suited, work hard to make their movements accord with his. Costumers can be invaluable in helping the girl to appear more boyish, and those who avoid shiny satins are to be commended. In some instances the flat-chested look is impossible to impart, but wide shoulders and distracting straight lines can do much to offset a generous bust, and even the knock-kneed effect can be disguised. The actress playing the role will negate all these efforts unless she has sedulously studied the boyish walk. With a good actress and singer in a good costume, and an audience willing to suspend its disbelief, Cherubino can be a delight instead of an embarrassment.

An audience may wonder why the Count, hearing Don Basilio's voice outside, has to hide behind the armchair. We have already been informed that Basilio is acting as a go-between in the Count's designs upon Susanna. Why hide from a go-between? We must assume that Basilio is talking to Figaro, and it is helpful if we hear Figaro's voice at this juncture. Figaro is looking for the Count, as we shall see when he leads in a band of peasants who scatter flowers as a tribute to the Count's gesture in abolishing the *droit du seigneur*.

If we actually hear Figaro's voice asking questions of Don Basilio outside, the Count's action is at once understandable. The armchair, if it has been used as suggested for Marcellina, needs to be turned around so that we can enjoy the full comedy of the Count's facial expression when he discovers Cherubino under the cloak or the dress or whatever is used, and we naturally wish to see the discomfited Cherubino also. A Susanna who from the opening scene has been well supplied with garments about the room can make the hiding of Cherubino in the chair itself look amusingly natural, and she can even hide him from the Count when the Count takes Cherubino's former place behind the chair. To bungle this comedy business is tantamount to bungling the screen scene in *The School for Scandal*.

In the second act, Susanna is asked by the Countess to take the guitar and play the accompaniment for Cherubino's "Voi che sapete." This is pretence, since the accompaniment is scored for flute, oboe, clarinet, bassoon, and two horns, with pizzicato strings to simulate the guitar. While the picturesque grouping showing Susanna's face is attractive, it is easier if she turns her back and closes the group informally, if less operatically. She has no lines, and we are less conscious of her fake playing. In all fairness, Susannas are generally more industrious in this matter of fake playing than Tannhäusers, most of whom are unconvincing.

The action aria of dressing Cherubino as a girl is often grossly overacted. Susanna's aria is charming and entirely functional; it has no trace of the concert hall about it and seldom if ever finds its way there. Although it is a song, it might just as well be recitative. All three participate: the singing Susanna, the amused Countess, and the rehearsing Cherubino. A stage director can demonstrate his taste and his light touch in his handling of this scene. If it turns into a contest between the singer and a gawky Cherubino determined to capture audience attention by his (her) silent acting, the director has failed.

The most complex scene in the opera is the scene preceding and leading into the second-act finale. The finale itself in its eight movements (*Allegro* in E flat, *Molto andante* in B flat, *Allegro* in B flat, *Allegro* in G, *Andante* in C, *Allegro molto* in F, *Andante* in B flat, and *Allegro assai* back in E flat) is a musical and dramatic marvel, and only an incompetent production can ruin it. Well sung and acted, it is one of the glorious half hours in the entire span of musical theatre.

The scene must be handled with dexterity and wit. The scenic essentials are a door to a dressing room, usually placed on stage right. The main door to the Countess's room is on the opposite side. Somewhere upstage is a door to Susanna's room. All the doors are equipped with keys. The dressing room door, however, has no visible key. It is, we may assume, somewhere about the room. This is the door that can be locked from the inside by a catch but not by a bolt. That is to say, someone inside can temporarily secure it, but if a key is applied from the outside, the catch may be moved aside and the door opened. Since much of the action depends upon the locked doors, a certain consistency must be respected. Often we are given a door which someone firmly locks from the outside only to have it opened from the inside with no explanation of how this can be.

The action is as follows. Cherubino is half-undressed, trying on his female costume. Susanna has gone out, presumably into the Countess's *gabinetto* (a small anteroom) to fetch a ribbon. The Countess is alone with Cherubino when her husband knocks on the main door to the room. It is locked and he is suspicious. Cherubino runs into the dressing room taking all his clothes with him, and locks it from the inside by slipping the catch. The Countess unlocks the main door, leaving the key in the lock. The Count enters. The Countess is noticeably confused and awkward in her lies. The Count hears a noise in the dressing room. Cherubino has clumsily upset something. Susanna enters from the *gabinetto* unobserved by Count and Countess. She stops short upon seeing or hearing the Count, and stands behind a screen. The trio, Number 13, begins. The Count orders the supposed Susanna to come out of the dressing room. The real Susanna remains silent, except for asides which we in the audience hear but which, by stage convention, the Count and Countess do not hear. Cherubino, locked in the dressing room, remains silent.

Since the supposed Susanna in the dressing room will not reply, and since the Countess will not produce a key to open the door, the Count threatens to force the lock. Prevented by the Countess from calling the servants and creating a scandal, the Count proceeds with extreme caution. He takes pains to lock the door leading from the *gabinetto* by which Susanna entered. He must, of course, take the key and pocket it. Insisting that the Countess accompany him to fetch a crowbar in order to avoid the possibility of trickery, the Count removes the key from the lock of the main door where the Countess left it when she opened the door to the Count, he ushers the Countess out, and we hear a distinct locking of the main door, the key to which he may or may not remove. Now if the supposed Susanna comes out of the dressing room she will find no way out. The door to the *gabinetto* is locked and the key removed. The main door is locked, and the key is on the outside or in the Count's pocket.

The little duet, Number 14, begins with Susanna's "Aprite, presto aprite" ("Open at once; open!"). This makes it very clear that the key is not in the door. Otherwise, Susanna could easily open it. She may know that the key is in the room, but if she also knows that by slipping the catch Cherubino can run out more quickly, there is little point in wasting time. Cherubino slips the catch from the inside and runs out. There being no way out except back again, he chooses the window and jumps down. We know it is an upper-floor room since Susanna says it is too high to jump, but Cherubino is athletic and he jumps. Susanna laughs at his jumping and running prowess, closes the window, and promptly takes his place in the dressing room. She slips the catch exactly as Cherubino had done and locks herself in. The Count and Countess are heard at the main door. The Count must unlock it before they enter. "Everything just as I left it," he remarks.

Some productions make the dressing room visible to us so that we can see Susanna behind the locked door. It helps us to understand why she does not prevent the Countess from confessing. Logically, if Susanna appeared immediately she would persuade the Count, and spare the Countess a great deal of tension. We would lose some rich music and comedy if she did, so it is necessary to keep her there somewhat longer. Perhaps she is waiting for the moment which will be the most effective. She has told us, "Let the braggart come. I'm waiting for him."

Almost too quickly, before Susanna can burst out to prevent her, the Countess confesses that it is not Susanna in the dressing room but Cherubino. Susanna has the trump card but is momentarily at a loss to know how to play it.

The opening of the dressing room door invites three possibilities. The Count has entered with a crowbar or some other implement for forcing the lock. The Countess has the key, either on her person or more probably somewhere about the room, perhaps in a drawer. In the Beaumarchais play the Countess gives the Count the key. In the opera he demands it, but it is not stated whether she gives it to him or not. Whether he obtains the key or uses a crowbar he is obliged to open the door, sword in hand (the sword is not mentioned in the play), and unless he is ambidextrous this is difficult and awkward. The best solution is to have Susanna open the door from the inside, surprising the Count standing with drawn sword, blustering but not really doing anything. Susanna has chosen the only way to undo the damage which the desperate Countess has done by telling the truth. Fortunately, the suspicious Count has to examine the dressing room just to make sure that Cherubino is not in its recesses. This gives Susanna the opportunity in a single line and a gesture toward the window to inform the Countess that Cherubino has made his escape. The remainder of the finale is simple. A good director makes sure that the Countess is in a favorable position to see Cherubino's commission, which the drunken gardener has given the Count, and Susanna must be between the Countess and Figaro for the warning line and the subsequent suggestion that the commission lacks a seal. Da Ponte made this clear earlier in the text, and only a very clumsy production fails to make capital out of this sequence.

In this entire scene the moment most ineptly handled is usually Cherubino's leap from the window. Few settings take the trouble to suggest an upper room, and few Susannas look down instead of straight ahead. Many Cherubinos, unwilling to jar the larynx, handle their leap from the window by stepping gracefully and visibly to the stage floor a foot below and seeking their confreres in the wings. A provincial German theatre solved the problem by having a deeply recessed window placed at the side instead of at the rear. As the shutters were flung open their shadow, which had decorated the opposite wall, was suddenly swept away and in the patch of sunlight Cherubino's shadow replaced it. The effect was so dynamic that the eyes of the audience were drawn to the shadow. Only the shadow's leap was visible, not the body's. When the shadow plummeted down, this Cherubino made a most believable crash into the flowerpots below, justifying Antonio's indignation and Figaro's simulated ankle sprain some pages later.

In Act 3 there is a single moment the handling of which may reveal skill or clumsiness. After her "Yes—no" duet with the Count, Susanna, overconfident, meets Figaro on her way out of the room and imprudently tells him, "You have won your case already." The Count, having almost walked into her trap, overhears, and in a soliloquy aria informs us of his pleasure in vengeance.

The awkwardness of this overhearing is made even more awkward by a conversation between the Countess and Susanna shortly before the duet. It is a conversation which takes place in the background, upstage, and we in the audience must hear it if we are to understand why the trick to send Cherubino dressed as a girl to meet the Count has been abandoned. In the Beaumarchais play, this conversation takes place at the end of Act 2, and we are clearly informed that the Countess is going to meet the Count and that she is going to be dressed as Susanna. Since the opera has avoided this anticlimax by ending Act 2 with a brilliant ensemble, this information must be imparted at the beginning of Act 3. Unfortunately, the scene begins with the Count on stage. After a short soliloquy for him, the Countess and Susanna enter, and their important conversation is supposedly not heard by the Count. He cannot leave the stage, however, since he punctuates their conversation with three interjections of his own.

There is an attempt to clarify the moment of audibility when the Countess exits and Susanna clearly overhears the last words of the Count's aside: "Figaro shall marry the old woman." Susanna, in a one-word aside, says "Marcellina." Then the conversation between Susanna and the Count proceeds normally and ends in the duet.

Since the overheard conversation has to be loud enough for us to hear the important change of plan, the line "You have won your case already" is often sung even more loudly, and Susanna's confidence becomes excessive.

A scene designer who provides a small library at one side is doing the director and the actors considerable service. The Count may think aloud, for his soliloquy at the opening of the act, with a book in his hand. Turned away from Susanna and the Countess his interjections sound quite natural, and since he is in a different room we can easily believe that he does not hear their revelation of the change in plan. As Susanna comes forward, the Count turns in her direction and his first aside is separated, as it were, from the others. This is the one which Susanna overhears and after which, to clarify matters for us, she says "Marcellina." The engaging little duet may be sung with decorative charm about a curved rococo staircase of four or five steps, at the top of which we see into the library.

If the Count had more time to exit, the scene which follows would go smoothly and convincingly. In the Beaumarchais play the Count tries to kiss Susanna, but she runs away from him, saying "Someone is coming." The Count goes off, saying "She is mine." Susanna then says, "I must go and tell the Countess," whereupon Figaro enters.

"Where are you running off to?" he wants to know, "after just leaving his lordship." Enough time has elapsed for the Count to be well out of sight by the time Susanna informs Figaro of her success. The Count reenters and overhears this remark.

In the opera, Da Ponte has not even given the Count an exit and reentrance. Most directors force one, or they have the Count pause unconvincingly behind a pillar or at the downstage wing of the scenery. Between the Count's aside, "She is mine for certain," and Susanna's "You have won your case already" are only an aside for her and four words for Figaro. With a library into which to step, the separation can be provided and Susanna does not have to overplay her line. The Count's facial direction informs us immediately that he can hear Susanna, just as Susanna heard him when he was facing in the same direction. If he were turned the other way, her words would be inaudible. It is not often that one sees this moment defined with absolute clarity.

Figaro is so close to perfection as a work that the lapses in the fourth act are more noticeable than they would be in a work less dexterous. Many audience members are unaware that in addition to the three solos they hear, Barbarina's, Figaro's and Susanna's, there are two others in the score, one seldom-heard aria for Marcellina (a soprano, not a mezzo soprano aria) and a seldom-heard aria for Basilio. Most productions omit both, on the grounds that the act becomes tedious if they are sung and that the arias are undistinguished. Neither has much to do with the opera at this point. Marcellina's, contrasting the tenderness of male animals toward females with the brutality of men, recalls for those who know the play Marcelline's speech on women's rights in the third act. Poorly placed in the final scene of the opera, it becomes what it is, an aria for the singer who up to this point has had none. Basilio's aria seems equally an afterthought, for the same reason. His elaborate story of the smelly ass's skin which saves him from the attack of a wild beast might have had some point earlier, but his part in the action is over and the aria is gratuitous. A producer will upon rare occasions include one of these two arias for an unusually gifted or aggressive soprano or tenor, but very rarely will both arias be heard in a stage production. They betray their lack of functionalism side by side with the remaining solos in the act. There is grave danger of tedium if the nonfunctional arias are retained, especially if the four-act structure with three intervals has been taken literally.

The complicated scene of disguises and confusions expectably presents singing and acting problems, but it also presents lighting and costuming problems. The moonlight must be very bright if we are to appreciate the misunderstandings, but some illusion of the dark garden must be retained. Most audience members will subscribe to the convention that the characters cannot see each other as well as those in the auditorium can see them. Contributing to the half-illusion required is a stage lighted with strong contrasts, where some positions are brightly lighted out of all probability and other places sufficiently darkened for a reasonable approximation of a Spanish garden by night.

There is no difficulty in understanding that because Susanna and the Countess have changed clothes, Cherubino makes love to the Countess under the impression that she is Susanna, while shortly thereafter the Count makes love to his own Countess under the impression that she is Susanna.

Most of us can easily follow Figaro's delighted determination to tease Susanna by pretending that she is the Countess and by making love to her, though we wonder why Susanna so readily believes him when he says he recognized her voice. If she were not deeply in love with Figaro, Susanna might well suspect him of quick thinking, a trait he has demonstrated several times. What is difficult and requires assistance is the sequence in which Susanna, dressed in the Countess's clothes, sings her lovely song of impatiently awaiting her lover. She knows Figaro is listening and sings to him in affectionate revenge. Figaro knows that it is Susanna, even though she is in disguise, and he furiously takes her impatience to be impatience for the Count. If he recognizes Susanna now, why does he take her for the Countess later? It must clearly be done with lighting and costuming. If, for the aria, Susanna removes a mask or in some other way reveals her face, she may place herself in a section of the stage which illuminates her face without calling attention to her costume. A few moments earlier the Countess had complained of the damp and could easily have put on Susanna's cloak as she departed, Susanna helping her. After her aria, with her face visible, Susanna may logically put on her mask and throw the Countess's cloak about her. If Figaro, lurking in the shadows, has by this time turned his back in a sulk, he might easily be unaware a few minutes later that the masked lady wearing the cloak (perhaps with recognizable insignia upon it) is still his own Susanna —especially just after he has jealously watched the Countess in Susanna's dress apparently luring the Count into one of the little summer houses. Susanna, of course, sings her aria in her own voice, but apart from a phrase or two of imitation of the Countess, Susanna sounds like Susanna to us and the Countess like the Countess, so that vocal disguise is impractical for long.

After the climax of this confusion there is no major problem. The emotional span of the finale, from the endearing "Pace, pace, mio dolce tesoro" through the sledgehammer threats of the Count, the trooping out of one of the summer houses, the Countess's appearance from the other, the delicious little staccato runs of apprehension, the heavenly "Perdono" sequence to the jolly "Corriam tutti" exhortation, with or without fireworks, is yet another glory in an *opera buffa* already brimming over with them.

There are few operas in which good scene design, costume design, stage direction, acting, and in one scene in particular, stage lighting are such an integral part of the totality that we take them for granted when they are present, or if they are absent, close our eyes and revel in the music. That a comedy should have such beautiful music as to make this second course bearable is astounding. That this course should so seldom be necessary is equally astounding and a tribute to Beaumarchais, Da Ponte, and Mozart, respectively, for devising the story and the characters, for compressing the complexities into musical theatre form and style, and for conceiving the music so dramatically that the work may with justification be described as celebrating not only Figaro's wedding but the wedding of music and drama.

The Ring: *A Matter of Illusion, Symbol, and Light*

DER RING DES NIBELUNGEN *Text and Music by Richard Wagner. First performed in its entirety at Bayreuth, 1876. Two of its four parts had been previously performed in Munich,* Das Rheingold *in 1869 and* Die Walküre *in 1870.*

What was Wagner rebelling against when he stood on the stage of the rococo opera house in Bayreuth and said No!? In the middle of the eighteenth century this beautiful theatre in blue and gold with touches of red possessed the largest stage in Germany. It had been built for entertainment in the *opera seria* tradition, full of mythological creatures, gods and goddesses, water nymphs, spirits flying through the air on especially constructed machines, serpents, dragons, horses, fine costumes, and lavish scenery. Scenes calling for floods and fires were especially popular.

The auditorium of the Bayreuth opera house was not large enough for Wagner. It was sumptuously decorated and intended to glorify the small and select audience more than the work being performed on stage. This did not suit Wagner at all and so he said no, and chose a spot on a hill just outside of the town. Upon this spot his theatre was to be built. Two sites were discarded before a final decision was made. A long struggle for money and support followed, and the theatre was at last built with assistance from the half-mad King Ludwig of Bavaria. It opened in 1876 with a trilogy preceded by a prologue, the whole stupendous work involving mythological creatures, gods and goddesses, water nymphs, spirits flying through the air, serpents, dragons, horses, and much of the rest of Baroque paraphernalia. Its final scene called for a flood and a fire at the same time.

Wagner never did anything by halves, and one feels that this show would have delighted Louis XIV if he had still been alive—until he heard the score, that is.

The differences are greater than the similarities. The mythological story and the assorted beasts are a small matter when set against the dramatic structure, the underlying philosophy, the fusion of word and tone, and the huge, ever-present orchestra commenting upon the action like a Greek chorus, and dominating the voices in a way no *opera seria* singer would have tolerated and no Baroque audience endured.

Wagner's idea of *Gesamtkunstwerk* stemmed from the unsatisfactory state of old-fashioned opera: unsatisfactory from the musical point of view because musical numbers, arias and ensembles, were simply excrescences upon an already determined sequence of action, and unsatisfactory from a dramatic standpoint because the speech and recitative between the numbers had been reduced to a perfunctory continuity which did only half as well what a spoken play was supposed to do.

In Wagner's judgment, the eighteenth-century reforms associated with Gluck had not really blended music and drama but had only moved slightly in that direction by opposing the pretensions of the singers. It was his ambition to dignify the musical part of music drama by giving it a unity impossible in an opera subscribing to separate numbers, and to dignify the dramatic part of music drama by freeing it from the external narrative action appropriate to a spoken play and giving it, instead, an internal action of ideas, ideas of magnitude and eternal truth.

All the visual aspects of movement, setting, and costume must contribute to this blend of music and drama. With words and music firmly wedded, neither music nor drama would be imposing their structures upon each other, symphonic on the one hand, dramaturgical on the other. Instead, Wagner's principle of using short associative phrases, called leading motives (*Leitmotive*, or in the singular *Leitmotiv*), served to unify an enormous work like the *Ring:* by the time he came to write this work they were used whenever they happened to be appropriate, from the first scene of *Das Rheingold* to the last scene of *Gotterdämmerung*. In addition, the resemblances among many of the *Leitmotive* themselves interlocked them in a much more subtle way and provided a deeper unity.*

Continuous melody took the place of the old-fashioned alternation of recitative and numbers, and the most expressive voice was that of the orchestra, not so much supporting the vocal line as surging forward with it and ahead of it, probing character, underlining thought and action, recalling the past, clarifying the present, and foretelling the future.

With a huge orchestra at his disposal Wagner made the most imaginative use of instrumental coloring, from the strings of magic sleep to the heavy brasses of striding giants, from the glockenspiel, harp, and piccolo flame-points to the French horn glow of the sunlight through water upon gold, transformed a moment later into trumpet brilliance.

Drama and music, supreme together, supported each other, and all the ancillary functions had to be unobtrusive. The movements of the actors were of paramount importance, since they were expressive of both the meaning of the drama and the music. For this reason the movements of the orchestra had to be rendered invisible, and at Bayreuth this was done by placing the orchestra in a sunken position beneath a curved shield, establishing direct communication between the characters and the audience over "the mystic gulf." Since the

---

* For a detailed analysis Deryck Cooke's *An Introduction to Wagner's Ring* is recommended. London Records RDM S-1 (three discs with booklet containing musical illustrations).

words of the singers were as important as the notes they sang, the submergence of the orchestra made the hearing of the words possible and put less of a strain on the singers, provided that their diction was good.

In opposition to the distracting scenic devices of old-fashioned opera, Wagner's scenery was to be "an unobtrusive practical background," a request which we cannot allow to go unchallenged since his own literal demands made it impossible to achieve.

The *Ring* occupied Wagner for a large part of his creative career, and remains to this day the most impressive demonstration of the security of his revolutionary techniques and the insecurity of his adjustment to the practical stage.

In spite of its lengthy narratives, sometimes of material we have already seen and heard, the *Ring* is intensely theatrical. Although Wagner wrote much about "the word" and much about the theatre, clamoring that he was first of all a dramatist, the general consensus now is that his verse-writing is mediocre, and that he was far more of a musician and far less of anything else than he cared to admit. He understood the drama, however, most thoroughly, and demanded the best acting by extraordinary singers gifted with that rare ability to radiate energy from poise. What he demanded scenically reveals a certain amount of confusion.

Ever since the first staging of the entire cycle at Bayreuth in 1876, productions of the *Ring* have been taken with desperate seriousness. Few of them would deserve the charges of irresponsibility that have been levelled, with some justification, at many productions of respected works in the standard Italian repertory.

The first production was staged by Richard Wagner himself, with settings painted by Josef Hoffmann (Plate 13). The Bayreuth stage tradition, jealously guarded by Cosima Wagner, made itself evident at the 1896 cycle, which she staged at Bayreuth after the Angelo Neumann productions had taken the works to major German cities and several foreign capitals, building up an eager audience for this astounding set of music dramas.

In 1895 Adolphe Appia had published *La Mise en scène du drame Wagnerien*, but Cosima Wagner, although acknowledging the validity of Appia's objections to the primitive approach to stage lighting, refused to accept his suggested changes. She pointed to the precise requirements for light intensity and quality in the text of the *Ring* as Wagner had written it, and declared herself interested mainly in carrying out the Master's wishes as he had made them known during the strenuous weeks of the 1876 production, and in the years following when the *Ring* was being produced out of Bayreuth.

Several seasons at Bayreuth under Winifred Wagner's management, with productions of the *Ring* from 1933 to 1942 with the exception of 1935, have been too long associated with Hitler's National Socialism to emerge untainted. It may be, however, that the staging of Heinz Tietjen and the settings of Emil Preetorius came as close to solving the problems as any before or since. The Reinhardt influence and the lavishness of the huge chorus were criticized by Friedelind Wagner, and in the case of Tietjen an imputation can be made of splendor uncomfortably paralleling Nazi self-glorification. In the work of Preetorius, however, who did not know Appia's work when he began to design for Bayreuth, there is a clear attempt to combine the opposing forces that must be present in any realization of the *Ring*, the forces of conscious illusion and subconscious symbol, of the tangible details of nature and the inner spirit of nature, of literal references and subtle suggestion. An indication of how close Preetorius came to Appia may be seen in a comparison of the famous Appia design for the third act of *Die Walküre* (Plate 15) with that of Preetorius. In Appia, to provide the mountain top, there are the sharp rock peak on stage right pointing stage left, a broken descent occupying the center of the stage and a hint of dark conifers at the left. In Preetorius the rock peak is stronger and straighter, extending to beyond the center, while the balancing conifer to the left is nearer and taller. The descent from right to center is easier to negotiate, less poetic in effect, more practical in performance, and instead of the sky at the rear accented with dark firs in Appia's sketch we are given by Preetorius a bluish rocky landscape beneath the sky and beneath the projecting rock, carrying the eye beyond the immediate scene. We seem to view the Appia setting from slightly below, as most probably in life. We seem to view the Preetorius setting from slightly above, as customarily in the theatre.

Lee Simonson, an admirer of Appia, designed settings for the *Ring* at the Metropolitan in 1948, adding the Preetorius straight lines but tilting his rocks more steeply. Six years after the end of the Second World War in 1951, Wagner's grandsons, Wieland and Wolfgang, broke with the tradition and startled the music lovers and theatregoers with the Bayreuth revolution. Many subsequent productions, especially in Germany, imitated the new style, and neo-Bayreuth was admired or vilified according to taste.

In 1954 a new *Ring*, directed by Rudolf Hartmann, with settings by Leslie Hurry and lighting by John Sullivan, appeared at Covent Garden.

In 1965 the first complete recording of the *Ring* was made public. While it did not aim to compete with stage productions, it was handsomely cast and scrupulously prepared. Having none of the visual problems to overcome, it nevertheless strove and to a considerable extent succeeded in visualizing the production for the enrichment of the listener in his home. Many music lovers living inconveniently far from the kind of opera house equipped to stage the *Ring* were given an opportunity to listen to and study the work, so that when they eventually attended a production of one part or all of the cycle they might come with greater familiarity and appreciation.

In 1967 Deutsche Grammophon recorded Herbert von Karajan's Salzburg production of *Die Walküre*. This was the beginning of a plan not only to record and produce in Salzburg the entire *Ring*, but to bring each part to the Metropolitan Opera House during the following season. While *Die Walküre* and *Das Rheingold*, in that order, made their appearance in New York, the labor troubles which shortened the Metropolitan season of 1969–1970 necessitated the postponement of *Siegfried*. The only happy note in this unhappy story is that by the time *Götterdämmerung* arrives in New York from Salzburg, enthusiasts will have had plenty of time to study two full-length recordings of the monumental composition.

A stage or a recorded production of this prodigious work is an expensive and time-consuming operation, made more difficult in these days of air travel by the unavailability of singers. Singers for the taxing leading roles in the *Ring* are scarce, and engagements for them, whether in Wagner or in other composers' works, are easy to obtain. Some years ago it was likely that the available few would be in the same country at the same time or at least in nearby countries, but while the time of travel has been greatly decreased, the geographical breadth of engagement possibilities has been increased and an urgently needed tenor or soprano may be in San Francisco, Milan, London, Buenos Aires, New York, or Vienna.

Considerable dedication usually goes into a production of the *Ring*, a dedication accounted for by an admiration for the scope of the work, the wealth of imagination and creativity involved, and the great beauty of much of the music. There are, nevertheless, those who genuinely dislike it intensely, and others who, not disliking it, resent for musical reasons the dominance exerted by the man's work, or for personal reasons resent the adulation of a man so unattractive and unprincipled. It is in some quarters considered a phenomenon that this self-centered and aggressive man concerned himself so devotedly to love and renunciation, and that such a detestable personality should have written music for which so many, in spite of themselves, have such a powerful affection.

Wagner made such demands of singers that many of them avoid his music altogether. Only a very few generously endowed vocalists make a career of Wagnerian singing, and even some of them in the leading roles show signs of exhaustion in the third act, a fact which draws a clear distinction between a recorded performance (with scenes sung on separate days) and a continuous performance in the theatre.

Wagner made such demands of scene designers and stage technicians that to this day there has not been an entirely satisfactory visual presentation of the *Ring*. Wagner himself was dissatisfied with the literal attempts of 1876, and there is an increasing dissatisfaction with the symbolic attempts since 1951.

It is in Wagner's requirement that scenery should be "an unobtrusive practical background" that most of the difficulty in Wagnerian production lies, and this requirement seems to have been the one about which Wagner himself was least confident. In choosing Josef Hoffmann to design the *Ring*, Wagner was moving in the direction of scenic artistry as opposed to conventional scene-painting, but he was not moving far enough. Although he wrote that the scenery should be unobtrusive, he confused his purpose by thinking in terms of the romantic literalism in vogue at the time.

The fashion in scenery and costumes in the 1860s was detailed picturesqueness and historical accuracy. Charles Kean, between 1852 and 1859, staged thirteen of Shakespeare's plays in London in this style. The Duke of Saxe Meiningen saw Kean's work, and in the late 1860s and for the next two decades the *Meininger* productions became the most progressive in scenic matters in Europe, just as the Vienna *Burgtheater* held first place for ensemble.

It is no wonder that Wagner, with his concern for breaking down the old theatrical traditions of bravura performance, should enthusiastically embrace the progressive theatrical modes of his day. Josef Hoffman's designs, attractive examples of detailed picturesqueness, are a far cry from "an unobtrusive practical background," especially when lighted in the bland nineteenth-century manner without the contrasts with which modern stage-lighting can match the contrasts of the music drama. This was exactly what disappointed Adolphe Appia when he saw Wagner's production of *Parsifal* and Cosima's production of *Die Meistersinger*.

Appia's musical training, and his perception of the connection between Wagner's music drama and the expressive potentiality of light and space, equipped him to be the foremost practitioner in the world during the first three decades of the twentieth century, the period during which Wagner was becoming widely established as a musical dramatist of the first rank.

The world, however, was not ready to receive Appia. His stage settings, costumes, and lighting for Toscanini's reading of *Tristan und Isolde* at Milan's La Scala were received with some hostility. Perhaps 1923 was too early for the austerity of the stage picture which, in a different form, caused a stir in Bayreuth as late as 1951. Perhaps, too, the experiment was attempted in the wrong country. Furthermore Appia, with his knowledge of Dalcroze eurhythmics, was not in charge of the stage direction and did not approve of what Ernst Lert had done with movement and grouping. Since for Appia movement and grouping were parts of the totally conceived picture and inextricable from stage forms and stage lighting, the result could not have been as unified as he so clearly wished.

Appia's projected scenery for the *Ring* at Basel was rejected by himself in favor of an even greater austerity and less romanticism, so that eventually an arrangement of steps and blocks against a sky drop and edged with dark drapes was chosen. This simplified staging, so familiar to most of us in countless productions of Shakespeare, was unfamiliar to audiences in 1924 and most of them disliked it. The remaining two parts of the *Ring* were cancelled. The *Ring* continued to be elaborately and literally staged until the years after 1945 when Wieland Wagner, before the Bayreuth revolution of 1951, was forced by circumstances to stage the work with a minimum of scenic effect.

Foremost in encouraging the older approach was Cosima Wagner. Her son Siegfried's productions, and those which followed at Bayreuth, improved technical standards without radical departure from the principles established by Wagner himself. The extreme conservatism stemmed from Cosima, who after her husband's death devoted herself to the promulgation of Wagner's ideas, although she was accused, mostly by Felix Weingartner, of imposing her own ideas upon or substituting her own ideas for those of the Master. She was a formidable woman, and she knew the music dramas and the mind of the creator so intimately that for twenty-three years she ruled Bayreuth and established a style of production which she insisted was the authentic and therefore the only style.

Geoffrey Skelton, writing far more understandingly and sympathetically of Cosima than most, points out the great difference between Wagner's devotion to the qualities of improvisation and spontaneity and the accurately timed movements and facial expressions which Cosima imposed upon singers and which she could perform herself in rehearsal. She fell victim to the temptation of teaching by imitation. She herself connected the inner urge with the performed movement, but she often failed to encourage the connection in others. In terms of contemporary jargon in matters of acting, Cosima was imposing a "technique" approach upon Wagner's "method." Her concern with detail and her fidelity to Wagner's insistence upon accurate note values and strong enunciation of consonants were admirable. She insisted also upon the anti-operatic advice which Wagner gave, that singers should sing to each other instead of to the audience, and in this she was on the side of the progressives.

Many accused her of pedantry, but no one could with justification accuse her of sloppiness. Not open to new ideas such as Appia's, since they seemed to her to be flouting the ideas of the Master, she nevertheless attempted to improve the settings and costumes for the 1896 production of the *Ring*. Wagner had already in 1876 found Josef Hoffmann's designs too pictorial, urging his own concern for the clarity of the events on stage in preference to picturesqueness. Doepler's costumes had been in 1876 wholly unsatisfactory. Cosima called them small-minded and tasteless, and for her 1896 production Max Brückner designed the settings and Hans Thoma the costumes.

They were a great improvement over the settings and costumes of the first production though even within the Bayreuth circle Max Brückner was severely criticized. They are, to the eye of today, far less like exhibits in an art gallery than Hoffmann's stately and detailed depictions. Viewed without prejudice, the Brückner designs (Plate 16) are remarkably theatrical, beautiful to look at, free of fussy detail, and as closely in harmony with the music and the drama as it is possible for romantic scenery to be. Even the prevailing greenish blue, of which there were complaints, supplies a unifying factor in a drama sweeping through the entire range of creation from the bottom of a river through the forests to the sky. Only by contrast to Appia's unobtrusive grays do they seem gaudy.

Wagner believed his music would overcome the illusionism of the stage scenery of his day. Brückner went some distance to meet his ideas by reducing detail and by dramatizing his settings, but he did not go far enough. Appia, in going further, promoted a wholly different approach which Cosima considered an affront to the Master. A close friend, Houston Stewart Chamberlain, tried to persuade her to Appia's ideas, but Cosima was adamant. When Appia published his *Die Musik und die Inscenierung* in 1899 he did so with a dedication to H. S. C., "who alone knows the spirit that I capture in these pages."

During the years between 1896 and 1951 the rest of the world either imitated the Bayreuth tradition or, especially in the second half of the period, moved uneasily in the direction of something less literal, a style described in some quarters as impressionistic. In the United States as early as 1916 Carl Van Vechten wrote in the *Musical Quarterly*, "There has never been a production of the *Ring* which has in any sense realized its true possibilities."

Lee Simonson's respect for Appia, and his statement that his own designs stemmed from the knowledge of Wagner's dissatisfaction with the 1876 attempts at setting and costuming, encouraged the employment of the technical advances of the twentieh century, especially in the science of stage lighting. Jonel Jorgulesco's 1936 settings at the Metropolitan, with a jagged peak in Act 3 of *Die Walküre*, moved in this direction but not as boldly as Lee Simonson's of 1948. Lee Simonson clearly understood the conflict in Wagner's artistic personality and the difficulty of reconciling the meticulous realist and the mystical poet. He was aware that when Wagner was preparing for the final dress rehearsal of *Siegfried* for King Ludwig of Bavaria, a strictly private occasion, he was as concerned about the arrival and effect of the mechanical bear and the dragon's neck as about the poetic music he had written for the magical scene in the forest. Simonson was in favor of ignoring the realistic business insisted upon by Wagner and concentrating instead upon the poetic unity of the work. He cited Ludwig Sievert's staging in Hannover around 1925 as characteristic of the newer approach. Geoffrey Skelton, in *Wagner at Bayreuth*, cites Sievert, Roller, and others (Roller as early as 1903) as insisting upon finding the visual form for the music drama within the words and the music rather than in the written stage directions. The Wagner grandsons, in 1951, sought the visual form in the music, claiming that with the passage of time the words had become somewhat old-fashioned.

Alois Nagler, in an essay for Leroy Shaw's *The German Theatre Today* (Austin, Texas, 1963, p. 20) makes specific reference to the Appian spirit of the Tietjen productions at Bayreuth in the 1930s, with designs by Emil Preetorius. Preetorius was concerned with the designer's responsibility to supply what Wagner wanted when he demanded " an unobtrusive practical background." Restraint, simplicity, an avoidance of strong contrasts in color, and close attention to the value of lighting for the purpose of achieving subtle mood changes were his guiding principles, the last of which he based on his belief that of all the media involved, light was the one most nearly related to sound.

The Tietjen-Preetorius production of the *Ring*, with Tietjen conducting alternately, or almost so, with Karl Elmendorff, was last performed in 1942. The Bayreuth Festival continued for the next two summers with Furtwängler conducting *Die Meistersinger*, after which there were no festivals until the 1951 resumption with Wieland and Wolfgang Wagner in charge.

The Bayreuth revolution, as it was called, was shattering to traditionalists. The aim was to return to the philosophy though not to the literalism of Wagner's text, and to the expressive vitality of his music, by sweeping away the incrustations of more than half a century, many of them initiated by Wagner himself.

In the early 1950s critics and commentators concerned themselves more with what had been left out than with what had been put into the music dramas. Every vestige of realistic scenery, every painted backdrop, and even every built-up rock was eventually discarded, although for the 1951 and 1952 seasons there was some tangible contact with prewar and wartime productions. Beginning with 1953, a huge disc was placed on the stage floor and tilted toward the audience in the manner of a raked Baroque stage. Upon this disc the participants stood or strode (Plate 17). One critic referred to it as a muffin. Another complained in *The New Yorker* that Brünnhilde lying upon its edge at the close of *Die Walküre* looked "no more imposing than a dead fly on a stove lid."

Conservatives bewailed the disappearance of breastplates, horned helmets, and eagle wings. Progressives applauded the uncomplicated tunics and the avoidance of comedy moments with bears, horses, and dragons, all of which were banished. It took audiences time to grow accustomed to a beardless Wotan, and those who knew their Wagnerian texts and their mythology objected to the replacement of Wotan's missing eye and the discarding of his hat, when the lines in Act 3 of *Siegfried* specifically referring to them were retained.

The greatest advantage of the new approach was that it freed singers from the need to compete with the orchestra in expression—

in their case the visual action which Cosima had taken such great pains to rehearse. Separating gesture and facial expression from specific lines and instrumental entries gave the singers as actors a richer opportunity to project a total character. By these means such detail as was appropriate was applied last, instead of the character finally achieved consisting merely of already established details.

Projections on the cyclorama were in many instances very effective, as when the wide blue sky covered the bare disc, with only Siegfried and Brünnhilde in all the hugeness of space. In other instances, as in the burning of Valhalla, a vulgarity of projection effect was simply a different sort of vulgarity (and a much easier one to produce) from the vulgarity of steam pipes, electric fans, silk ribbons, and red light.

During the first few years there was much complaint about the dimness.* Projections are less effective on a brightly lighted stage, and there was a tendency to favor the projections over general visibility. As a consequence, one of the faults of the 1876 production was repeated, though in a totally different way: detailed scenery distracted from the actors in the older production, better-lighted projections distracted from poorly lighted actors in the newer. There is an argument in the fact that if the stage is bare there is not much to light except the actors, and if spotlights perform that function both the projections and the actors can be seen. However, spotlights on human figures moving about a murky vastness of stage are not wholly satisfactory, and tend to suggest a return to the old-fashioned principle of scenery behind the actors rather than scenery around them. Dimness about the actors makes the audience wonder where they can tread with safety, and the mere concern is distracting. Following faces in small spots of light rapidly produces visual exhaustion.

It has been suggested that the new Bayreuth style was conditioned by financial considerations more than is usually admitted. Dimness has the financial advantage of reducing the need for scenery and furnishing, and a further advantage of mercifully obscuring

---

* *Theatre Crafts* for September 1969 contains a valuable essay by Dr. Glenn Loney called "And Wagner Said! Let There Be Light—But Not Too Much."

action which might be irreverently greeted if seen in full light. Scenes, however, intended to represent bright daylight and treated sunnily in the music are not only unsatisfactory in themselves when dimmed, but ruin the intended effect of contrast between bright light and the darkness of night or storm or a cave. Later in the 1950s there was some movement toward stronger illumination, but this had the disadvantage of making the huge stage look bare and dull until it became filled with people. At the one extreme in 1876 we have scenery distracting attention from the all-important actors. At the other in the middle 1950s, we have, apart from the projections on the cyclorama, nothing much to look at except the actors, and ironically enough, actors who move comparatively rarely and who stand quite still for far longer periods than the actors of 1876.

Where Cosima had painstakingly matched action to the music, Wieland Wagner deliberately discouraged action, preferring the music to speak for itself and permitting actors a greater freedom of interpretation. Relieved of the mechanical necessity of providing what Cosima called the correct gesture, the singers were encouraged to enrich their characterizations by probing them psychologically. For those who succeeded in doing so, Wieland Wagner's approach was beneficial. For those who did not, it foisted a dramatic oratorio stasis not much to the liking of many of the audience, for the characters achieved stronger contact with the audience than with each other.

From 1953, when Wieland Wagner placed the action on the disc, until 1958, the basic approach did not change, although details were altered and the movement toward a greater measure of illumination was welcomed. In 1960, after a season in which the *Ring* was not given, Wolfgang Wagner presented his version of the *Ring* with a disc which was shaped like a dish and which came apart symbolically during the action, to be restored to its unity at the close of *Götterdämmerung* when the ring was returned to its proper guardians in the Rhine. Hunding's hut in *Die Walküre* consisted of a phallic tree penetrating the cleft of a roof, which was the other half of the disc, and the disc, split into further sections, became rocks for subsequent scenes. (See Plate 18.)

The symbolic productions of the Wagner grandsons cleared

away a great deal of musty realism, traditional and poorly staged effects, and stimulated a reconsideration of the text, the action, and the music. Wieland Wagner's willingness to reconsider details and add improvements was, in addition to exciting curiosity and publicity, deserving of genuine respect, and many singers proclaimed him a perceptive and sympathetic stage director. It was generally felt that Wolfgang Wagner was not his equal, and a tension became evident during the 1960s which was not resolved when Wieland Wagner died and Anja Silja broke her connection with Bayreuth, declaring that she did not want to be a part of its decline. Whether the 1970s, with the unavoidable centennial frenzy of 1976, will be a decade of mediocrity remains to be seen. If it is, the fact will in no way diminish the contribution of the vital 1950s.

Alois Nagler, while appreciating the effectiveness of some of the Wagner brothers' originality, urges a reconsideration of productions using painted scenery. Feeling that Wagner was in harmony with the best the nineteenth-century stage had to offer and had only objected to the less than good, he takes issue most convincingly with those who ignore Wagner's stage directions and substitute symbolic meanings "for what emerges from the score for the normal listener." He accuses the new Bayreuth productions of forcing upon the spectators and the audience interpretations which have "lost all belief in the music," and declares that "the Wagner Renaissance is still to come" (Shaw, *German Theater Today*, p. 25).

If productions at Bayreuth in the next few years decline into sterility, more theatregoers will ally themselves with Nagler and hope, not for a return to the 1876, 1896, or 1936 approaches, but for an investigation of what could now be done with the painted scenery of romantic opera with free use of three-dimensional pieces, with all the advantages of modern lighting, with properties and costumes as prescribed by the dramatist, with illusionistic realism in the handling of masses, and a thoughtful "method" to take care of the emotional expression reflecting what is so clearly stated in the sound of the orchestra.

In acting Wagner a singer would have to avoid the mechanical compliance with the tradition urged by Cosima Wagner's knowledge, authority, intuition, and even, when memory occasionally failed her, invention. He would as sedulously avoid the oratorio withdrawal, which allows the music to say everything in sound and refuses to offer visual competition. Instead, a singer would attempt to find the point of contact, with no gaps, where sound and sight reinforce each other. If Wagner's music were entirely literal a conflict would arise at once, but it is not. It is possible to complement the music with visual action, without repetition and without competition. Each can express the other half of the thought or the emotion, the one in sound and the other in sight. A smooth adjustment has to be made, by the singer, from the passages in which his expression is partly vocal and partly physical to the passages in which he does not sing but is free to use facial expression and more controllable action.

We expect singers to convince us while they are to some extent hampered by the mere process of singing, and this is asking a great deal. From some it is asking more to expect a slow, controlled mime during the sometimes lengthy orchestral passages. It demands considerable skill. An old-fashioned opera makes little attempt to blend the two. Conversational passages are "acted" and lyrical passages are "sung" and while being sung are given concert treatment, and the audience is fully accustomed to adjusting from one to the other. This will not work for Wagner, although it has been used in performances of *Tannhäuser* and *Lohengrin* which are, in part, old-fashioned. Continuous melody requires continuous acting, and continuous acting requires continuous believing.

By the time the vocal requirements for Wagner's leading roles have been satisfied, it is a matter of astounding good fortune if the singers are capable enough and dedicated enough to sustain their roles without lapses. Since there are comparatively few singers available at one time for the heavier Wagnerian roles, several of them are persuaded to devote most of their attention to these roles, which they may sing in Europe, North America, and South America without having to add non-Wagnerian roles. An ability to sustain a role in this style is more likely to be achieved by such a singer than by one who occasionally performs Donner, if a baritone, or Gutrune, if a soprano. Wagner specialists are likely also, wherever they may be singing, to find themselves on a stage with familiar colleagues with whom they have often acted the role they are singing. It is not surprising that under these conditions something resembling an ensemble is readily established .

Subjective drama has the advantage of seldom looking ridiculous when a lapse in acting occurs. The worst that happens is a patch of dullness which the music may go far to covering. It is the drama of external action, resembling melodrama, which provokes laughter when the actor lapses. There are dangerous moments in the *Ring,* but most of them, like the Rhinemaiden swimming or the piling up of the gold, are technical matters. The most dangerous nontechnical scene is one of the most popular in the most popular work, *Die Walküre.* Only exceptionally sensitive directing, costuming, and lighting, together with a faultless team of eight all of whom can move with swiftness and grace, can provide the Ride scene with what it must have to match its musical vitality. The slightest hint of unathletic scurry, of middle-aged housewives running for a bus, and the illusion is ruined.

The Wagner renaissance, when it comes, will respect the contrasts in light which are clearly demanded by the text and by the music. Although we in the audience are aware of the safety value of dimness and the advantages of it to the handling of satisfying projections, we are nevertheless disturbed to frustration when there are textual references to light accompanied by gleaming music, both of which are flatly denied by the murkiness on stage. Many German productions during the 1950s and 1960s have given the impression that the *Ring* is enacted in gloom, with an occasional scene in half-light which seems bright by comparison. On the contrary, many of the scenes in the *Ring,* some of them long ones, take place in bright daylight, and the dark scenes are comparatively short. There are about as many dark scenes as light scenes, since an alternation carefully devised for contrast sets the pattern, but even in dark scenes a single light source is usually provided. Firelight and moonlight are obviously to be given sufficient theatrical exaggeration so that faces can be adequately illuminated.

A dingy half-light throughout a production does as great a disservice to the dark scenes as to the light. The half-light effect is implied mostly for transitional purposes, superbly matched in the music. The contrasts are sometimes quite suddenly achieved, and the music tells us even more plainly than the stage directions how gradually or how swiftly the light increases or fades. Light intensity is as clearly indicated.

For the opening of *Das Rheingold* a greenish twilight of the Rhine waters, dark below but lighter above, lasts an almost unbearable thirty pages of vocal piano score but matches the slow-motion unfolding of the obsessive E flat opening. The sun strikes the gold at this point and the yellow light streams into the water. Twenty pages of golden light follow and brightness is essential for all its physical revelations, since a point is made of sudden thick darkness when Alberich tears down the gold.

The change to the dawn is gradual since an entire change of scene is indicated. The transition, with no characters visible and no one singing, except for Alberich's mocking laughter from the depths, lasts three pages.

"Increasing brightness" is indicated on page 55 of the Schirmer score and, by the sixteenth bar, even glittering. Many pages later Fasolt refers to its brightness, and since the sun is now fully up there is no reason for the gods and giants to be in half-darkness. Forty-eight pages later, for a dynamic effect, a gray mist fills the stage, and the gods, deprived of the goddess Freia and the youth-preserving properties of the golden apples in the garden she tends, begin to look old and wan. Two pages cover Freia's departure and Loge's observation of the phenomenon.

Singing ends eight pages later for the transition to Nibelheim. A dark red glow is called for during the striking of the anvils. It is presumed that enough light remains for the following scene, since we must see well enough to note Alberich turning into a column of mist and to appreciate the fact that while Mime could see him a moment ago he cannot see him now. The quality of the light is referred to by Loge when he and Wotan enter: "How the fiery sparks glow through the pale mist." Later in the scene, Loge reminds Alberich that he would be in total darkness in his caverns unless he, Loge, had provided him with fire for his forges. The scene is a long one, forty pages of score, too long to play in near darkness for the purpose of handling conveniently the difficult dragon and toad appearances, the first generally being too vague to discern and the second merely imagined.

The transition to the final scene takes place in the reverse order, as the three characters pass from the ruddy glow of Nibelheim, past the clanging anvils, to the pale gray light of the mountain top, pale gray because of Freia's absence and the inability of the gods to rejuvenate themselves.

After Alberich's curse and departure the mist is dispelled, and the whole foreground is restored to brightness when Freia is brought back by the giants. The background remains dim, however, so that Valhalla may remain invisible until the closing moments.

The heaping of the gold in scene 4 takes place in bright light, not in semidarkness. It is a temptation to dim this scene for two reasons. One critic referred to the gold as usually "looking like a pile of old suitcases," and the technical problems of enacting this passage convincingly are somewhat diminished by dimness. The radiant Freia, however, and the gleaming gold lose much of the visual impact intended if the producer plays for safety. A second source of temptation is that Erda's appearance from below, in a rocky crevice suffused with a bluish light, requires darkness, and this darkness is indicated in the text. It is a theatrical direction, and darkening the stage somewhat earlier draws attention from its obviousness. The original stage direction "bis zu halber Leibeshöhe" demands that Erda rise to the height of her waist. Not only is this difficult to achieve with dignity, but on a brightly lighted stage the bluish light would be almost impossible to manage. There is no real reason for a weather change at this moment, and although the clouds are still concealing Valhalla they have not yet gathered about Donner. We must assume that the solemnity and portentousness of the earth mother's appearance justifies all creation turning sombre.

Experiments have been tried with Erda inside a rock which fronted with scrim reveals her gradually. The lower half of her body can be concealed by a section of rock not fronted with scrim, so that Wagner's effect can be achieved without the trapdoor device. The contemporary association with rising elevators in public buildings makes the use of this device in solemn moments unwise for the rest of time.

Erda is required to appear at one side of the stage. If she addresses Wotan she sings less imposingly, since she must face somewhat sideways, and to have her face front smacks too strongly of old-fashioned opera. There is no reason, however, why she cannot be placed a few feet upstage so that she can sing to Wotan and yet project her voice toward the audience. In Herbert von Karajan's 1968 Salzburg production Erda appeared far back at the center, very faintly lighted. It helped the direction of the singing but not its projection.

The bluish light naturally fades when Erda disappears. We are told that the background is still veiled in mists, which are to be dispelled when Donner, having gathered them about him so that he and Froh are quite invisible, strikes the rock with his hammer. Six bars in B flat follow, and at the modulation into G flat the rainbow bridge becomes visible "mit blendendem Leuchten" ("with blinding radiance"). The fact that the sun is setting has persuaded some producers to make an evening scene of it, but Wotan's words read "Abendlich strahlt der Sonne Auge, in prächtiger Gluth prangt glänzend die Burg" ("in the evening the sun's eye gleams; the castle shines radiantly with a glorious blaze"). It is true that Wotan later says "Es naht die Nacht" ("the night is near"), but it has not yet arrived and the sun, very low over the horizon, is shining brilliantly.

The Salzburg production provided merely a blotchy dullness. Mist seemed to rise, but no bright sun shone on Valhalla. The music seems to call desperately for it.

In *Die Walküre* the first act, from a lighting point of view, is composed of firelight and the full moon. There are explicit directions as to when the fire in Hunding's hut collapses to spurt a bright glow and when the fire fades. It is totally extinguished by the time the door flies open and a full moon brightly illuminates Siegmund and Sieglinde.

The second act takes place in a wild and rocky pass. No stage direction indicates the quality or intensity of the light. It must be bright enough for Brünnhilde to see down into the valley. The stage grows dark only after Brünnhilde's warning of death, about seven-eighths of the way through the long act. The darkness is oppressive at this point, and all the more so if the bulk of the act is well lighted. Heavy storm clouds gradually hide the cliffs, but for the fight between Siegfried and Hunding there are dazzling flashes of lightning, and another glare above for Brünnhilde's appearance in the air. A reddish glow illuminates Wotan's appearance. Brünnhilde is seen rather indistinctly going towards Sieglinde (this obviously also covers a technical problem) but for the moment of Hunding drawing his spear out of Siegmund's body he is described as *deutlich*—clearly visible. Thunder and lightning end the act.

The third act, beginning with the celebrated Ride, makes use of occasional clouds flying past an open sky, but the clouds gather for Wotan's arrival and the peaks are enveloped in black clouds. The stormy dimness lasts somewhat over half the length of the act; for the climactic scene of Wotan and Brünnhilde, fine weather returns with the gradual fall of the dusk. The darkness of night at the end is essential in order that the fire, conjured by Wotan's spear, may flicker more effectively against the dark sky. The stage directions ask for ever-increasing brightness from the magic fire until the fall of the curtain.

Siegfried shows the same careful alternation of light and darkness, with the darkness lighted by various kinds of directional lighting. Although much of the first act takes place in a cave, one-fourth of the stage represents the wood outside, to which there are two exits, letting light into the cave. Mime curses the brightness and stares into the sunlit wood outside. The darkness of one part of the cave is illuminated when Siegfried blows up the fire at the forge.

Act 2 begins in the gloom, and its darkest spot is the entrance to Fafner's cave. As soon as the Wanderer enters, which is not very long, the clouds part and he is easily visible in the moonlight. When Siegfried and Mime enter, day breaks. The rear of the stage remains in shadow, shrouding the lair where the dragon lies sleeping, but the sun brightens the middle of the stage and the rest of the act takes place in morning light. The familiar forest murmurs take place at noon: Siegfried clearly informs us of the fact.

The third act runs the gamut from the blackness of stormy night, through Erda's bluish halo, moonlight for the Siegfried-Wanderer scene, rolling fire for the scene change, and beautiful blue sky and fine weather. Brünnhilde's waking words greet the sun, and its radiance is undiminished to the final triumphant notes.

Götterdämmerung begins at night with the magic fire at the back against which the three Norns are silhouetted. Day dawns upon

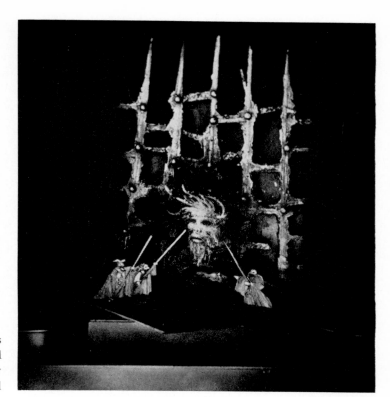

1   Verdi's
Macbeth, model
of setting by
John Ezell

2   *The
Threepenny
Opera*, model
of setting by
John Ezell

3 Interior
of
Drottningholm
Palace Theatre

4 (*right*) Interior of
Hamburg State Opera

5 (*below*) Interior of
Wuppertal Opera House

6 *Dido and Aeneas*, rendering by Donald Oenslager, Yale, 1953

7 Interior of Central City Opera House, Colorado

8 Exterior of Glyndebourne Opera House, Sussex, England

9 (*left*)
Figaro at
Stratford,
Ontario
1964

10 (*below*)
Figaro at
Glyndebourn
1956

11   *Così fan Tutte* at Stratford, Ontario, 1967

12   *Così fan Tutte* at Glyndebourne, 1956

13 *Das Rheingold,*
design by
Josef Hoffmann,
Bayreuth, 1876

14 *Il Trovatore,*
renderings by
Timothy Dewart

15 *Die Walküre,*
design by
Adolphe Appia, 1892

16 *Götterdämmerung*,
design by Max Brückner,
Bayreuth, 1896

17 *Wieland Wagner's Siegfried* at Bayreuth, 1954

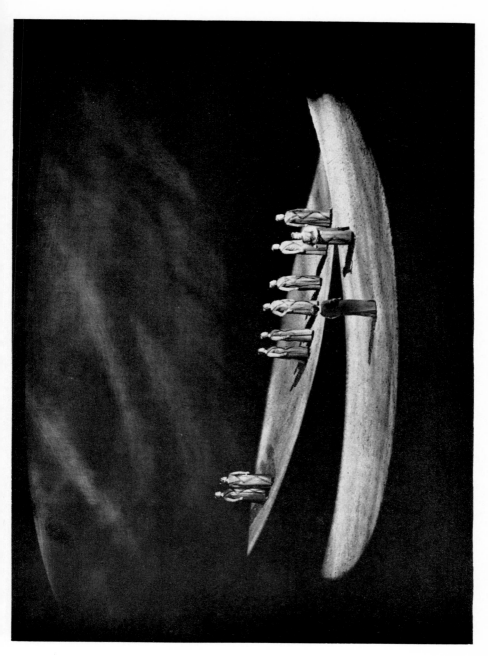

18 Wolfgang
    Wagner's
    Walküre at
Bayreuth, 1960

19 (*right*) *The Merry Widow* at Central City, 1967

20 (*below*) *Oklahoma!* in New York, 1943

21 *A*
Midsummer
Night's Dream
English Opera
Group, 1960

them and the fire gradually dies down. The first scene of the first act is obviously a daytime scene. Siegfried arrives by boat, not usually a nighttime occupation in olden times, and Siegfried and Gunther depart by boat at the end. Hagen, left to guard the house, is a black figure in bright light, not what we are sometimes given, a spotlighted figure in Stygian gloom.

The second scene takes place on the rock, with Waltraute riding in among the clouds. At her departure a brightly lighted storm cloud sails away. It is now evening and the firelight from below increases, the flames darting upward until Siegfried, in Gunther's likeness, strides through them. The flames sink, and the scene of Brünnhilde wrestling with Siegfried is mercifully performed in partial dimness.

The second act begins at night with moonlight on Hagen and Alberich. It is a short scene, and at the end of it the sun rises and is reflected in the waters of the Rhine. For the rest of the act it remains day.

The scene of the Rhinemaidens, at the beginning of the third act, takes place in the afternoon. The huntsmen gather for refreshment in daylight. After Siegfried is struck down by Hagen, the dark begins to fall; Wagner called for it to begin as the ravens flew above. After Siegfried's death the moon breaks through clouds and illuminates, with increasing brightness, the funeral procession. This shining of the moon is most poignantly timed for the music associated with the love of Siegmund and Sieglinde. Mists rise at the end of the scene, to disperse gradually and reveal moonlight glittering on the water for the beginning of the final scene, a cold light that is soon turned into the beginning of the fiery ending to come. Torches are brought as men arrive on the scene and at Brünnhilde's command a pyre is erected. When the torch is put to the wood, the flames blaze up. A splendid minor contrast is inserted at this point. The flames of the pyre seem to seize upon the hall of the Gibichungs and then dense smoke takes its place. The Rhine has welled up and the Rhinemaidens recover the ring from Hagen. The dense cloud at the rear now glows with a fiery light. As the smoke disperses we see the half-burned shell of the hall of the Gibichungs, and beyond it in the sky we see all Valhalla burning. It is still blazing away as the curtain falls.

In spite of the technical difficulties involved, the ideal production will pay close attention to Wagner's lighting requirements. Clumsily attempted in his day, most of them can now be quite smoothly achieved. The temptation to darken the stage in order to simplify other technical problems must be overcome, and other ways found to solve these problems.

The severest problems come at the beginning and at the end of the *Ring*. A producer who can present the opening scene in the depths of the Rhine convincingly and rise to the grandeur of the final conflagration need fear little in the twelve and a half hours between. If the production is illusionistic and Fricka's rams, Brünnhilde's horse, and Siegfried's bear are real, a much likelier event fifty years ago than now, they will be seen only briefly and they will not remain in full view of the audience for any length of time. The modern audience is accustomed to doing without them, and very little is gained by restoring them. More, indeed, is lost, since not only are they distracting in themselves but we have now come to associate the presence of animals with tasteless and spectacular productions of *Aida* and *Carmen*.

The fire in *Die Walküre* is disappointing if literally attempted and clumsily executed, but equally disappointing when evaded altogether or merely hinted at by means of moving projections. Downstage flames are very difficult to achieve, but fire and smoke at some distance, partly screened by rocks and fir trees, could like the witch's oven in *Hänsel und Gretel* prompt us to supply the remainder from our imaginations. A smoke effect harmful to the voice must obviously be avoided. It is the movement of smoke which is evocative, however, not so much its actual presence, and this is where projection technique can be mixed with bolder and more tangible devices. A tongue of flame darting upward from behind a rock at an unexpected point will never be clearly seen but its movement will be felt, and the slow drifting of the cloud above, projected, will leave enough in between for our imaginations to create. A projection giving the effect of the inside of a gigantic oven is as far from achieving a persuasive result as the old visible ribbons, always the same length and always in the same place.

The fight with the dragon in *Siegfried* would be an almost insuperable problem if it were to be taken quite seriously. Mime's spite and Siegfried's contempt are in a light vein, and although Mime is plotting to kill the lad we are as sure he will not succeed as we are that the witch will not eat Hänsel. The world of the brothers Grimm is not far distant and we accept the potential horrors complacently. The dragon is a fairy-tale dragon and the whole scene is given the iridescent quality of sudden changes of mood. Siegfried jars the loveliness of the sunlit forest with his amateurish pipe squeaks; his heroic horn call is jarred by the appearance of the dragon. The dragon almost laughs when he declares that he came out for drink only to find a tempting morsel of food. Siegfried makes fun of his teeth and the fight follows promptly, with movements that Wagner described in detail, a dance duet of clumsiness and agility ending when the sword pierces the dragon's heart. Fault has been found with the confidential, informative dying dragon, but the swift change from the boastful clatter of the fight to Fafner's realization of the wasted years of encircling the accursed gold and his resignation in the face of destiny is curiously poignant in the music and must in some way be as evident visually. It lasts only a moment, since Siegfried has an exasperated reaction to the dragon's inability to finish his story. A similar iridescent quality pervades the curious scene in which Mime flatters Siegfried and unwittingly vocalises his murderous thoughts. Siegfried, who has tasted the dragon's blood, can not only understand the forest bird's song but also hear what is going on in Mime's mind. Appia's dappled setting of moving leaf shadows matches to perfection the quality of the music of this light-hearted scene, shot as swiftly with the portentousness of the legend beneath the fairy tale as Mozart's *Cosi* is shot with true feeling beneath its rococo hilarity.

The most embarrassing moment in the *Ring* is without a doubt Siegfried's "Das ist kein Mann" ("That is no man") when he cuts Brünnhilde's corselet and reveals her in her woman's dress which is, however, a warrior maiden's dress. The forest bird has fully informed Siegfried that Brünnhilde lies sleeping on the fire-girt rock and that only the one with no fear can win her. Siegfried receives corroboration from the Wanderer and plunges on toward the rock, fully expecting to find Brünnhilde and only Brünnhilde there. It is true that he has never seen a woman and has only heard about his mother

Sieglinde from Mime, but the words, following the most beautiful ethereal music, are unfortunate.

The greatest problems remain the first and the last, Alberich's theft of the gold and the scene of the ring's return to the Rhinemaidens. Both Bayreuth and Salzburg have improved upon most earlier attempts to create the underwater illusion, and their projections upon scrim with wavering spots of light catching the moving maidens have avoided the crudest realism, while not falling back upon an easy and totally unconvincing suggestion.

Whether there are three Rhinemaidens or six Rhinemaidens (three non-singers to increase the fishlike, darting movements, but with never more than three altogether appearing at the same time), the spots of morning light reflected from the gold look quite believable as they move through the water to brighten triumphantly when the sun pours directly upon the heap of gold at a most effective musical moment. A silent turntable can be an advantage in this scene. A large stage is a necessity. On a small stage with three inhibited maidens, inhibited because constricted by insufficient space, waving their arms but otherwise remaining still, the scene fails, and Alberich's attempts to reach the gold within a few feet of him become ludicrous.

Height as well as breadth are required. The eyes of the spectators must be engaged by a flash of light to one side, by a swift movement on the other, and by the increasing luminosity of the gold near the center. Only in this way can twisting, turning, darting, rising, and sinking resemble swimming. One wishes that the entire rock face were of gold, so that the heaving from behind by Alberich would send it tumbling forward and for once persuade us that an enormous vein has been dislodged, to be converted into treasure in the caverns below the water. The little lump with which Alberich so often departs looks pitifully small for the payment. Gold is known to be heavy, but Alberich ought to be an immensely powerful dwarf. A plunging rock would create its own darkness, in which we could imagine Alberich plunging after it; instead we merely see him hurry into the wings with a package. This is not to recommend a return to early-nineteenth-century stage effects which dealt as a matter of course in cascades, fires, and volcanic eruptions, but where depiction is strong in sound, visual reticence seems unnecessarily timid.

The closing scene of *Götterdämmerung* would by no means have daunted the technicians of the Paris Opéra some forty years earlier. It is not so much that the effects cannot be achieved. It is that the audience reaction to them has changed, so that a thorough and lifelike depiction of Rhinemaidens swimming close to the pyre in order to seize the ring calls attention to itself as something of a technical triumph. On the other hand, a retreat toward symbolic gesture and formal placement aided by dimness is quite as noticeably an evasion and is furthermore contradicted by the music.

The extremes of literalism and symbolism have been reached. It only remains to find the compromise which will reveal without description and which will suggest without evasion.

Der Rosenkavalier: *A Matter of Taste and Proportion*

Text by Hugo von Hofmannsthal. Music by Richard Strauss. First performed in Dresden, 1911.

Der Rosenkavalier, the second collaboration between Hugo von Hofmannsthal and Richard Strauss and the most popular of Strauss's theatre scores, has also the distinction of being the most recently composed work to have secured a firm place in the western repertory. The date of its first production is a dismaying commentary on public operatic taste and the economics of the repertory and *stagione* systems.

Many works written after 1911 have been acclaimed but soon neglected, except for too-rare revivals. There are not nearly enough opportunities of attending such distinguished works as Berg's *Wozzeck*, 1925, Hindemith's *Cardillac*, 1926, Křenek's *Karl V*, 1938, Britten's *Peter Grimes*, 1945, Poulenc's *Les Dialogues des Carmélites*, 1957, Stravinsky's *The Rake's Progress*, 1951, and Henze's *Der Prinz von Homburg*, 1960.

Der Rosenkavalier is safe for many years. An urbane, literate play of wit, tenderness, and charm receives music drama treatment with scrupulously detailed orchestration. The orchestra is large and the general tone of the work is at variance with the eighteenth-century rococo settings and costumes, but two of the chief characters are memorable and the third, that of the rose cavalier, is a surprisingly successful freak.

Dramatist and composer achieved a remarkable blend. A Viennese poet, sensitive almost to the point of effeteness, is wedded artistically to a Bavarian musician with a vigorous physical appetite and a fondness for creamy orchestral textures, to the point of greedy vulgarity. The tastes of the two met in an appreciation of a tender melancholy touched with wry humor, a nostalgia born of the consciousness of the rapid passing of time and the fading of youth and beauty. This sweet sadness, fashionable in Robert Herrick's seventeenth-century England, was fashionable in late-nineteenth-century Vienna, as anyone familiar with Schnitzler's plays is aware. *Der Rosenkavalier* caught it just before it became unfashionable again.

It is a skilful mixture of modish realism and warm, appealing romanticism. The conversational style alternating with bursts of vocal and orchestral lyricism is new-fashioned enough to seem natural and old-fashioned enough to appeal to the general, tune-loving audience. Characters sing to each other or they reflect alone or in the presence of others, but their reflections are carefully motivated to appear natural and there is an avoidance of direct address to the audience in the manner of eighteenth- and nineteenth-century arias. At first it seems as if there are ten pages of realistic speech-song for every rewarding short passage of lyricism, but upon a closer study of the score or after repeated hearings, all sorts of felicitous little touches rise to the surface to be looked forward to and recognized the next time we see and hear the work in the theatre. As in Wagner, passages which seem opaque, at first, yield more rewards at a second hearing, and at a third, still more. In this age of recordings, it costs far less to become acquainted with the musical felicities of such a work.

The text has been criticized for being too detailed, too like a spoken play, for effective musical setting, the score has been criti-

cized for being too long, too lush, and in places too vulgar, and both
text and score have been blamed for dragging out the Baron's wooing and wounding in the second act and his humiliation in the third,
making it a very long evening. It is occasionally desperately literal
(the less-than-completely housebroken little dogs, for example, and
the stopping of the clocks in the middle of the night), and one can
all too frequently hear the Belasco clutter in Strauss's music as
plainly as one could see every expected article in the restaurant on
stage in the otherwise unremarkable play of 1912 called *The Governor's Lady*.

Yet both story and score beget affection, and the Viennese
ambiance is at its most powerful. If we have a weakness for French
horns, running snatches of woodwind, and soaring soprano voices
which seem to scorn to pause for breath, we are lost. The opera
seems also to have worked its magic on certain well-known singers,
who in turn have worked their magic on willing audiences, and in a
curious way the singers' personalities have become a part of the
roles, just as the roles no doubt became irremovable elements in the
singers' personalities. One can hardly think of the Marschallin without thinking of Lotte Lehmann, nor of Lotte Lehmann without
thinking of the Marschallin. To a degree, for Europeans, Elisabeth
Schumann was long associated with Sophie and Richard Mayr with
Baron Ochs. Other singers have been associated with a few specific
roles during their careers, but seldom with such warm personal
attachment.

It is well known that at first the opera was to be called *Ochs* and
that the title was then transferred to the young rosebearer, and that,
for all practical purposes, it might as well be changed to *The Princess*
or *The Marschallin* or *Marie Thérèse*, since both leading soprano
and general public now regard her as the heroine.

There is an obvious symmetry to the story, two sides, as it
were, of a rococo medallion. A mature man is sexually interested in
a very young girl and even more strongly in her money, though for
the Baron Ochs this is saying a very great deal. A young rival, the
rose cavalier, gets the girl instead and while doing so makes a fool
out of the older man, and we are happy, in a merry Viennese way,
to see justice being done. That is the way of the world. A mature

woman is sexually interested in a very young man. A young rival, Sophie, gets him instead and while doing so furnishes the older woman with an opportunity of showing how good breeding and dignity can turn what would otherwise be humiliation into a resignation touched with nobility. And we are melancholy, in a sad Viennese way, to see justice being done. It is again the way of the world, *der Lauf der Welt*. We know that the great lady is wise to give up the young man and she knows it too, but it saddens us in a highly pleasurable way to contemplate her renunciation and we come out of the theatre feeling ourselves ennobled, as if somehow we had had a hand in it.

The charming sentiment, the lovely music, and our admiration for Lotte Lehmann conspire to make us seem to ourselves even coarser than the Baron if we are tempted to view the Marschallin as the Blanche Dubois of Old Vienna. She is a married woman in her thirties, and from the little we hear of the Marschall he sounds a more satisfactory husband than Blanche's. Yet while he is shooting bears in Croatia she is in bed with a seventeen-year-old boy when the curtain rises, and we are quickly given to understand that this is not the first time, nor he her first lover. She was once almost caught, we are told. One would like to see the great ladies of the stage handle *that* moment in the lady's life with aristocratic dignity.

The realistic picturesqueness of Strauss's stormy prelude is dispelled by discreet costuming and innocent attitude, but the opening is a mite uncomfortable for all that and especially so when we discover, unless we already know the opera, that the young man is a mezzo soprano or soprano. After a stab of distaste at this juxtaposition of realism and stage convention, we proceed to more pleasurable matters. There is tenderness in the relationship which, once we become adjusted to the convention, we understand, and there is genuine comedy when the libidinous Baron Ochs paws the young man who is dressed as a chambermaid. By this time, although we know that Ochs is making a mistake by thinking she is female when she is male, we also know that she is really female or she could not be singing soprano or mezzo soprano so successfully. There is almost no convention we will refuse to accept if it is properly established. After the first nervous moments of this one, all goes well.

We understand the necessity for the female voice. Only an extremely young boy with an unbroken voice could fool the Baron into taking him for a girl, even in the dim light of the suburban Viennese tavern in which he proposes to seduce her. There is a large bed for the purpose concealed in an alcove. Needless to say, he does not succeed.

It is inconceivable that this curious mixture of half realism and outrageous convention, of sentimental tenderness and noisy foolery, of psychological refinement and coarse suggestion, of lengthy chatter and melting *cantilena*, of whipped Viennese cream and heady Munich beer *(Pschorrbräu)* should ever emerge as a satisfactory unified whole, but for many people it does. Faults may be found (in text and music) by specialists, but for thousands of operagoers it is a rich experience, and audiences for it after half a century seem to be increasing. Faults are not noticed, or if noticed are forgiven, even the fault of its prodigious and unnecessary length. Every bass baritone with a wide vocal range and a sense of comedy longs to play Baron Ochs. Most mezzo sopranos and many sopranos, if their figures are suitable, have their eyes on Octavian, and high sopranos see the role of Sophie as a splendid one in which to make an effect. There have been singers who, like Lotte Lehmann, have started with Sophie, changed to Octavian, and made yet another change when they assumed the role of all roles, that of the Marschallin. *Der Rosenkavalier* is a work difficult to view dispassionately. For some it is a pretentious bore. For others it is their favorite, their very special opera which touches them more deeply and gives them greater pleasure than any other.

No one who attends the opera house needs to be informed that *Der Rosenkavalier* is one of the most difficult and expensive operas to produce. In addition to footmen, couriers, maids, waiters, and children, it asks for twenty-two singers, of whom half a dozen must be of the very first class. The title role of Octavian, whether mezzo-soprano or soprano, demands a physique and impetuous male movements at the disposal of only a few, the physique by good fortune and discipline, the movements by assiduous study, all this in addition to the voice which we in the audience tend to take for granted.

Octavian sings extensively in all three acts, the range is wide, and the orchestra is large. No singer of the role can risk exhibiting exhaustion in the taxing phrases of the love duet at the very end of the third act. On the other hand, an Octavian who is not warmed up by the second phrase of the role, marked *feurig* (ardently) in the score, is placed in the unenviable position of trying to recover favor with the audience, not only for the remainder of this long scene but through the duologue at the close of the act. Octavian, as well as being a convincing young man, must be a *comédienne* in Viennese dialect for a brief section of the first act and an extended sequence in the third.

The Marschallin, in addition to being a beautiful singer, must be an actress of distinction and, as fashion now decrees, something of a personality in addition. On stage throughout a long first act, she is absent for the entire long second act, to reappear only after two-thirds of a long third act have been played. The music accompanying her reappearance is unforgettable. If the singer possesses something less than a strong personality, the contrast with her forgettableness is damaging. The universal and sentimental appeal of the role, everyone's battle with the passing of time, the peculiarly endearing music written for her, and the association with the commanding personalities who have made this role their personal property, albeit shared, have all contributed to making the Marschallin the leading character in the mind of the popular audience. Octavian has the title role and Octavian is thematically the leading character, although Ochs and the Marschallin demonstrate the opposing methods of capitulating to the forces of tempestuous youth, with ridicule or with dignity. Both Octavian and Ochs have longer roles than that of the Marschallin, but the Marschallin is expected to dominate in the third act renunciation. For this she has had a long rest, her only theatrical advantage except for the role itself, which is a gem.

Ochs must be a bass with a phenomenal range, and he must also be an accomplished comedian. If he is a clumsy one he quickly becomes a bore and we wait impatiently through two-thirds of the last act.

Most theatres do not even consider staging *Der Rosenkavalier* unless they are assured of these three singers, but there are others. In many productions the least satisfactory singer and actress is Sophie. In earlier days Elisabeth Schumann invested the role with radiant charm and the kind of bourgeois enthusiasm we would expect from the daughter of a man who had made his money selling oats for cavalry horses. Her high soprano of marked individuality gave an edge to the character, correctly boding some trouble in the years ahead after the fall of the third-act curtain on an unlikely happy marriage. Without seeming to compete, she was never pushed into the background by the strong personalities of Octavian and the Marschallin, whoever they might be. Many a Sophie is made to seem uninteresting and disappointing, and some have even been outclassed by their duennas. Some have also looked older than the Marschallin, a tactical error in casting, lighting, and costuming. An ill-fitting wig can turn a potential teenager into an inappropriate middle-ager more readily than can a full life, at least on stage.

Sophie's father Faninal has what for many is an ungrateful role with a cruel *tessitura*. He is called a high baritone and he alternates between solicitous flattery and near hysteria, mostly the latter. For a comedian of unusual ability possessing the requisite voice, like Erich Kunz, the part can enrich Hugo von Hofmannsthal's picture of parvenu Vienna and, in aping the manners of the aristocrats, contrast delightfully with the Baron Ochs, whose lapses are a mixture of fashionable "rakery" and the permissible crudity of a country squire. Faninal, nevertheless, remains a difficult role to establish, and the subtleties are often lost. Annina and Valzacchi are rewarding roles for a contralto and a tenor *buffo*, and they are usually played with competence.

The Italian tenor has only a brief appearance but it is an important one. Some leading singers have disdained the role, but in fact it requires a voice of high calibre. At the Metropolitan during the 1940s Kurt Baum, a frequent Radames and Manrico, was not too proud to sing the role of the Italian tenor. For most tenors it is a brief display of spectacular singing. For Richard Tauber it was an opportunity to make a satirical point about Italian tenors, which is what author and composer intended, a satirical point that was made again recently at the Metropolitan by Nicolai Gedda.

Der Rosenkavalier is not well proportioned in all parts and is altogether too long. Even those who treasure a great deal more than the famous numbers and the agreeable waltz sequences find the first act sagging somewhat before the scene of the levée. The second takes an inordinate length of time to travel from Octavian's delight in Sophie to his wounding of the Baron, and the practical joke display in the third act could have been reduced to half its length with some musical loss but considerable dramatic gain. Orchestrally the work is very rewarding, and a listener in his home may profit from the playing of an uncut recording, perhaps one act an evening for three successive evenings. In the theatre it can be exhausting, and some of the overlong scenes present visual problems. If these remain unsolved the scenes seem even longer.

The lack of a stage director's hand, applied with good taste, is nowhere more noticeable than in the overacting of a minor role, pushing the performer into prominence at the expense of the production. In a well-directed and well-rehearsed scene involving a dozen or more characters, emphasis on meaningful business can go from character to character in turn and the audience can easily be made to look at what is important and to ignore the remainder as general background. One of the most revealing scenes is the Hogarthian levée in this opera.

The Baron Ochs, a major character, has no lines for eleven pages of vocal score, but he is presently to be extremely vocal. It is assumed that the steward, the footman, and the old *Kammerfrau* make no bid for attention, although, as occasionally directed, if the *Kammerfrau* carries a chamber pot she cannot help being noticed. Entering one after the other are a notary, a chef followed by a scullion with the menu, a milliner advertising a Pamela hat (as worn in Samuel Richardson's novel and in plays and operas derived from it), a scholar with a large volume, an animal salesman with small dogs and a monkey, two Italian intriguers, a widowed aristocrat with three daughters, a professional singer, and his accompanist on the flute. Before the three orphans depart with their mother, the Princess returns to the stage from behind a screen and a hairdresser enters.

While the Princess dominates the scene, she does so almost in silence. For twenty-six pages of vocal score she has five short phrases, the first, less than four bars, introducing her notary to the Baron, the second and third short, angry rejections of the gossipy intriguers, the fourth the touching four-bar reproof to her hairdresser for making her look old, and the fifth merely three words of dismissal to the crowd. The orphans have a tiny trio and then depart. The milliner and the salesman have one or two short lines at the beginning of the scene but remain until the general dismissal. The notary has an earnest colloquy with the Baron, the tenor sings two verses of an aria, the second not quite to the end, and the hairdresser is given elaborate business as the flute is playing the introduction to the tenor's aria.

When this scene is well directed, we are made aware even of the characters with no lines and we are not made too aware of the hairdresser. The characters with few lines stay in character throughout and do not distract attention at times when the attention should be on others. The Italian intriguers must visibly decide upon a plan of action in pantomime, without distracting from the hairdresser's desperation and without in turn losing attention to him. Every bar has to be scrutinized, inventive touches brought into focus or blotted out as the action demands, and the whole presented as a single piece of complex action, perfect in detail yet more perfect as a whole.

When in a poorly handled production the levée is a muddle except for the hairdresser, who dances his role and makes it the *pièce de résistance* of the scene, the original purpose of the entire scene is discounted.

To complain that a work is too long is a wholly different matter from cutting it once it has been performed and published. Strauss and von Hofmannsthal could undoubtedly have improved the work if they had excised and reshaped it as a unit. They did not choose to do so, and Strauss was rightly angry with Ernst von Schuch, the Dresden conductor, who made cuts in *Der Rosenkavalier* after the premiere. Later, however, Strauss confirmed cuts made at the Metropolitan performances of the opera. George Szell, who conducted the opera there in the 1940s, wrote that he asked Strauss to open a cut in *Elektra* because of the beauty of the passage usually omitted in performance, but Strauss forbade it on the grounds that to restore it would check the dramatic impetus. Strauss is reported also to have found *Der Rosenkavalier* inordinately long when he conducted it.

Today a conductor may accept the traditional cuts, a choice which makes the stage director's work somewhat easier, or he may insist upon presenting the entire score. Complete recordings have undoubtedly had some effect upon a conductor's choice. Musicians who study scores are naturally aware of cuts, but most members of the average audience are easily deceived until their ears become accustomed to a complete recording. For many years the only recorded *Der Rosenkavalier* was an abridged version. Long sections of the opera were omitted, and even in the disconnected passages recorded there were cuts which today would scarcely be condoned. In the 1930s it was thought so remarkable to have presented as much as the recording did of a long and difficult opera that it was treasured as a phenomenon in recording, in addition to being treasured for the performances of Lotte Lehmann, Maria Olczewska, Elisabeth Schumann, and Richard Mayr. Following the arrival of long-playing records, three recordings were made in the 1950s, under the direction of Erich Kleiber, Karl Böhm, and Herbert von Karajan. Two of these recordings were absolutely complete, but the third was marred with short cuts, some of them almost meaningless. Now, especially with the additional Georg Solti recording, far more audience members need no score on their laps to detect the major cuts when they occur.

Der Rosenkavalier is so much a conversation piece that the big ensemble scenes, unless imaginatively directed, seem stylistically alien, and the numbers which often seem purely musical tend to interrupt the continuity, instead of blossoming out of the action and being the subjective, reverse side of that action.

The first of these is the celebrated monologue of the Marschallin, especially effective since it almost immediately follows the busy levée scene with its numerous characters. Its springboard, as it were, is an enchanting line from the levée scene itself. The Marschallin has not uttered a word since the departure of the three orphans and their importunate mother. When she does so it is as if a cloud had passed over the face of the sun. Looking into her mirror, she gently reproves the hairdresser, knowing very well that it is not really his fault: "Mein lieber Hippolyte, heut' haben Sie ein altes Weib aus mir gemacht" ("My dear Hippolytus, today you've made an old woman of me"). Her face, we are told in a stage direction, remains dejected. She dismisses the levée, but she has disagreeably been made aware of the passing of time. When she is finally alone it all comes out in a soliloquy, but a soliloquy addressed to herself, not directly to the audience. It is an admirable example of good proportion. It is not long. It begins with a description of the Baron which spirals out of his courtly heaviness, a little figure describing the flourishes of his bowing, and it moves simply to a similarity between the convent-bred Sophie to the convent-bred older woman who is remembering her youth and seeing age ahead of her: "die alte Frau, die alte Marschallin." The remainder of the brooding over the inexorability of time is reserved for the conversational sequence between the Marschallin and Octavian.

The second sequence is one of the most famous in the opera. It is the first meeting of the young couple, who instantly fall in love. The awakening of their love is in tender contrast to the parvenu pomp of the ceremonial in Faninal's *Stadtpalais*, where all is supposed to go according to plan and most assuredly does not. Sophie and Octavian blend their voices to the different words of their personal reactions, which symbolically end with the same "den will ich nie vergessen bis an meinen Tod" ("which I don't want to forget until my death").

The chattiest of confidential scenes follows, succeeded by the Baron's exhibition of coarse behavior and his retinue's exhibition of even coarser as a preparation for a duet, the overt statement of the love they felt only individually during the ceremony of the presentation. This is a lovely piece, with the musical direction to be sung throughout in *mezza voce*, but it is in reality an old-fashioned set number. Octavian takes Sophie in his arms and they remain in this position until the Italian intriguers creep up to them and capture them. Each sings to the other without listening to what the other sings, but we are to assume that physically and musically the tender sentiments are clear enough. The words are not easily distinguished although we catch a few in the clear, mostly words of small significance. Fortunately, the dramatic situation has been made perfectly clear in the conversational sequence preceding the duet, so we do not feel that we are missing anything. Their singing and the orchestra express mutual love, and we really do not care whether we hear the words or not. We have, however, returned to a technique not unlike the *opera seria*, which tells us the facts of the situation rapidly and then broadens musically and statically while it embroiders the situation without advancing it. The duet is a hundred bars long, although for over forty of them the Italians are visible and bearing down upon the lovers, obviously waiting for their cue to spring upon them. The number is a curious mixture of a purely musical method interrupting the dramatic conversational method, only to be itself interrupted by dramatic pantomime. Even a good Annina and Valzacchi find it difficult to behave convincingly without distracting attention from some of the loveliest phrases of the duet. The clumsiness is accentuated by twenty-five almost impossible bars of luckily very fast music during which the two intriguers hold on to Octavian and Sophie, singing as they do so. Sophie and Octavian, both determined young people, are supposed to struggle in attempts to free themselves, but they are given no lines at all, not even cries of surprise or anger, and if they struggle too resolutely Annina and Valzacchi will not be able to detain them, occupied as they are with their words and their cues. The scene seldom comes off with any kind of persuasiveness.

The most celebrated numbers, after the formal presentation which, being a ceremonial, imposes its own most effective stasis on the scene, are the trio and the duet which close the opera. Musically and dramatically this entire final scene is prepared in the most astute and stylish manner. The farcical scene of the baiting of Ochs is over, the police commissioner has investigated matters, and Octavian has become a young cavalier again. The Marschallin has made her grand entrance, the chorus has punctuated the proceedings with raucous outbursts, and the scene has been consistently conversational, very rapid, like a play. The trio is hinted at before it begins in earnest. Several pages before the opening phrase (which is a noble transmogrification of the farcical one leading to the dialect phrase "Nein, nein, nein, nein! I trink kein Wein") the Marschallin repeats her warning of Act 1 to Octavian, "Heut' oder morgen" ("today or tomorrow"), a poignant repetition, since when she first sang it all seemed well with their affectionate relationship except for the sadness induced by thoughts of the passing of time. Now her prophecy has been fulfilled, and all too soon.

This passage, however, grows out of the conversation and swells into an ensemble so subtly that for most of its very brief length only two of the three are singing across each other. It is only slightly over fifty bars long and is strictly a trio for only six of these bars. Furthermore, after a passionate climax, it trails off over seventeen bars to return to natural conversation. With this fore-taste of a trio, we are ready for the lyrical interweaving of the three female voices, this time singing together almost throughout, the rests for each singer very brief except for one of eight bars before the Marschallin's "Da steht der Bub" ("There the boy stands"). Be-gun by the Marschallin's half-whispered "Gar nix" and the trumpet introduction, and ending with her confident "In Gottes Namen" followed a dozen bars later by the radiant modulation from D flat to G natural, the whole sequence is concocted of the most artful theatre, and yet so effectively done and so inviting to beautiful singing that it continues to be the triumph of the opera. Its most remarkable feature is that with its careful preparation, its emotional appeal, and its brevity, it is wholly acceptable as lyrical expansive-ness in a conversational piece, though in performance it could in-variably be improved by the position of the three singers. It is true that they are expressing their innermost thoughts, but the isosceles triangle with all three exactly parallel with the footlights is visually crude and unsuited to the subjective music.

The use of the vulgar little waltz tune for the crowning trio is not an accident, nor is it an instance of Strauss showing how clever he could be. William Mann, in *Richard Strauss*, concedes that "it binds the act more closely and creates stronger connexions between farce and serious emotional portrayal" (p. 141). It does even more. It points up the symmetry of the story, the two sides of the medal-lion, the merry Viennese jest of the older man's absurd attempted seduction with its consequent humiliation, and the sad Viennese wisdom of the older woman's resignation with dignity. "Sind halt aso, die jungen Leut' " ("It's always that way with young people"). But with older people there are differences and they have just been demonstrated.

The closing pages of drama and music are in excellent proportion. The soaring trio is brief, the modulation to G major is soon followed by the simple duet, which is sung twice with a short E major passage separating the two parts and treating with tenderness the moment in which the Marschallin sets the seal upon her renunciation of Octavian. The purely lyrical and static sequences are brief and there is dramatic action between them, with the decorative final touch of the little black boy's search for the dropped handkerchief, his finding of it, and his disappearance. If Strauss can be accused of prolixity in each of the three acts, he must assuredly be respected for his unerring judgment in timing the closing pages of each. He was astute enough to know that much is forgiven when much has been forgotten.

THE RANGE
OF
MUSICAL
THEATRE

Introduction: Sense, Sound, and Sight

Any work of the theatre considered for production today must first be viewed in the light of the period in which it was written and the audience it was designed to please. That is the only way in which it can be fully understood. The musical director and the stage director must therefore be historians.

To be merely historians, however, is not enough. The producers of a musical drama have the obligation to make the work viable in the theatrical climate of today, professional or amateur, *stagione* or repertory. To display a mummy does credit neither to the work nor to the producers of it. The work must be presented as living musical drama.

This requires effort on the part of the production staff. It also requires effort on the part of the audience. A willingness to become acquainted with musical dramas of all kinds can, it is hoped, lead to enlightenment, critical discrimination, and increased enjoyment.

Offered here in Part Two is an historical perspective, with fourteen representative works from the Renaissance to 1960, each an example of a characteristic genre, all successful at different times and in different ways, and here considered as theatre pieces. These works are analyzed to illustrate the stage director's and musical director's concern with the nature of the work they are producing for the musical theatre. While the three works discussed in Part One were treated in greater and more specific production detail, the fourteen works in Part Two are discussed with approach and intrepretation primarily in mind.

The works appear in chronological sequence and have been chosen to illustrate the impressive range of musical drama. Only such connective material as was deemed necessary has been placed between these fourteen studies, and the emphasis, in each case, is upon the responsibility of the stage director to his production staff, to his singers and actors, and to his audiences, that responsibility being to understand the work, to arrive, with the agreement of the musical director, at a point of view about it, and to exert his energies to present that point of view to the audience so that the work makes unified sense and gives pleasure in the theatre.

Two of the fourteen works are seventeenth-century pieces. Monteverdi's *La Favola d'Orfeo* is generally regarded as the first great opera, and Purcell's *Dido and Aeneas* has been described as "the first tragic modern opera."* There are three operas from the eighteenth century, four from the nineteenth, and five works from the twentieth—two operas, two musical comedies, and one operetta.

In selecting only fourteen works from three hundred and fifty years of musical theatre, not every genre could be included and certainly not every country represented. It was not intended to slight masterpieces nor to affront nations. The omission of great works does not imply that the fourteen works chosen are greater. They simply perform their function in this study more conveniently, having been selected, in each case, as representative of a genre which, at a specific time in a specific place, served a musical and dramatic purpose and served it with distinction.

Serving dramatic and musical purposes at the same time has never been easy. The demands of speech and the demands of song are often in conflict with one another. Add the demands of the visual elements and the conflict becomes a war lasting several centuries. It is this blend of the appeals of sense, sound, and sight which has attracted and fascinated audiences since the earliest performances of lyric drama.

The essentials for such performances, in addition to the presence of an audience of spectators, are as follows:

1. the text for listening: words, sung or spoken, and the silences between
2. the text for watching: action, and the immobility between

* Robert E. Moore, *Henry Purcell and the Restoration Theatre*, Cambridge, Mass., 1961, p. 42.

3. the aural surroundings: musical instruments
4. the visual surroundings: costumes surrounding the participants individually, and the setting surrounding the participants as a group.

Dance customarily does without the text for listening. The spoken play customarily does without the aural surroundings, and uses spoken words in preference to words sung.

In forms of musical drama, a significant number of the words are sung instead of spoken. As for the aural surroundings, a single musical instrument or a group of instruments may play while the performers are singing, while they are speaking, or while they are doing neither.

There are mixed forms. Dance has upon occasion used a text for listening, and the spoken play has used dance, song, and instrumental music. While the wholly sung music drama at one extreme and the wholly spoken play at the other are readily distinguished from each other, there are pieces which are a blend of the sung and the spoken, the accompanied and the unaccompanied. If the music used is considerable and functional, the qualifications for inclusion as musical drama are considered to be present.

While song may be more forcefully projected than speech, and under difficult acoustical conditions the sense may be easier to grasp, there is no doubt that the chief advantage of singing over speaking lies in the heightened emotional pleasure derived from the sound. When the intellectual pleasure of the recognition of shapes and repetitions in sound is added, together with the emotional and intellectual pleasure associated with rhythm, the pleasure is involved and intense.

The attainment of a wholly satisfactory blend has not been without difficulty. In some forms of musical theatre, sense has so dominated sound that music and the singing of it have suffered. In other forms, sound has encroached upon sense to an equal point of domination, so that sense has all but disappeared. The reasons for the dominance of one force over others must be sought in the social structure of the times and in the ever-changing literary, theatrical, and musical fashions.

In the fourteen works under scrutiny the appeals of sense,

sound, and sight are blended in strikingly varied proportions. That the musical and dramatic purposes are in each instance so different is a tribute to the range of the lyric drama. That the works have given pleasure many miles from the first audiences for whom they were written and for many years after the time for which they were written may be taken as a tribute to their internationalism and durability.

6

Drama for Music

Much of our ancient theatre seems to have been cast in the lyric form. The Athenian drama of the fifth century B.C. is now generally conceded to have used some kind of declamation for the verse dialogue, and more formal lyricism for the choral odes. For these there are no extant musical scores except for a fragment from the *Orestes* of Euripides, first published in 1892, but there are over forty texts by the dramatists Aeschylus, Sophocles, and Euripides.

For the choral odes, speeches, and dialogues declaimed in open-air performances before large audiences, it is obvious that the softer, more intimate, more rapid, and more realistic end of the vocal range would be less practical than strong projection at a more measured pace with chanting and singing.

The first complete notations of words and music together in the history of drama intended to be sung are those of the liturgical drama of the Middle Ages. These plays, which brought to life the Bible stories, were performed first in the churches themselves and later in the open air. They employed the four essentials of musical drama, namely the text for listening, the text for watching, the aural surroundings, and the visual surroundings.

The words and the notes to be sung are in the manuscripts. The stage action is indicated in directions placed before and between passages of dialogue, and frequently involves walking some distance from one part of the church to another, sometimes with instrumental accompaniment. Instrumental accompaniment was also provided for monologue and dialogue.

Costumes of a special nature are implied when a character is described *in similitudine Sauli* (in the likeness of Saul), and in the Rouen play of the shepherds many boys are required to appear in the roof of the church *quasi angeli* (as if they were angels). In the same play two clerics are clothed in dalmatics as if they were the midwives who officiated at the manger. Women's roles were played by men and of necessity required special costumes.

The setting was the church, cathedral, or monastery itself, with acting areas prescribed with an eye to using a great part of the building. *Herod*, sometimes known as *The Adoration of the Magi*, written for the Abbey of Saint Benoit sur Loire, demands four main areas at some distance from each other. A fifth area aloft is occupied by the angel who addresses the shepherds below.

Medieval music drama began with dialogues in song. The earliest example, from the ninth century, consisted only of one question by the angels at the sepulchre of Christ, the simple reply of the three Marys, and a single statement by the angels announcing the Resurrection.

During the course of five centuries there were developments, the most expectable being the movement from exclusively Latin words to a mixture of Latin and the common language of the people, the movement from wholly sung drama to drama partly sung and partly spoken and eventually mostly spoken, and the movement from plainsong, which is unmeasured music with the subtle rhythms of speech preserved in the singing, to the measured, metrical music which developed in the twelfth century, the kind of music employing whole notes, half notes, quarter notes, and other subdivisions, the kind of music with which we are most familiar.

A musical encroachment took place in the Middle Ages. While the single melodic line of ancient music encourages the Gregorian chant approach to sung words, any attempt at two or more voices moving along together is eventually going to encourage the establishment of carefully measured music with regular accents.

An added voice proceeding at the same pace and exactly as the first voice may sound more interesting than a single voice, but only slightly. An added voice singing several short notes to each long note of a slow chant sounds even more interesting. Most interesting of all, musically, is the stage of advanced polyphony; then two, three, or many voices start and stop at different places, moving freely and weaving threads of melody as they move.

With the unison singing of the early Middle Ages, the problem of meaning by hearing was not a serious one. With the development of polyphonic music the problem became more acute. It has perhaps been exaggerated. It is possible to catch the general drift in polyphonic music and we actually enjoy the alternation of passages which are "in the clear," with elaborate polyphony affording a different kind of pleasure. For reasonable clarity, however, there must be much repetition, and for this reason the pace is likely to seem inadequate for a forward-moving drama.

A dramatic encroachment took place in the Renaissance. Toward the end of the sixteenth century a scholarly group met at the home of Count Giovanni Bardi in Florence to discuss the possibility of recreating the direct word communication and strong dramatic action of ancient Greek drama, the directness and strength to be projected by the singing voice, supported by instruments. Although they yearned after the vitality of Aeschylus and Sophocles, it is not surprising that for a while they stayed in the familiar territory of the aristocratic drama of the period, the pastoral play.

The Italian plays of the sixteenth century intended for cultivated audiences seem, when read today, conspicuously dull. It is not much pleasure to read what was mainly a show. In their own day the visual elements came first: perspective scenery and astounding machines were the chief attractions, with the delight provided by the dancers only a little less. Sound was by no means neglected, since there were large orchestral groups, with choruses, madrigals, and solo songs to be heard. Sense came last. One pastoral play with its shepherds and shepherdesses, its passionate declarations and its disappointments, was much like any other pastoral play, and one could be reasonably sure that a misunderstanding which came near to causing a suicide would be resolved and the suicide averted by a handy god or goddess.

The new, sung pastoral plays had two distinct merits, one dramatic and one musical. The extra urgency and beauty of the singing voice competed with greater success against the visual elements of scenery and machines, while the adoption of monody as opposed to polyphony guaranteed the utmost in clarity of word.

A treatise by Vincenzo Galilei, father of the astronomer, advocated a single vocal line following the natural accents and inflections of the words with close attention to the proper expressiveness. At the same time he criticized the polyphonic style for its inability to follow the emotions exactly, for its unnecessary complexity, and for the obvious difficulty of hearing the words clearly. By 1602 there had been court performances of a pastoral drama for music entitled *Dafne*, of two with the title of *Euridice*, and another treatise on the subject of the new musical style of monody, this one by Giulio Caccini.

There had, of course, been songs in plays before this, but a song does not as a rule describe an immediate experience. Its connection, indeed, with the drama itself may be very slender. Even a song with a stronger connection generally represents a looking backward, a retelling, a consideration, a recollection less agitating than the experience itself, a summing up, a statement of adjustment, or simply a narration of past events. The really new feature of the New Music was its dramatic potential, its concern with the immediate.

The setting of words to music poses a problem of proportion. How expressively close to the word should the sung sound be? If it is very close, as in a Hugo Wolf song, we are in a different realm from musical drama, in that of the exquisitely painted miniature. In the realm of musical drama the sung sound may come just as close but it cannot afford to stay there. The subtle touches must be balanced by the broad strokes appropriate to the stage. The constantly changing dynamics of the spoken play contribute greatly to the holding of attention, in addition to setting up a series of contrasts which, rhythmically and temporally related, give the play the patterns of its shape. These patterns, fused with skill, provide the feeling of unity and totality. In musical drama a similar closeness and distance, literal expressiveness and the formal considered expressiveness, must also alternate so that, in addition to dynamic patterns, extraverbal patterns are imposed upon the texture and an even more involved and fascinating shape is given to the whole.

Recitative, the discovery of the Renaissance monodists, is stiff and dull when, like a poor reader or actor, it clings too closely to the expressive potentiality of a single word and neglects to take account of whole phrases or the emotional content of an entire passage.

The earliest operas partook too largely of this dullness and it is by way of contrast that Monteverdi's writing, with recitative spilling into *arioso*, with strophic songs, madrigals, choruses, and *ritornelli*, commands attention. Its recitative is easily articulated so that the story is advanced and the expression of emotion understood, but recitative is not permitted to predominate to the exclusion of other forms. We have, instead, what we have in the most successful lyric dramatic works, a satisfying relationship between the rates of progress in the various elements. Our interest in the drama is stimulated and our desire to hear music is satisfied, sometimes at the same time, but if separately, with enough alternation to avoid dramatic or musical tedium.

In the earliest operatic experiments, sense was respected at the expense of sound. Monteverdi's *La Favola d'Orfeo* displays an admirable balance between the two.

The Story of Orpheus

LA FAVOLA D'ORFEO *Text by Alessandro Striggio. Music by Claudio Monteverdi. First performed at the ducal palace of the Gonzaga family in Mantua, 1607.*

The operagoer of today, accustomed to the fiery proceedings of *Carmen* and *Aida*, will upon first hearing or first attending *La Favola d'Orfeo* find it static. Most of the dramatic action is contained in the second, third, and fourth acts, the first and the fifth providing the pastoral framework.

After a short orchestral introduction, the Spirit of Music sings a strophic song, with a lovely *ritornello* before and after each strophe.

Some of her admonition might be listened to and acted upon by twentieth-century operagoers.

> I am the Muse of song. My loveliness
> Of sound can calm the troubled spirit,
> And now with splendid rage, now gentleness,
> I can inflame those who are cold and frozen.
>
> Now, as I sing my songs of joy or sorrow,
> Let not a single bird move in the thicket,
> Nor let the lakeshore hear the lapping water;
> Let every little zephyr cease its motion.

The first act takes place on the wedding morning of Orpheus and Eurydice. The lovers have a single solo apiece. Everything else is for nymphs and shepherds, alone, in pairs, and in chorus. The love lamentations of Orpheus are over and joy has taken the place of sorrow. Nothing really happens. The first act is simply a statement and a pastoral setting.

In the second act, sorrow takes the place of joy. As soon as the mood of the first act has been reestablished in the second act, climaxed by a strophic song for Orpheus, the Messenger enters to announce Eurydice's death. Orpheus has a ten-line lament and declaration of purpose, and grieving nymphs and shepherds end the act. Added touches of drama are provided by the Messenger's inability at first to reveal the fact of death, and by her self-reproach for having brought such evil news.

A faint note of comedy is struck in the third act episode with Charon. Orpheus appeals to Charon in five stanzas of three lines each, to end his appeal with a sixth in four lines, fully accompanied. Charon is affected by the sweetness of the music but remains adamant in his refusal to allow Orpheus to cross. Like a bourgeois concertgoer, however, he falls asleep, and Orpheus reaches the authorities of Hades, Pluto and Proserpina.

We are denied the pleas of Orpheus which Pluto has apparently refused between the acts, and at the beginning of the fourth act Proserpina is persuading Pluto to relent. He does so, Eurydice is delivered to Orpheus, and sorrow is once more turned to joy. It lasts a

very little time. When Eurydice is lost to Orpheus a second time a
chorus of spirits sings the moral:

> Orfeo vinse l'inferno e vinto poi
> Fu degli affetti suoi.
> (Orpheus conquered Hades and then
> Was conquered by his own desires)

The fifth act begins with a lament for Orpheus, echoed by
Echo, another superhuman character of pastoral literature and one
much favored by composers as a musical device, condemned as she
was to become a disembodied voice. While Orpheus continues his
lament, his father Apollo makes a happy-ending appearance, and
both rise to heaven as they sing, presumably using the machine
which was often in evidence in the production of pastoral plays.
Sorrow has once more turned to joy, as the shepherds say in song.

Even the greatest enthusiasts find the happy ending unsatisfactory, both dramatically and musically, but there are treasures aplenty
in the work, and the more closely one listens and studies, the more
there are to be found.

What perhaps is most astonishing is how little several characters
who leave a most powerful impression actually sing. Even Orpheus
sings for only slightly over two minutes in the first act and somewhat over three minutes in the second.

The leading character in the first act is La Musica, singing the
prologue, making slight variations in the melody as she sings the five
strophes over what is virtually the same bass. Her words and her
tunes are haunting, but what welds the opening scene together so
strongly is the six *ritornelli*. One carries them in one's memory
through all the Arcadian revelry, and even through the scene in
which the Messenger brings the news of Eurydice's death. Then, at
the very end of the second act, after the shepherds' repeated and
searing lament, softly and once only comes the *ritornello*, last heard
almost two acts ago, assuring us that behind all is still the great power
of music. Two acts later at the beginning of the fifth act, when
Orpheus has lost Eurydice for the second time, we hear the *ritornello*

for the eighth time and realize that so long as there is music, sorrow will once again be replaced by joy.

The leading character of the second act is the Messenger, and her entire short role is like a play with a beginning, a middle, and an end. It takes her five statements before she can bring herself to utter the word *morta* (dead). After the cry of *Ohimè* she recounts in a calmer, more controlled mood every detail of the event, much as Gertrude in Shakespeare's *Hamlet,* reverting to the pastoral style, recounts the drowning of Ophelia. Her final act is to curse herself passionately and to depart to spend the rest of her life in solitude.

Orpheus comes into his own, vocally speaking, in the third act when he pleads for over twelve minutes with the lumpish Charon, and the tiny wordless passage in which Charon falls asleep is most beautiful.

La Speranza (Hope) has only a single passage to sing, the climax of which is the unforgettable "Lascia ogni speranza, voi ch'entrate" ("Abandon hope, all ye who enter here"), which she repeats at a higher pitch. Charon himself has a two-minute role which is equally unforgettable. Pluto's role is not much longer, but his bass voice and his accommodating nature make him most agreeable, and Proserpina, a model of queenly tact, sings an endearing little passage glorifying the rape which elevated her to the throne.

Eurydice has only two passages to sing, both short, the first of less than a minute in the first act, and the second slightly longer in the fourth act as she is dying. Apollo, although he actually sings for longer than Eurydice, La Speranza, Charon, Pluto, and Proserpina, emerges as only the most shadowy of characters. Even Echo, with her three tiny responses, is more memorable.

The richest qualities in the score are perhaps the imaginative variety of forms and styles, the control of that variety into a splendidly organized whole, the expressiveness of the recitative, and the moving tensions and releases of the orchestral texture.

Although a concert reading or a modest production can reveal the many beauties in an atmosphere more conducive to enjoyment than the mere listening to a recording, *L'Orfeo*, to open up fully in its Renaissance glory, needs the extravagance, the cloud machines, the pastoral vistas, the boat upon the Styx, and as many of the fires

of hell as can be safely crammed onto the stage. Unless a rich enthusiast donates a generous budget for such a production, this "first
great opera" will probably continue to hide its considerable light
under the bushel of textbook study and recording, a luminous fly
embedded in academic amber.

7

Baroque Opera

Before the year 1637, opera productions were given not for the general public but at courts of princes and dukes, usually for a single occasion such as a birthday or a wedding.

In 1637 Benedetto Ferrari and Francesco Manelli opened the Teatro di San Cassiano in Venice with a performance of their opera *Andromeda*. This was the first public opera performance in Europe. Monteverdi's successors, encouraged by public taste, moved in the direction of works dominated more by sound than by story. Smooth, attractive melodies were more appealing than subtle recitative, and by the middle of the century, with five new opera houses in little more than a decade after the first, recitative was showing the danger signs of simply filling in the necessary story material between one number and the next. With dramatic expressiveness decreasing in importance, its place was readily taken by the display of singers' voices. The pleasures afforded by scenery and costumes were still competing, but the main attraction of the Baroque *opera seria* was the vocal display.

The often totally undramatic and exhibitionist aria can be blamed to some extent upon the popularity of the castrati singers, and their popularity can in some measure be blamed upon the Roman Catholic Church. To discourage immorality there was a ban on public performance by women. There was also a ban on human castration, but with male sopranos and contraltos doing useful vocal work in church choirs, this ban was more ignored than respected.

When boys are castrated before puberty, the unthickened vocal folds are capable throughout life, until affected by age, of extraor-

FIGURE 4 A prima donna and two castrati: a caricature. The drawing, originally attributed to Hogarth, depicts a scene from an *opera seria* with Francesca Cuzzoni as prima donna. The ungainly physique of the castrato, one of the results of the operation, is outrageously emphasized.

dinary purity and agility. The combination of the boy's high voice and the man's lung capacity invited and received a special kind of vocal writing. The natural and deeper male voice, much prized today, was because of its inferior agility relegated to minor roles. The admiration for the castrato voice also obtained where women were permitted to sing and act publicly, and in mixed casts a classical hero might well be singing in the male soprano register, while his heroine might be a female mezzo-soprano with a lower voice than the hero. (See Figure 4.)

As melodiousness and vocal demonstration took the place of Monteverdi's expressive recitative, the drama in musical theatre received a setback. As Baroque ornamentation cluttered the melodious-

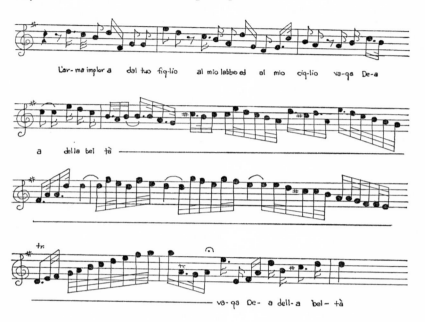

FIGURE 5 A *roulade* from Handel's opera *Alessandro* (*Alexander*),
1726, an example of florid writing. The famous Faustina Bordoni
made her London debut in this opera, singing with her rival
Francesca Cuzzoni, and playing her rival for the love of Alexander.
John Gay burlesqued their rivalry in the characters of Polly and Lucy
in *The Beggar's Opera*. Drawn by Deborah Dryden.

ness and the *da capo* aria became longer and more elaborate, the
drama received an even greater setback. For the benefit of the bravura singer the *da capo* (back to the beginning) aria was in three
parts, the second in contrast to the first, and the third a repetition of
the first, with added embellishments. A contrasting section and a return to the opening mood can have dramatic validity, but most *da
capo* arias were merely showpieces, constructed without regard for
emotional motivation. The repeat with added embellishments could
seldom be accounted for dramatically, and each of the twenty or
more arias became a concert number followed immediately by the

exit of the singer for the encouragement of applause. (See Figure 5.)

This constant interruption of the dramatic continuity successfully prevented any competition from the dramatist. Between the long bravura arias, *recitativo secco* (sung conversation to a sketchy accompaniment) explained the involved action, but since many scores were written to the same familiar texts, not much attention was paid to this dry recitative by either composer or listening public. The arias were far more important. Most important of all was their vocal execution.

In foreign countries, where the classical stories were not as familiar, translations were made of the recitative sections but the arias remained in Italian, because what the singers said while singing was of little consequence and because Italian was the natural language of *bel canto*. England first tried out *opera seria* in English translation throughout, then it tried the bilingual performance, only to capitulate finally to Italian opera in Italian.

In the Baroque period most of the courts north of the Alps as far as Russia employed Italian composers, conductors, singers, and designers, so that Italian domination of opera was almost complete. In France, however, Lully (originally the Italian Lulli) shrewdly adapted Italian styles to French Baroque taste. Lully's respect for the words of a drama kept the French contribution to musical theatre better balanced between drama and music than the Italian. His recitatives, instead of being *secco* and perfunctory, were orchestrally accompanied and partook of the declamatory vigor of the Hôtel de Bourgogne, the distinguished spoken-drama house of Paris.

His operas also provided opportunities for the chorus and the ballet. Castrati singers were not much admired in Paris. The French air was shorter than the Italian aria and did not interrupt the dramatic continuity as disastrously. The French were better dancers than singers and Lully was an accomplished choreographer, which means that interruptions in a French Baroque opera are those of the *divertissements* involving crowds and festive dances. These were sometimes convincingly motivated, but at other times they were present only because the ballet had to be kept busy and the audience's desire to see plenty of dancing had to be satisfied. The French resistance to Italian domination extended into the eighteenth century and Rameau's *tragédies lyriques,* the first of which was written in 1733, further with greater refinement the characteristics of Lully.

English resistance to Italian domination capitulated with Handel's arrival in England in 1710 and the successful production of his opera *Rinaldo* in 1711. Before this, Italian opera had made little headway in that country, and the prevailing style in Henry Purcell's theatre music (Purcell's compositional life covers the fifteen-year period between 1680 and 1695) derived from the English masque, a court entertainment combining poetry, music, spectacle, and dance, with an occasional excursion into drama. *Dido and Aeneas,* 1689, has much more affinity with Jacobean masques and the French lyrical ballet entertainments than with Italian *opera seria.* It was also, like court entertainments, intended for a single production only. Its superiority to most masque operas lies in its dramatic urgency, of which Purcell made the most potent musical use. *Dido and Aeneas* and almost any *opera seria* stand at opposite ends of the Baroque spectrum. In Purcell's work the music springs fully armed, as it were, from the dramatic impetus. In an *opera seria* the vocalism was of the greatest importance and the music was subservient to it. The drama, such as it was, merely provided the framework.

Today's repertory displays Baroque operas infrequently, although many of Handel's operas have been revived, mainly because of the high quality of their music. Modern audiences put up with the inadequate drama and the stereotyped characters for the sake of the music, not always fully understanding the prodigious difficulties put in the way of the librettists of the eighteenth century. With bravura singing preeminent, librettists had a hard time planning a convincing story around two dozen arias, making sure that each aria contrasted suitably with other arias written for the same singer and that each aria came at the close of a scene, or arranging matters so that the singer could leave the stage to the gratifying sound of applause. When each aria intentionally brings the dramatic action to a halt, a dramatist has to be as adaptable as a present-day television script writer who plans commercial breaks with much the same regularity and for much the same purpose—the display of merchandise.

Dido and Aeneas.

*Text by Nahum Tate. Music by Henry Pur-
cell. First performed at Josias Priest's Boarding School for Young Gentlewomen in Chelsea, London, 1689.*

Dido and Aeneas is not in the professional repertory, although it has
been staged in small professional theatres and frequently by amateur
groups. It has been avoided by large professional theatres and has
never been produced at Covent Garden nor at the Metropolitan. *La
Serva Padrona,* which is much smaller in scope, has been seen at both.

Dido and Aeneas was written specifically for amateurs, and first
performed at the Great School House in Chelsea to which Josias
Priest, dancing master, had moved in 1680. Priest was a choreographer attached to the theatre in Dorset Garden, and his name is
mentioned in connection with the dramatic opera of Macbeth altered
by William Davenant from Shakespeare and staged after Davenant's
death.

Priest seems to have been a capable and rather distinguished person, and it was no impertinence for him to secure the services of
Nahum Tate as librettist for his school opera, a man who three years
later was appointed poet laureate. For a composer Priest turned to
the best possible, Henry Purcell, who for several years had been the
keeper of the King's wind instruments, had written official compositions for King and State, and was the organist of Westminster Abbey.

Because *Dido and Aeneas* is a short opera it is sometimes called a
one-act, which it is not. Often performed by amateurs and usually
done continuously, it can seem like a rather long one-act lasting
about seventy minutes. It is frequently performed with a minimum
of scenery and with not always very well designed or constructed
costumes. To be quite frank, since it is royalty free and the orchestra
consists only of stringed instruments and the staging *can* be simplified, it has become "a cheap show to do," and since it is at the same

time one of the great musical theatrical works of all time, it has become irresistible.

It suffers from misrepresentation. *Dido and Aeneas* is a Baroque
masque-opera originally intended for performance by aristocratic
young ladies with rich, influential, and in all probability theatregoing
parents. A. K. Holland comments upon the simplicity in range and
style, but refers to the limited resources as responsible for the modest
bounds within which the instrumentation and stage requirements are
kept. It seems logical that with young voices to be projected, the
choice of a small band of strings was a wise one. It may be questioned
whether the production was visually as simple as is generally supposed.

The opera is in three acts and in the text there is a prologue. Because no music for the prologue exists, it is often stated that Purcell
did not set the prologue to music. Whether he did so or not, the fact
remains that the prologue was written, and that in itself has some
bearing upon the production style of *Dido and Aeneas*. The preface
by William H. Cummings to the facsimile libretto states in a foot-
note: "Purcell probably did not set the Prologue to music. We know
that on other occasions he exercised a similar discretion in the treatment of stage drama." This is true, but *Dido and Aeneas* is not a
stage drama in the usual seventeenth-century definition of stage
drama. The semi-operas of the period are stage dramas with long
sections of spoken dialogue. What we have of *Dido and Aeneas*,
however, employs no spoken dialogue and seems to have been intended from the beginnning as a through-composed opera.

There are three possibilities. The first is that William H. Cummings and others are correct and that although Nahum Tate provided him with a prologue, Purcell chose not to use it. The second
is that, because no vocal music was written for it, the prologue was
performed in speech and the necessary dances were borrowed from
already written dance music, probably by Purcell. The twentieth
century rejects this immediately as stylistically unsound. However,
seventeenth-century style was less rigid, and speech and song were
teamed where we today would be disinclined to team them. Few
producers today would follow a through-composed opera with a
spoken epilogue of twenty-nine lines. For the production of *Dido*

and Aeneas, Tom d'Urfey wrote a special epilogue which was delivered by Lady Dorothy Burke.

The dances could have been composed for the occasion and the manuscript lost, but if nothing was composed for the prologue it would not have been impossible to borrow from Purcell's store of compositions. The overture to *Come, ye sons of art away,* an ode for Queen Mary's birthday, was used in the following year in Dryden's and Howard's *The Indian Queen.*

The third possibility, too tempting to be accepted without caution, is that the prologue was as fully set to music as the three acts which follow, but that the music has never been discovered. Some encouragement to this theory is given by the fact that the first published edition in 1841 omitted music which was later found. Twentieth-century productions have added material for the abrupt ending to the second act. In the London Mermaid Theatre production which opened on September 9, 1951, a welcome song for His Majesty on his return from Newmarket October 21, 1682, was supplied for the six lines not composed (or composed but lost) and clearly demanded by the libretto. In addition, an air from *The Virtuous Wife* provided a dance. The Mermaid Theatre, designed by Michael Stringer and C. Walter Hodges and built in an old school, was the setting for the famous production which cast Kirsten Flagstad as Dido, Maggie Teyte as Belinda, Edith Coates as the Sorceress, and Murray Dickie as the Attendant Spirit. This Mermaid Theatre should not be confused with its offshoot, the Mermaid Theatre built out of a warehouse on a wharf on the north bank of the Thames.

When the music for the finale of the second act is missing and six lines and a dance are called for by the text, it is not unreasonable to raise questions, at least, about the prologue.

A. K. Holland in *Henry Purcell* makes no mention of the prologue. Surprisingly, J. A. Westrup in *Purcell* makes no mention of it either, although (p. 135) he links *Dido and Aeneas* with John Blow's *Venus and Adonis,* which has a prologue of a similar sort. Robert E. Moore, in *Henry Purcell and the Restoration Theatre,* dismisses it as "a short pastoral prologue, perhaps suggested by Blow's *Venus and Adonis*—Phoebus, nereids and shepherds appear—in which Purcell apparently took little interest and never set" (p. 41).

The prologue cannot correctly be described as short. Counting lines of verse is no satisfactory clue to length of scene, but if the prologue had been set to music and performed it would probably have consumed a third of the performance time. With eighty-two lines, it is longer than any of the acts which follow, and the whole piece would then have run something over an hour and a half.

Westrup and others make reference to the modest nature of a school performance, Westrup going so far as to state that "the resources of a boarding school were inevitably more limited than those of Dorset Garden." A more limited production than some of Dorset Garden could range, however, from simplicity to considerable extravagance. Shadwell's *Psyche*, which had been staged at Dorset Garden more than a dozen years earlier, asks for a deep walk in a mighty wood, a temple of Apollo, a fire, a rocky desert with precipices, a high rock from which characters leap into the sea, a palace of Cupid with little cupids flying about the columns, a group of Cyclops forging vases of silver, balconies thick with people, an altar which breaks apart, a vanishing garden of statues and orange, lemon, and pomegranate trees, together with a palace, a marsh full of willows, rising and descending furies, plunges into a river, a descent of Venus with Cupid flying up and descending with her from the clouds, and in Act 5 an elaborate scene in hell followed by an equally elaborate scene in heaven.

Beside all this, the requirements of *Dido and Aeneas* are modest enough but by no means unextravagant.

Even if we assume that the prologue was never set to music nor performed, *Dido and Aeneas* calls for more than "modest facilities" and it was, after all, being staged and choreographed by Josias Priest, who was associated with Dorset Garden. Usually performed today in a single setting, the demands in the text of the three acts are a palace scene, followed by a cave scene which changes in mid-act to a grove. (The word *grove* in texts of this period should often be read *groove*, meaning stage groove. Here it actually means grove.) There is the probable appearance of clouds (a favorite device of the period), the sound of thunder and rain, the descent of the sorceress as the attendant spirit, a port scene with ships, the appearance of a tomb with cupids appearing in the clouds over it, and for the finale a dance of cupids. It is not clear from the text whether at the close of the opera the direction "Cupids dance" means simply that cupids enter and dance, or whether the cupids above in the clouds are required to descend and dance. Descents and ascents of this kind were frequent and popular in the Baroque era.

If the prologue were performed, with or without song, the technical requirements would be as follows: "Phoebus rises in his chariot over the sea, the Nereids out of the sea. Venus descends in her chariot. The Tritons out of the sea." One scene change is required.

The unlikely event that the prologue was performed in speech instead of in song, with music for the dances, would have offered one considerable advantage. In a production intended for influential parents and friends, whom it was important not to offend, the young ladies with no sense of pitch or with poor singing voices could be tactfully used in a striking and beautiful prologue.

Westrup points out that Tate, although he based *Dido and Aeneas* upon his earlier *Brutus of Alba,* given at Dorset Garden in 1678, wrote virtually a new libretto for Priest and Purcell, rather than an adaptation. It is noted that he appreciated the conditions under which the performance was to be given. If Nahum Tate had seen the facilities in the Great School House and discussed the project with Josias Priest, it seems remarkable that he wrote the work as he did. It would have been simpler and far more tactful to write a straightforward libretto without adding stage directions for effects not possible of achievement. One may well imagine that the idea was more ambitious than the execution. Most American musical comedies are forced to cut out numbers during the out-of-town tryouts, if only to reduce the length of the first act. Perhaps Mr. Tate asked for too much. Perhaps he was not given all he wanted.

He wrote the text, however, with the requirements and the school hall in mind. He also wrote it with the sophisticated audience in mind, most of whom were the parents of the sophisticated girls in the Chelsea School. Tom d'Urfey's epilogue, spoken by Lady Dorothy Burke, was intended to set them all laughing (the customary procedure, after the tragedy, in the professional theatres of the day). Its sly references to innocence, the school's regulations discouraging the attentions of the lewd fops of the town, and the trick of slipping a note into an orange bought from an orange wench at the theatre were a direct address to those "in the know." Prologues and epilogues in the period were racy, convivial, satirical, and topical. Quite young girls added a fashionable titillation by speaking unladylike words and phrases. Lady Dorothy's lines, considering the author of them, are ostentatiously respectable, but at the close she smilingly promises an end to this Chelsea world of innocence: "And in few years we shall be all in tune."

With such an audience and such a cast, with the theatrical reputation and choreographic skill of Josias Priest and memories of Dorset Garden productions, and presumably with full knowledge of the school's facilities, Tate wrote his text, which begins with the prologue.

It is by no means an irrelevant pastoral. It is in three parts, the second and third descending, respectively, in gravity and in social consequence. The first character to appear is Phoebus, rising in the chariot over the sea while the nereids rise out of the sea. The effect is a spectacular one of the rising of the sun, and the two motions have a visual choreographic value.

A few lines later Venus descends in her chariot and the Tritons come out of the sea to perform a dance. The theme of all-powerful love, the major theme of the drama, is now touched upon, and although Venus protests her harmlessness, pointing out her blind archers, Phoebus retorts: "Blind they are but strike the heart." Venus, more gently, replies: "What Phoebus says is always true. They wound indeed but 'tis a pleasing smart."

Phoebus, impressed, pays homage to Venus, and the chorus pays homage to them both. There is a dance of nereids, and the first part of the prologue is over. Phoebus continues on his way and Venus retires. The young man we are shortly to see, Aeneas, is the son of Venus by Anchises, a mortal struck blind for boasting of his intimacy with the goddess.

The second part of the prologue overlaps the first, as Spring comes to welcomes Venus before the gods depart to soft music. Spring sings an inviting ditty and the second part ends with yet another dance of nymphs.

At this point country shepherds and shepherdesses enter, obvi-

ously more rustic and realistic to contrast with the Arcadian characters in the company of the semi-divinity, Spring. There is a dialogue
contrast too, and a "He and She" duet ending with a choral reference
to intoxication and a country maids' dance that may well have used
the grotesque attitudes of drunkenness for comic effect.

The familiar first act begins with the entrance of Dido, Belinda,
and the royal train. The lovely "Peace and I are strangers grown"
strikes the serious note which was prophesied in the prologue. Dido
has been wounded by one of love's arrows, and the object of her passion is the son of the goddess herself:

> Whence could so much virtue spring
> What storms, what battles did he sing?
> Anchises' valour mixed with Venus's charms
> How soft in peace and yet how fierce in arms.

Belinda and others cheer Dido by telling her that the hero loves
her as she loves him, and Aeneas arrives to support the contention. A
triumphing chorus and a triumphing dance end the first act.

Just as the opera began with superhuman figures of the eternal
forces of goodness and life, the second part of it begins with the
forces of evil and destruction. The scene is a cave, and the sorceress
and her enchantresses are plotting against the lovers. In spite of a
certain sinister quality in the orchestra the witches sound a jolly lot,
and every critic has marvelled at the oddly artificial nature of Restoration theatrical convention. The witches are really intended more
as good fun for the more sportive girls of the Great School than as
any credible representation of wickedness. Their conjuring leads to
the musically picturesque device of an echo chorus:

> In our deep vaulted cell the charm we'll prepare,
> Too dreadful a practice for this open air.

This in turn leads to an echo dance of enchantresses and fairies, a
splendid invitation to choreographic display.

The scene changes to Diana's woods, and there is a dance to
entertain Aeneas, who has successfully killed a boar. The storm
magically induced by the witches now interrupts the hunt and the

party hurries off to shelter. Aeneas is prevented by the Sorceress, disguised as Mercury, and agrees to Jove's command that he instantly set sail for Italy in order to found Rome. It is at this point that the music to the end of the act is missing. The requirement consists simply of music for a chorus of enchantresses and a dance danced by the young girls of Carthage.

The third act begins in the port. It is simply described as "Scene the Ships," which probably meant that the back scene or shutters depicted the port viewed from the city of Carthage. A jolly sailors' chorus and dance provide yet another relief from the prevailing tragedy, and the enchantresses gleefully sing:

> Destruction's our delight, delight our greatest sorrow,
> Elissa dies tonight and Carthage flames tomorrow.

There is another dance, and with no change of scene noted, since Aeneas is on his way to his ship, the final scene opens. After an introduction in which Dido refuses the counsel of the court, it consists only of an exchange of eight speeches between Dido and Aeneas. It is a compact little scene. Aeneas tries to convince Dido that he is powerless to disobey the gods. The merriment induced in the twentieth century by the couplet

> Thus on the fatal banks of Nile
> Weeps the deceitful crocodile

is unfortunate. In the seventeenth century the reference was no funnier than a reference to a hydra or a dragon. Dido accuses her lover of perfidy. Aeneas is suddenly of a mind to stay with her and defy the gods, but he has not reckoned with the pride of a queen, and the entire court is present for this confrontation:

> No, faithless man, thy course pursue,
> I'm now resolved as well as you.
> No repentance shall reclaim
> The injured Dido's slighted flame
> For 'tis enough whate'er you now decree
> That you had once a thought of leaving me.

The chorus comments:

> Great minds against themselves conspire
> And shun the cure they most desire.

Realism is utterly abandoned as Dido welcomes death. There is no stabbing, as in one of the legends, nor a pyre as in another, and in Christopher Marlowe's play and Metastasio's later *opera seria*. Nahum Tate has already informed us that there will be no pyre until the next day when all Carthage burns. Against the ships in the theatre candlelight appears a tomb, or more probably shutters are drawn to blot out the ships, and on these shutters might be painted not only the tomb but the cupids in the air above.

Whether the tomb is solid or painted, the music assures the proper mood for the sad but decorative Baroque ending. Even those who find the mention of crocodiles hilarious are generally hushed by the chorus or by Dido's recitative leading into her lament:

> Thy hand, Belinda, darkness shades me,
> On thy bossom let me rest
> More I would but death invades me
> Death is now a welcome guest.

The words of the air itself have drawn praise, even from those who are grudging in their appreciation of Nahum Tate's contribution:

> When I am laid in earth may my wrongs create
> No trouble in thy breast,
> Remember me, but ah! forget my fate.

The stage direction for cupids to appear in the clouds above is placed at the side of the recitative. It would be in the Baroque scenic tradition to lower cut-out cupids to hang before the painted cupids on the shutters. It would also be perfectly acceptable to float live cupids against the painted cupids on the scenery. The superb lament, with its passacaglia bass, is well known outside the context of the opera. The chorus makes specific reference to cupids scattering roses on Dido's tomb, and the cupids dance slowly and mournfully. The opera is over.

It is possible to scatter roses from dancing positions on the stage floor, but more effective, perhaps, to scatter them from above, whether from live cupids or by some device from constructed ones. Joseph Kerman, whose interests are almost exclusively musical, shrewdly comments that *"Le merveilleux* was as imperative in a school play as at the court of Louis XIV" (*Opera as Drama*, p. 60).

Most productions of *Dido and Aeneas* will continue to be simply staged, and it is far better that they be simply staged than not staged at all or badly staged. A more decorative production than usual was done by Elemer Nagy at the Yale Drama School in 1953, with settings and costumes by Donald Oenslager (Plate 6) and with Heidi Krall singing Dido.

If Purcell actually wrote music for the prologue and that music were one day discovered, some enterprising producer might be tempted to accord it the Baroque panoply to which it is entitled, complete to the plumes upon the helmets and a chariot for Phoebus, a production as professional as the one with which Josias Priest surrounded Lady Dorothy and her schoolmates.

Dido Deserted

DIDONE ABBANDONATA *Text by Pietro Metastasio. Nearly forty musical versions, the first, with music by Domenico Sarro, performed in Naples, 1724.*

Didone Abbandonata was written by Pietro Trapassi, later called Metastasio, in 1724 when the author was twenty-six years old. He had written a tragedy, *Il Giustino*, when he was fourteen, and when he was twenty-three a birthday piece for music called *The Gardens of the Hesperides*. The kingdom of Naples, where he worked, had been ceded to Austria in 1713 and was not returned to Spain until 1735. At the age of thirty-two Metastasio succeeded Apostolo Zeno as poet laureate to the Emperor Charles VI, and thereafter lived in Vienna.

Metastasio was a specialist in the *melodramma*, a play written in verse for the express purpose of being supplied with music, vocal and orchestral. *Dido Deserted* was first set to music by Sarro in 1724, and through the remainder of the eighteenth century and well into the nineteenth received nearly forty musical settings, the last one Karl Reissiger's in 1823. It is significant that Metastasio himself composed and played the harpsichord, both valuable accomplishments for a writer of *melodramma* texts. A later Metastasio drama is *La Clemenza di Tito*, which had been set to music half a dozen times before Mozart used Mazzolà's adaptation of the drama in 1791. It must be noted that there were no copyright laws at this time and that Metastasio's dramas were not always set as he had written them. Handel did not set a Metastasian drama to music, but he set several texts which had been altered and adapted from Metastasio.

Metastasio drew his subject matter from ancient history or legend, and since he wrote with stage production in mind, he subscribed to the fashions of the day, some of which resemble our present-day fashions and others of which are entirely different.

The Baroque era inherited the Renaissance passion for splendid scenery and effects, frequently painted by first-class artists, like Raphael. The visual splendor had little to do with realism. What one saw on stage was not trying to be like life. Everything was bigger and better than in life, more colorful, more concentrated, more compelling, and more astounding. Nor was what one heard like life. It was equally varied, colorful, concentrated, compelling, and astounding.

The words artificial and contrived have acquired unflattering connotations, but all art is artificial, and to contrive means first to think up and then to make or construct. Good contriving produces results which are solid and satisfying. Baroque art is highly decorated but well contrived; that is to say, its foundations are solid, and the decorations, though lavish, are an integral part of the total design.

A Baroque church interior first astonishes the viewer by its profusion of objects and colors. Little by little the profusion seems to shift into place, and finally he sees that profusion is not confusion but that there is a total plan of which the curving planes, the gilded statues, and the carefully arranged vistas are all a part. In keyboard music of the Baroque era one hears the sonic counterparts of the curving planes, gilded statues, and vistas, and once again one is at first more aware of the decoration than of the firm structure of which the decoration is a beautifully modelled and rhythmic exten- sion. A dramatic piece, combining sight and sound, is all this and more too. The solid scenery and static decorations resemble the church interior, and many of the motifs used are similar, but there is moving scenery, scenery which opens and closes before the eyes of the audience, clouds which descend from the sky, chariots which roll across the stage, and demons who rise from below on coils of smoke.

The eighteenth century, in addition to its addiction to spectacle, was the age of bravura singing, with male sopranos and altos showing off their skill in *legato,* ornamentation, dexterity, power, sweetness, breath control, and vocal dramatic intensity. The purpose of a Baroque opera was to set a great variety of opportunities for singing, supported by orchestra, against a background of candelit and lamplit spectacle.

The necessity of displaying several leading singers in a succes- sion of contrasting arias, each aria summing up, as it were, the emo- tions aroused by the action and recitative dialogue of the short scene leading to it, presents obvious dramaturgical problems. Insofar as such problems are soluble, Metastasio solved them. He supplied scen- ery enough, with a perspective view of Carthage being built, the temple of Neptune, a seaport with ships preparing for departure, and a royal palace with a perspective view of Carthage in flames. For the four leading singers he supplied eighteen arias, and an additional six for three minor characters. Every number of the twenty-four is an aria. There are no duets or larger ensembles of any kind, and no chorus. No character has more than two arias in each act.

The action is handled mostly in dry recitative. Of the twenty- four arias in *Didone Abbandonata,* twenty-three are what are usually called "exit arias." Dido has one entrance aria and a splendid immo- lation scene at the end.

As the opera opens, Aeneas has been instructed to leave Carthage and to found Rome. Unable to tell Dido, he confides in her sister Selene, who is secretly in love with him. Iarbas, King of the Moors, is a violent rival suitor for Dido but is refused. At the end of the first act Aeneas tells Dido that he must leave her. Intrigue complicates the second act.

In the third act, climax mounts upon climax, both visually and dramatically. Iarbas matches Dido's righteous anger with his own evil rage. Sending guards to pile wood upon the flames to make them rise higher yet, he promises that Carthage will be laid in such ruins that those who pass the site of it will not even know it was there. Dido's immolation solo is written not as an aria but as a dramatic recitative ending with the words,

> Precipiti Cartago
> Arda la reggia, e sia
> Il cenere di lei la tomba mia.
>
> (Let Carthage fall,
> Let the palace burn
> And let its ashes be my tomb.)

She throws herself into the flaming ruins and is lost to sight in flame and smoke. At the same time, the sea on the horizon swells up and comes slowly toward the palace. Heavy clouds hang in the sky, and the dramatist suggests loud music. There is a fierce fight between fire and water. Water conquers.

Suddenly the sky clears. Gentle music is now called for. The realm of Neptune shines placidly and Neptune himself appears, seated on a shell drawn by sea creatures and surrounded by nereids and sirens. There is an odd foreshadowing of Rhinemaidens and of Wagner's blue sky and bright weather which follow his raging personal and natural storms.

The final aria, which is for Neptune, a new character, asks for all the realms of the sea to return to peace and calm once more, and so the opera ends.

It is small wonder that nearly forty composers found it worth their while to spend time and energy on this text. Half their work had already been done for them in the alternation of fury and tenderness, villainy and nobility, with words beautiful in themselves, yet not overdecorated to rival the music which they might inspire.

Opera seria is not in fashion, and much scorn has been heaped upon these "stop and go" operas with their worship of castrato singing and their preoccupation with sensational effects. It is not surprising that some dramatists of the period gave up and threw together shabby pieces of formula, but this is also the way many modern plays, films, and television scripts have come into being. There are countless shoddy scripts but there are some good ones, good in spite of the straitjacket format. Metastasio's first drama for music is good. A careful assessment of it will conquer prejudice and stimulate imagination.

8

Ballad Opera

Side by side with the solemnity and stateliness of the Baroque there was laughter. One cannot have serious entertainment for the educated without a more spontaneous and popular entertainment for the less-educated or wholly uneducated. This is not to imply that the well-educated did not enjoy comedy. Many probably preferred it, but the working classes had little in common with lofty classical stories, elegant pastorals, or works entailing, for their full appreciation, some technical knowledge of music and the art of singing.

Laughter is popular. As soon as anything is taken too seriously, someone pokes fun. One can also laugh simply for the joy of living. The musical comedy of the Baroque period was either burlesque of pretentious opera or it took the form of country jigs, acted ballads, or farces laced with songs. Sung comedies in Italy used the recitative so readily adapted to the Italian language, and two short ones were often performed as *intermezzi* between the acts of an *opera seria*. Pergolesi's *La Serva Padrona* (*The Maid as Mistress*) had its first showing with the same composer's *opera seria, The Proud Prisoner*. Metastasio wrote *intermezzi* for the intermissions of *Dido Deserted*, and these little skits, with their contemporary situation-comedy and backstage scuttlebutt, must have been refreshing after a long bout of castrato warbling and posturing.

Sung comedies in France, Germany, and England used spoken dialogue between the songs, and the form was called respectively *comédie en vaudevilles* (later *opéra comique*), *Singspiel*, and *ballad opera*. John Gay's *The Beggar's Opera* was not quite the first of the genre, but it was easily the most distinguished.

The Beggar's Opera

Text by John Gay. Music chosen by John Gay, arranged by Dr. Johann Pepusch. First produced at Lincoln's Inn Fields Theatre, London, 1728.

There could scarcely be a greater gulf between two works of the musical theatre than the one between the two most famous early English operas, *Dido and Aeneas* and *The Beggar's Opera*. The first is a moving treatment of a classical love story, dramatically perfunctory but musically sophisticated and yet at the same time deeply felt, the last of a genre which died almost as soon as it had been born. It was intended for amateurs and planned for a single performance.

The second is all mockery and cynicism, dramatically sophisticated and musically perfunctory, yet functional in its brazen appropriation of excellent and attractive popular tunes, this one nearly the first of the ballad opera genre which was to be, in one form or another, popular for a century or more. It was intended for professionals and played by them over a hundred times in its first two seasons at Lincoln's Inn Fields Theatre.

It is as natural to refer to John Gay's *The Beggar's Opera* as it is to refer to Henry Purcell's *Dido and Aeneas*, forgetting that in the first instance we are referring to the dramatist (and we would scarcely presume to use the term librettist in reference to Gay) while in the second instance we are referring, as we so often do, to the composer. Both Nahum Tate, the dramatist-librettist of *Dido and Aeneas*, and Dr. Pepusch, the musician who assisted John Gay, are comparatively minor characters. Dr. Pepusch, music director at Lincoln's Inn Fields, composed almost nothing for *The Beggar's Opera*. Even the little overture he wrote is largely based on Air 47, "One evening having lost my way" (Lucy's "I'm like a skiff on the ocean toss'd"), and it was possibly Gay's idea that the overture should be unpretentious, based on a song from the drama. Originally the songs were to have been sung without accompaniment, but the inadvisability of this soon became evident, and Dr. Pepusch supplied basses for the tunes. These are printed in the 1729 edition, together with the overture scored for two oboes and string quartet. *The Beggar's Opera* is seldom in a repertory program. Even in its first season it upset the repertory system by running more than sixty consecutive performances.

Today it presents a number of serious production problems. The tunes, with few exceptions, are no longer familiar to every member of the audience. A modern audience, therefore, is hearing attractive old tunes instead of popular street songs. The audience of 1728, accustomed to the words to which these tunes were generally sung, responded enthusiastically to the piquant new words which Mr. Gay had provided. We can compare the words associated with the tunes to Gay's altered words, but we no longer appreciate the connotations of the day and we are conscious of being left out of the joke.

Air 67 is the charming tune of "Greensleeves," very familiar to almost everyone. Even the words are fairly familiar:

> Alas, my lord, you do me wrong
> To cast me off discourteously,
> And I have loved you so long
> Delighting in your company.
> Greensleeves was all my joy
> Greensleeves was my delight,
> Greensleeves was my heart of gold
> And who but Lady Greensleeves.

A hint of the extra dimension many of the songs in *The Beggar's Opera* must have provided for the audiences of Gay's own day may be appreciated by singing to Gay's almost Brechtian words the tune of "Greensleeves" and recollecting the personal regret in the sentimental original. Macheath sings the song as the last of ten short ditties in the condemned hold where he stands in a melancholy posture, drinking wine and brandy in preparation for his execution:

Since laws were made for ev'ry degree
To curb vice in others as well as me,
I wonder we han't better company
Upon Tyburn tree!

But gold from law can take out the sting,
And if rich men like us were to swing,
'Twou'd thin the land such numbers to string
Upon Tyburn tree!

The tunes in *The Beggar's Opera* are attractive enough and Gay's words piquant enough for enjoyment in the theatre by a modern audience with no knowledge at all of the eighteenth-century associations. What must be resolved by the stage director and the music director is the prevailing style of the work, its reduction in length, and precisely what kind of singer, actor, or singing actor is required in each role.

The musical style of the work ought to be related to the abilities of the cast and the size of the auditorium in which the piece is to be performed. It can easily be accompanied by a single harpsichord, by a chamber ensemble consisting of flute, oboe, string quartet, with an added double bass and the occasional use of older instruments such as the viola d'amore and the viola da gamba, or by a somewhat larger orchestra.

The setting and costuming style may range from the brilliant colors and stylized cleanliness of the Claud Lovat Fraser designs of the 1920 production, through adaptations of Hogarth, to the dingiest realism.

If the stage director is an academic pedant who insists upon doing everything as written with no deletions, *The Beggar's Opera* is going to be rather too long for the average audience. This is a pity, since most of the dialogue is lively and the songs, all brief, are appealing and excellently contrasted. Several times a single character will have two in succession. Mrs. Peachum has her three in succession, an E minor piece of sadism about young men about to be executed, a D major warning, at first graceful in a passage comparing maidens to moths and then a positive upward scale passage of an octave leading to the "what I dare not name" joke, and the third a cynical, rippling ditty proclaiming the adage of the Restoration period a half century earlier that becoming a wife is a general invitation to licentiousness.

Macheath has twenty-two solos, counting his snatches in the condemned hold, and a few are dispensable. In spite of the "nice impartiality to our two ladies that it is impossible for either of them to take offence" as claimed in the introduction, Polly has eleven solos and nine duets, while Lucy has ten solos and five duets.

It should be noted that several of the numbers called duets are strictly speaking not duets at all, but simply two solos using the same tune, one singer singing the first verse and another the second. Twentieth-century arrangers have revised some of them so that the singers sing together for at least a brief passage. It has been the custom, also, to change a solo into a duet or even a trio, in order to end an act with an ensemble rather than with a solo.

Air 16, "Were I laid on Greenland's coast," is a sequence of solos for Polly and Macheath, but it generally is given a line or two of duet singing. Air 17, "O what pain it is to part," is given to Polly, but in many productions is turned into a duet and ends the first act. It makes a satisfactory mock-touching finale, but necessitates the dropping of the original ending with the double simile song, "The miser thus a shilling sees" for Macheath and "The boy thus, when his sparrow's flown" for Polly, an engaging tune of Scottish nostalgia set to the most preposterous of similes. This ridicule of similes promised in the introduction—"I have introduc'd the similes that are in all your celebrated operas"—achieves little audience reaction today, since we are less familiar with the word content of Handelian *opera seria* arias than the audiences of 1728, who had been listening to them for seventeen seasons.

It is in this respect and in the string of solos that the burlesque of Italian *opera seria* is displayed. The songs themselves, being mostly folk songs, are simple, direct, and unadorned, the very reverse of the *da capo* arias of *opera seria* and therefore a sort of burlesque by contrast. We have no means of knowing with what familiar castrato or prima donna mannerisms the singers of these simple songs stepped forward to utter their inappropriate similes or reveal the ludicrous shallowness of the emotions they were expressing.

This reverse burlesque is paralleled in the story and the characters. *Opera seria* concerned itself with classical and mythological love-and-honor plots set in exotic countries, kings and queens, the capture of noble prisoners, and the fall of empires. *The Beggar's Opera* turns this operatic world inside out by substituting the underworld of contemporary London, lust and dishonesty, highwaymen and whores, the only capture that of a gangster and the only empire that of the rogues and vagabonds—an empire which shows no sign of falling and, with the example of corrupt government, never will.

Polly and Lucy, obviously intended to be burlesques of Francesca Cuzzoni and Faustina Bordoni, the rival *prime donne* of the Italian opera, have no opportunity to ridicule the decorative excesses of Italian singing except briefly in "Why, how now, madam Flirt," in which Handelian "divisions" are placed (seventeen of them) on the most uneuphonic English word *dirt* in the first stanza, and less aptly on *made* in the second.

Polly is invited to trill on her section of the last song in Act 1, and it may be that Lavinia Fenton and subsequent Pollies of the eighteenth century and early nineteenth century accepted this as a general invitation to decorate penultimate or antepenultimate syllables in other songs. This would naturally depend upon their vocal ability and mastery of florid singing. An untutored singer would burlesque herself rather than an operatic prima donna if she attempted ornaments she was unable to perform. The modern audience for the most part cares little about the amount or the nature of the operatic satire in *The Beggar's Opera*, as it cares little about the Walpole-Townshend political satire, or the literary satire implicit in the dialogue and the gentlemanly hero and the sentimental heroine. The casting problem remains.

How well must the music be sung? The first production used the regular members of the Lincoln's Inn Fields acting company, and while many actors and actresses sang adequately for plays, they were not professional singers of the caliber of Catherine Tofts and Anastasia Robinson, who themselves were modest performers beside the international Cuzzoni and Bordoni and even Dr. Pepusch's own wife, Margherita de l'Épine.

By the time Mary Ann Paton was singing Polly in the 1830s and Sims Reeves was singing Macheath in the 1850s, the nature of the piece had somewhat changed. The musical interest in the opera is purely melodic. There are no complexities or felicitous touches of orchestration and few subtleties, but to hear forty or fifty good tunes in a single evening at the theatre is an experience not to be missed, and if the tunes are well sung the pleasure is considerable. This pleasure is increased if the contrast between the beautiful or jolly tunes and the prosaic, almost doggerel, and sometimes biting words is clearly presented.

Singing ability alone, however, is not enough. The inappropriateness of a vocally ladylike Mrs. Peachum may have a comic effect, but if several characters give the impression of inconsistency, singing sweetly and speaking coarsely, we have in performance something in the nature of the several recordings of the work which have tried to solve the problem by using a double cast, one of singers and one of actors.

On the other hand, acting ability alone is not enough. The dashing Macheath who pipes thinly when he sings is as unsatisfactory as an unsteady Polly or a reedy Lucy. Although *The Beggar's Opera* is not generally classified as an operetta, it shares the casting problems of operetta in its demand for actors with more than usual singing ability and singers with more than usual acting ability.

The Coronation Year film of *The Beggar's Opera* which appeared in 1953, directed by Peter Brook, used the professional voices of Adele Leigh, Jennifer Vyvyan, and John Cameron, but without their appearance. Edith Coates, an operatic singer of many years of distinguished service, played the small role of Mrs. Coaxer, and Stanley Holloway, with quite enough voice for Lockit, sang and acted his own role. Dorothy Tutin, as Polly, and Daphne Anderson, as Lucy, did not sing theirs, but Laurence Olivier, with no singing voice, sang Macheath. The result was chaotic.

In 1952 there was a radio broadcast by the English Opera Group, and in the following year, with some cast changes, a stage production which solved the problem by using singers with considerable acting ability and experience, including Peter Pears as Macheath, Gladys Parr, Norman Lumsden, and Monica Sinclair. When such singing actors can be found, this would seem to be the most satisfactory solution. Unfortunately, not many lovers of *The Beggar's Opera* were able to attend the Taw and Torridge Festival in Barnstaple, Gay's birthplace, and in any case such singing actors are all too rare.

Productions with mixed casts, with the singers showing up the actors and the actors showing up the singers, are not likely to be satisfactory. Academic productions treating the work with the musical care with which Handel is approached are not successful entertainment, and a musical comedy approach, while catching the vigor of the early Georgian period, wholly misses its elegance. It is the happy juxtaposition of easy gentility and cold-blooded crime, with a seamy gleam of coarseness as a highlight, which so often eludes the producer. Unless this note is struck with urbane confidence, productions of *The Beggar's Opera* will risk the likelihood of seeming fumbling, awkward, and dated.

9

Comic Opera: Rococo
and Biedermeier

If the first half of the eighteenth century was dominated by *opera seria*, the second half brought to a head the opposition to it.

As early as 1733 Jean Philippe Rameau, at the age of fifty-five, produced his first opera, *Hippolyte et Aricie*, and by humanizing the tortured characters of Theseus and Phaedra, anticipated the celebrated reforms of Christoph Willibald Gluck in Vienna. It is worth noting that Rameau was operating in Paris where there was little danger of Italian bravura excesses. The danger in France was one of indiscriminate use of choral and ballet *divertissements*.

The reforms of Gluck the composer and Ranieri Calzabigi the librettist are frequently referred to without mention of one who was perhaps the chief instigator, Count Giacomo Durazzo, a Genoese, and the Intendant of the Vienna court opera. Durazzo, however, could not have proceeded so far or so rapidly without Gluck's predisposition and ready understanding.

In 1755, Durazzo had adapted a libretto for Gluck with the specific aim of deriding and dethroning Metastasio. Fourteen years later there appeared the celebrated Dedicatory Epistle to *Alceste*, text by Calzabigi and music by Gluck.

Dr. Charles Burney, in *The Present State of Music in Germany, the Netherlands and United Provinces* (London, 1773), quotes the main points of the epistle. Briefly, they are to divest the music of the abuses of vain singers, to discourage superfluous musical ornament, to delete the repeated sections of arias, to use the instrumental accompaniment in the service of the drama, and to aim, in general, at a noble simplicity.

Gluck's *Orfeo ed Euridice*, of 1762, is the most frequently revived of the reform operas today. Although it impressed Dr. Burney with its novelty and sincerity, it not only retains the Baroque male alto for the leading role (now assumed variously by mezzo sopranos, contraltos, tenors and baritones) but a conventional Baroque happy denouement with a set of festive dances in the French *divertissement* manner. It also seems, to post-*verismo* eyes and ears, extremely static. The beauty of the music, however, is striking, and after a bout of *opera seria* listening one cannot fail to appreciate the substitution of meaningful *arioso* for matter-of-fact *recitativo secco*, or to welcome expressive arias in the place of elaborate singers' pieces. It is little wonder that Gluck spent most of the 1770s in Paris where the climate was more favorable to the new kind of lyric drama.

Bravura arias did not die. Although Mozart benefited greatly from his study of Gluck (as *Idomeneo* especially reveals) he wrote scores of bravura arias (*da capo* and all) and the romantic triumvirate of Rossini, Donizetti, and Bellini readily checked the dramatic action for purposes of vocal display.

While comic opera in France, England, and Germany used spoken dialogue between musical numbers and was comparatively unpretentious vocally, Italian *opera buffa* competed with the more serious genre, used *recitativo secco* well into the nineteenth century, and became more and more addicted to *da capo* arias, some of them requiring a prodigious vocal technique.

In other respects *opera buffa*, triumphant in the second half of the eighteenth century, altered its nature both dramatically and musically. The *commedia dell'arte* stock characters gave place to realistic, closely observed contemporary and local characters. In Mozart's operas, especially, a tenderness and psychological profundity turned merry comedy into half-serious comedy and sometimes into near tragedy. It was a part of the increasing humanitarian and sentimental concerns of the eighteenth century.

Audiences who considered themselves refined sighed over the tender raptures of tearful drama and musical plays. The lesser tradesmen and their loud wives still preferred musical farces, but it was a mark of breeding to be a person of sensibility. The rococo ambiance is a delicate mixture of laughter and tears difficult if not impossible for coarse palates to appreciate.

The growing concern for people encouraged the involvement of characters on stage, and the old Baroque string of solo arias had to be cut down somewhat to allow room for the duets of affection, teasing, and quarreling, the trios and quartets of intrigue, and the lengthy ensembles of complexity and perplexity. Some of Mozart's predecessors had already established the elaborate act finales offering continuous accompanied singing for an entire scene, but no greater examples can be found than in the Lorenzo Da Ponte and Mozart finales of *Figaro, Don Giovanni,* and *Così fan Tutte.*

Tenderness became a middle-class European fashion, with or without an admixture of comedy to blend laughter with tears. In the French language, the operas of Philidor, Monsigny, Grétry, and Boieldieu carried the fashion into the early nineteenth century. In England, rural pieces like Isaac Bickerstaffe's *The Maid of the Mill,* with music arranged by Samuel Arnold, and Frances Brooke's *Rosina,* with music by William Shield, fused sentimental stories with comedy passages of relief, using the ballad-opera format. In Italy, Niccolò Piccinni seized upon the sentimental excesses of Samuel Richardson's bestselling novel *Pamela* to concoct his half-serious, half-comic *The Good Girl* (*La Buona Figliuola*), and in Germany Albert Lortzing wrote both text and music for bourgeois comedies in *Singspiel* form, following Mozart in his fondness for duets, trios, quartets, and ensemble numbers. The most successful of them was *Tsar and Carpenter* (*Zar und Zimmermann*).

Così fan Tutte

Text by Lorenzo Da Ponte. Music by Wolf-gang Amadeus Mozart. First produced at the Burgtheater in Vienna, 1790.

The peculiar rococo mixture of frivolity and sensibility is nowhere more apparent than in *Così fan Tutte* where it also is rather puzzling.

Even the straightforward *Figaro*, written four years previously, has one recent critic describing a song as "an outburst of rage and jealousy" while another calls it "a patter song, light in tone."

If *Figaro* stumbles now and again into ambiguity, *Così* may be said to be based upon it. Some commentators imply that Da Ponte wrote superficially and that Mozart glorified his barely adequate lines with superb and profoundly felt music. Edward Dent accords Da Ponte a great deal of credit. Others imply that Mozart must have been responsible for most of the good things in the libretti, and Joseph Kerman goes so far as to contrast Da Ponte's "miserable material" with Mozart's "revelation" (*Opera as Drama*, p. 108).

Without claiming for Da Ponte more than he deserves, it should be noted that his work has been shoved into far brighter light than the occasional flicker which illumines the writing of his librettist contemporaries. Ordinary words and phrases have been invested with glory, and the glory is undeniably Mozart's, yet it should be remembered that less glorious words are a better springboard for glorious music than more competitive ones, and most of Da Ponte's served Mozart well.

On the surface, the text of *Così fan Tutte* deserves Joseph Kerman's description of it as "a clever comedy, which is satirical, witty, superficial, and unworthy of Mozart" (p. 113).

Two young men, Guglielmo and Ferrando, are the ardent lovers of two sisters, Fiordiligi and Dorabella. Their bragging confidence in the fidelity of the ladies irritates their bachelor friend Don Alfonso, who proposes a wager. If the men do as he says for a day he will show them that, like all women, these two are inconstant. The young men comply. Following his plan they suddenly depart on active service to return almost immediately in outlandish disguises. Don Alfonso has bribed Despina, the ladies' chambermaid, to urge them to entertain the strangers. The men overconfidently pay addresses to the wrong sisters. Dorabella capitulates to Guglielmo. Ferrando is furious but continues his wooing of Fiordiligi until she, too, succumbs. Don Alfonso has won the wager. The men return "from active service" as themselves and the ladies realize that they have been duped. They protest eternal fidelity thereafter.

Anyone attending or listening to a performance of *Così fan Tutte* is made aware of the great gulf that lies between the sym-

metrical, artificial, sophisticatedly cynical plot and the music, a part
of which seems to be in agreement with Da Ponte and merely derides
the expression of insincere or exaggerated emotion and another part
of which gives in completely to emotion which we can only accept
as genuine and deeply felt. The characters are at one moment *buffo*
puppets and at another human beings in a semi-*seria* opera.

There is naturally some disagreement as to precisely where these
parts lie, but the first act finale and the Despina frivolity, together
with Don Alfonso's bachelor cynicism, are very clearly of a different character from Fiordiligi's second-act aria, a desperate determination to be constant, and from her touching capitulation, with
the duet that follows it. Her first aria, with its excessive leaps and its
coloratura in the wrong part of the voice for most sopranos, Dorabella's theatrical show of desperation, and the elaborate protestations
in the second finale are generally accepted as satirical, but what is one
to say of Ferrando's first aria, which most audiences accept for its
intrinsic tenderness and beauty but which Otto Jahn insists is so
effeminately overplayed as to be wonderfully funny?* And how
seriously are we to take Fiordiligi's second aria, a rondo with a two-
horn obbligato of ravishing beauty? And who can explain being
moved almost to tears by the canon for three voices which follows
the toast at the wedding, while a fourth voice wishes that the ladies
were drinking poison, a number which precedes by only a few seconds a preposterous scene in which the chambermaid dons her
second male disguise and pretends to be a wheezing old notary?

Most contemporary productions of *Così fan Tutte* follow the
course of playing the work as an *opera buffa*, a musicalized artificial
comedy letting the moments of real feeling act as serious relief (to
borrow Eric Bentley's term in his illuminating study of *The Importance of Being Earnest* in *The Playwright as Thinker*†), and the
result can be very satisfying in the theatre unless an overstrenuous
stage director or a group of undisciplined singing actors give in to
the easy reactions of a provincial audience and play the delicate
absurdity as slapstick farce.

It would require extraordinarily good singing actors and a most

* Otto Jahn, *Life of Mozart*, trans. Pauline Townsend, 3 vols., London,
1891, 3:255.
† New York, 1946, p. 176.

perceptive director to play the work progressively, to point up the contrast between the fashionable, pretended affection at the opening and the growing realization of something deeper and more genuine when the two ladies fall in love with the disguised young men, the wrong way around. It would not be impossible to keep the comedy of intrigue in balance with the theme of emotional awakening, and this would be to the advantage of both. Alternating genuine emotion with a recurring pretence to which the ladies had always been accustomed is certainly true to nature. The pretended struggles with the real throughout this work, and even though it ends on the artificial it has disclosed the genuine. The early protestations are false enough. The sense of loss at the departure of the young men is real. The trio "Soave il vento" is deeply felt, and audiences invariably react with discomfort when amusing business is allowed to distract from the music at this point.

Jean Gascon's 1967 production at the Stratford Festival, Ontario, Canada, was a richly satisfying one, thoughtfully respecting the ambivalence of *Così fan Tutte*. Neither comedy nor sentiment was slighted, but the farce was controlled and sedulously prevented from upsetting the total balance. The result was a triumphant evocation of the spirit of rococo. (See Plates 11 and 12.)

To judge by the usual approach of stage directors, few go so far as to attempt the expression of what W. J. Turner calls "the anguish of separation, the horror of infidelity, the ruthlessness of nature, the unexpectedness of one's own natural behaviour, the tortures of jealousy, and the differences in human characters even when fundamentally they are subject to the same iron laws of nature. . . . *Così fan Tutte*," he avers, "is a tragicomedy and the most profound and terrifying work of its kind that has ever been written" (*Mozart, the Man and His Works*, p. 327).

Joseph Kerman points out that while Da Ponte had no thought of real feeling, Mozart was greatly concerned with it. The divergence of the music from the text leads to some difficulty when, for the purpose of the calculated cynicism of the ending, the girls return to their former lovers. It is too pat, and Don Alfonso has won his wager too predictably. All is not lost if we think more of the "learning to love" theme than of the simple exchange of lovers and their reexchange before the final curtain. No one with any sense would conclude that for these youngsters the second change is necessarily final. They still have more growing to do, but the first lesson they have had, and we were in on it.

If this were a wholly serious opera Fiordiligi, having learned to love, would have to stay with the man she had learned to love, Ferrando. If not quite semi-*seria* it is at least semi-*buffa*, and we must accept at the close a Fiordiligi who at first was protesting a conventional love because she as yet had not found the right man. Faced with deprivation and temptation she then discovered real love (and real love is only final love in the most extravagant romances), but this time she had the wrong man. It would be unnecessary and wearisome to have felt obliged to write an extra act to show how Fiordiligi found real love again with Guglielmo, and this pedestrian course would have ruined the comedy.

The finale to the opera presents a problem, the only satisfactory solution to which is to accept it as a kind of dramatic-musical shorthand dispensing with inessentials in order to avoid the anticlimactic. This finale is a part of the comedy framework to what Turner calls "a work of iron realism" (p. 328). To accept a stage convention of this sort is just as easy as to accept the preposterous deception of the Albanian disguises. Anyone who boggles at such conventions should begin to question the three-inch tears coursing down the five-foot faces on our motion picture screens, before declaring less extravagant conventions to be unacceptable.

A perfect production of *Così fan Tutte* may be impossible, but in recent years there have been productions sufficiently good to provide satisfying evenings in the theatre and to stimulate argument after the performance is over. No two people will agree on the shape this composition of mercury should assume.

Tsar and Carpenter

ZAR UND ZIMMERMANN *Text and music by Albert Lortzing. First produced in Leipzig, 1837.*

Thirty years ago, *Zar und Zimmermann* was among the top half dozen favorites in the theatres of Germany. Today it remains in the top half dozen. It is over one hundred thirty years old. Unlike its close rival, *The Bartered Bride* by Smetana, it has never been produced at Covent Garden nor at the Metropolitan. *The Bartered Bride* began as a *Singspiel* with spoken dialogue but was later turned into a comic opera with recitatives. *Zar und Zimmermann* still retains its spoken dialogue, but so do *The Magic Flute, Fidelio*, and *Der Freischütz*, all of which have been staged at the world's great opera houses.

Why is it perennially successful in Germany and far less so elsewhere? It is not to be accounted for by its Germanness. *Der Freischütz* is far more German. *Zar und Zimmermann* is set in Holland and its chief character is a Russian emperor.

Zar und Zimmermann belongs to the early period of *Singspiel, opéra comique,* and comic opera in which unmistakable operetta characteristics are quite evident a half century before the Viennese made operetta a household word, and more than thirty years before Offenbach's *opéra bouffe* declined into the *opérette* of Lecocq, Planquette, and Audran.

Zar und Zimmermann has a pleasant but not a cloying sentimentality, it is historically set, it is picturesque in its shipyard locale and with its Dutch costumes and clog dance, it is decoratively pretty, it provides every major soloist with gratifying music and most of them with opportunities for comedy acting, it is generous to the chorus, and each act closes with an extended finale. It contains a famous *Bombenrolle* (showpiece role) in the character of the Burgomaster of Saardam, its plot and dialogue are expertly handled, and its music runs the gamut from piquancy to tenderness and from satire of pomposity to a work song, a drinking song, and a wedding song in the popular tradition. The riotous commotion with which the second act ends may have given Wagner a part of the idea for his second act *Meistersinger* riot.

The story of Peter the Great was popular in plays and musical pieces from about 1780 to the 1850s. The first operatic version had appeared in 1780 under the title *Peter der Grosse*, written by Christoph Hempel. In 1790 a Paris production with music by Grétry appeared as *Pierre le Grand*. In Germany Joseph Weigl's *Die Jugend Peter des Grossen* and Karl von Lichtenstein's *Frauenwert oder der*

Kaiser als Zimmermann told the same story. Donizetti wrote *Il borgomastro di Sardam* in 1827 and was followed by the musical treatments of Adam, Flotow, Lortzing, and Meyerbeer.

There were also plays on the subject in the late eighteenth century, but the most important in the nineteenth century was the one by the Frenchman Mélesville, who with two collaborators wrote *Le bourgmestre de Sardam ou les deux Pierres*. The success of this encouraged a German version, and the English version by James Robinson Planché called *The Czar, or A Day in the Dockyards* which was produced in London in 1819.

Albert Lortzing wrote his own texts and sang and acted in his own operas when he was not conducting them. The first production of *Zar und Zimmermann*, which was based on the French play, was at Leipzig in 1837, but it was the excellent production at the Berlin Hoftheater in 1839 which started the work on its road to wide success.

The story was inspired by the fact of Peter the Great having worked in 1697 and 1698 in the shipyards of Zaandam, the correct name of the Dutch port which in the opera is known as Saardam. A Tsar in disguise as a laborer is a piquant idea for a play, and even before being written is a potential middle-class success. In the decades following the French Revolution, middle-class and working people's themes were especially popular. The Russian Tsar was not too proud to work among common men, an attitude which at the same time dignified the common man and humanized the Tsar. With admirable restraint, Lortzing did not write a Student Prince story that would have had the Tsar falling in love with a Dutch girl and tenderly discouraging her, or accepting the girl's noble renunciation of him at the end so that he might return to rule his people. Peter Michaelov is not involved with a girl. Another Russian Peter who happens to be a deserter from the army, Peter Ivanov, provides, with the Burgomaster's niece Marie, the love story. This, however, is not in the least degree sentimentally treated; as a matter of fact, Peter Ivanov is a jealous young man who becomes extremely agitated when any other man admires Marie, and since Marie is very pretty, this happens often. The two young people are obviously in love, and Marie actually declares that she will jump into the canal if her uncle prevents her from marrying her beloved Peter. Peter, not to be outdone, says that he will jump too.

"That's settled," says Marie, "We'll jump in a duet."

This is characteristic of Lortzing, who was so perfectly at home in the theatre that jokes joining the backstage world with the audience world came naturally to him. His most famous joke of this sort in *Zar und Zimmermann* has become a musical-theatre cliché. The Burgomaster when singing a bass aria implies, going down the scale, that he is to sing a low F. He does not reach it. Instead he shapes his mouth, and a bassoon plays the note. The Burgomaster acknowledges it with a slight bow and "Danke sehr, Herr Kollege." It is a simple, middle-class joke, but in the theatre, especially one attended by the middle classes, it encourages *Gemütlichkeit.*

The sentimentality in *Zar und Zimmermann* is patriotic and paternal, and this may be a reason for the enduring popularity of the work in Germany. Peter the Great is for the most part a serious character, and although he is involved in the misunderstandings and false accusations he is never made ridiculous. When he is ordered to be bound, he frightens his captor and emerges with dignity.

He sings material which seems designed to endear him to hero worshippers. Between two parts of the opening chorus he sings a vigorous and masculine exhortation (foreshadowing with his ax blows the sword smiting of Siegfried), and when he hears news of rebellion in Moscow he bursts into an angry recitative on the subject of a people's ingratitude. The aria is at first concerned with his leadership of the people and his attempt to win them with gentleness and love, but it moves to a second part in which he declares that for those who have spurned this parental solicitation the only answer is death, "so that they may die in expiation and the Fatherland may flourish."

His best-known song, skilfully placed between a burlesque scene of a welcome cantata and a comedy duet, is just as paternalistic and sorrowful, with the added sentimentality of the loneliness of eminence. It is crowned, rather unfortunately, with a sanctimonious reference to the mutability of earthly greatness and his happy acceptance of the child's estate in heaven.

It may well be that the sentiments expressed in this song have done much to hinder the popularity of *Zar und Zimmermann* outside Germany. It should be remembered that the work appeared in the year Queen Victoria came to the throne of England and that the temper of the times was sympathetic to jingoism in countries some distance from the Prussian domains of Frederick William III.

The workers of Zaandam, together with their wives and their girls in the three settings of the shipyard, the tavern, and the town hall, form the background to the story. This chorus, besides performing the customary function of a chorus, participates in the action far more than most choruses. It is given three extended opportunities in the first act, about as much in the second act, and a bravura scene of the cantata rehearsal in the third. It takes part in all three finales.

The Tsar, in addition to his two arias, sings a solemn address to the townspeople just before the end of the opera. He sings no duets, but he is active in the male sextet of political intrigue in the second act. While some contact with the people and the intrigue is necessary, it is clear that the world of the Russian sovereign is to be separated from that of the Dutch people. The songs and duets allotted to Marie, Ivanov, and the Burgomaster are comedy pieces, with the sole exception of Marie's charming bridal song.

Lortzing is especially skilful in the placing of his musical numbers. After the vigorous drinking chorus opening the second act the French marquis, at Marie's request and to take attention off the Tsar, sings the lovely "Lebe wohl, mein flandrisch Mädchen." An involved conversational sextet is admirably and most theatrically organized to smooth, precise, and conspiratorial music. This is immediately followed by the simple bridal song and, after a short passage of dialogue, by the brilliant finale which exposes the Burgomaster's mistakes one by one, a hilarious scene in which three ambassadors are falsely accused, each one clearing himself by identifying himself until, to the astonishment of the chorus, the tavern seems full of ambassadors. When the two Peters are arrested, the joke becomes a brawl and a musical one of considerable ingenuity.

Lortzing modestly ascribed a part of the phenomenal success of his opera to the fact that it is simple to produce. It is, indeed, easy to stage and plentifully supplied with opportunities for the actors. The scenic requirements of three settings by no means discount the possibility of lavishness but it takes very little ingenuity to simplify them, and many productions, using brown wood and blue decorative tile, make little attempt to depict a realistic shipyard, tavern, and town hall. The ship hull and masts at the rear can remain to be viewed from the windows of the two interiors.

Two tenors are needed, but Ivanov is a *buffo*. The Tsar is a baritone, the Burgomaster and two of the ambassadors are basses. The widowed proprietress of the shipyard has only a small role and is expectably a mezzo soprano. Marie is usually sung by a soubrette, and since her love affair is not treated seriously she has no sorrowful moments and therefore no emotions to express lyrically. An operetta cast can play it well. The only luxuries required are a lyric baritone for the Tsar and a lyric tenor for the marquis, and a good operetta cast possesses these already.

A ballet is not necessary. When the clog dance is done as a ballet display, as it often is, it immediately becomes a *divertissement* for the audience instead of the small-town entertainment it is intended to be. Six children in clogs can provide a much more authentic effect.

There is always the danger that van Bett, the Burgomaster, will be in the hands of an overenthusiastic comedian. It is the risk that must always be taken with a *Bombenrolle*. Played with skill and taste it can be a triumph of comedy acting. There is another danger, that the lyric baritone singing the Tsar's role may be only a singer and no actor. For the very reason that he is separated from most of the rest of the characters, he must be one of them when he makes contact. If he is merely an assisting soloist the piece fails as a drama.

Zar und Zimmermann has held its own against the competition, after 1874, of Viennese operetta, and the powerful attraction exerted by the works of Strauss, Millöcker, Zeller, Lehár, Fall, Straus, and Kálmán. It appeals to the same audiences and like the operettas it is reasonably successful when sung by modest forces, but it responds, like them, to more expert vocal and instrumental treatment. It owes its continued success, in part, to its excellent text, beside which many operettas seem trite. Its tunes can stand comparison with most of the Viennese favorites.

In an operetta repertory it gains by being different. Its simple nature enhances the Viennese sheen of its rivals. It is bourgeois German, hearty, and masculine. It has no ballroom scenes or displays of wealth, and the flirting is minimal. The common people are not patronized. The hero is not in love. In accordance with operetta tradition the hero is in disguise, but his purpose in being disguised is political. There is no leading pair of lyrical lovers. The soubrette and the *buffo* tenor have taken their places, but their behavior has remained soubrette and *buffo* and their music is to match.

Beside the dazzling Strauss and the suave, exotic Lehár, Lortzing seems rather homespun. This, in countries devoted to operetta, is perhaps the secret of its longevity. After evenings of *Fledermaus, The Merry Widow,* and *Countess Maritza,* Lortzing's *Zar und Zimmermann, Waffenschmied,* and *Wildschütz* are gusty and refreshing, and we go back to sophistication with appetites renewed.

It may be that *Zar und Zimmermann,* although not usually described as an operetta, needs an operetta audience and an operetta repertory in which to lead a healthy existence. In the favorable climate in which it now thrives, it will soon be a century and a half old. Unless Europe changes greatly at the turn of the century, it may reach its two-hundredth birthday and still go on delighting the workers of the world.

IO

Romantic Melodrama

Romantic indulgence, providing an escape from the monotonous regularity and dullness of daily life, surged most strongly at a time when regularity and dullness were being firmly established by the industrial revolution. The development of romanticism coincides with the gradual passing of the aristocratic theatres of the sophisticated courts and the growth of bourgeois consciousness. Side by side with the literary penchant for romanticism was the theatrical penchant for melodrama.

Some of the great operas of the early nineteenth century fall into the category of romantic melodrama, a form which aims less at tragic profundity than at pathos and excitement. A melodramatist is more concerned with immediate effect in the theatre than in recollected thought or emotion after the curtain has fallen. If action is occasionally unmotivated or exciting events insufficiently explained, it is because the melodramatist considers it his primary job to provide the excitement rather than to account for it. So long as audience attention is maintained, no questions are asked until the piece is over, and often not even then.

Beethoven's *Fidelio*, to a text by Joseph Sonnleithner, 1805, was taken from a French play of the revolution-rescue school, and in one scene the composer actually employs the established French technique of *mélodrame*, music between and sometimes under spoken dialogue. Its hero is a political prisoner immured in a dungeon, its heroine a woman who impersonates a man in order to be near and to rescue her husband. The villain, about to murder the hero in the dungeon, is threatened with a pistol by the desperate wife and promptly brought to justice in one of the popular traditions of romantic melodrama.

The enthusiasm of its conception and the nobility of much of its music have brought it to the stage for repeated revivals in spite of its tawdry dialogue, the static quality of its set pieces, and the embarrassment of seeing a dramatic soprano in boy's clothes representing a married woman whose disguise fools not only a mature prison-keeper but his daughter, who falls in love with her, to be undeceived in the final scene. Her consternation, however, is not permitted to mar the general rejoicing.

Such is the power of Beethoven's music, and of melodrama, that this strangely flawed work has enough moving and exciting moments to bring it repeatedly to the stage, when a less-expensive oratorio platform would allow its undeniable musical grandeur to work its magic unhampered by the clumsiness of production, some of it unavoidable.

The great strength of Beethoven's only opera lies in the fact that the music *is* the drama, albeit by fits and starts and in an absurdly conventional genre. The music is not added to the story, but takes its emotional cues from the dramatic situations of the story and then proceeds to ennoble that story so that in the theatre we are often profoundly moved. Originating in a form which is content to achieve only pathos and superficial excitement and makes little attempt to touch us deeply, *Fidelio* unhesitatingly makes the attempt and triumphs.

It would be stepping into an academic booby trap to oversimplify cause and effect and to be too preoccupied with social, political, and popular influences, but it would also be a mistake not to observe the astuteness of the Italians Rossini and Donizetti in adapting themselves to the changing tastes of the postrevolutionary era by abandoning the moribund *opera seria* which Paisiello, Cimarosa, and others were still writing. They provided, instead, opportunities for a new generation of dramatic voices whose owners, in contrast to the *bel canto* concert-in-costume approach, responded warmly to the theatrical opportunities. To perform a role convincingly became important; the demonstration of vocal virtuosity alone was not enough. Forceful voices of considerable size were required for the extra dramatic thrust, the increasing interest in orchestral volume and in ensemble singing reduced the amount of gently supported solo singing, and the larger theatres, larger for commercial reasons, made vocal volume an absolute necessity.

Rossini, Donizetti, and their gentler, more elegiac compatriot Bellini still required bravura singing, but Rossini's tenor Arnold in *Guillaume Tell* (Adolphe Nourrit), Donizetti's tenor Fernando in *La Favorite* (Gilbert-Louis Duprez), and Bellini's soprano *Norma* (Giuditta Pasta) had to pay far more attention to the dramatic presentation of their roles than had their predecessors in the late eighteenth century, whose roles were primarily a matter of singing.

As early as 1797 Cherubini's *Médée* had fused dramatic, unornamented singing, symphonic richness, and a classical subject so successfully that Cherubini became the outstanding composer in Paris at the turn of the century. Beethoven studied his operas and declared, "of all living composers of opera Cherubini is the one I most respect." *Fidelio* bears testimony to his admiration.

Rossini and Donizetti have often been dismissed as superficial Italian melodists. While by no means reformers of Cherubini's zeal, they were perhaps the two greatest operatic composers to bridge successfully the gap between the *opera seria–opera buffa* world of Italy and the world to come, the world of Meyerbeer's "grand" opera in France, of Wagner in Germany, and of Verdi, an altogether new Italian, in Italy. Donizetti, before writing *Don Pasquale,* the last important *opera buffa,* in 1843, had written *Anna Bolena* (1830), *Lucrezia Borgia* (1833), and the French *La Favorite* (1840), precursors of the passionate, supercharged melodrama of which Giuseppe Verdi was to make such satisfying capital. One of the most characteristic and most successful of Verdi's romantic melodramas is *Il Trovatore.*

Il Trovatore

Text by Salvatore Cammarano, completed after his death by Leone Bardare. Music by Giuseppe Verdi. First performed in Rome, 1853.

It is ironic that the Italian opera which of all Italian operas has been chosen as the target for ridicule is *Il Trovatore*, one of the most successful of all works for the musical theatre. Those who are of the opinion that only the music in opera is of value, and that any dramatic excuse will suffice so long as the musical numbers are satisfying, have used *Il Trovatore* to back their argument. Even George Marek, who is certainly not of this opinion, makes an exception of *Il Trovatore* and *Madam Butterfly*, immediately after making the statement that "an opera with an out-and-out shoddy libretto cannot be properly considered of the first rank" (*Opera as Theater*, p. vii).

It would be idle to pretend that the libretto for *Il Trovatore* is as good as those for *Rigoletto* or *La Traviata*, the operas written immediately before and immediately after it, but for a melodramatic romantic story it is functional and it has an admirable swiftness, a headlong violence that is most effectively stemmed by slower, more reflective passages of great musical beauty. If Verdi had not provided the beauty the work would never have been the success it proved to be, but Cammarano must be given at least as much credit as Nahum Tate for pointing the way to his composer and then keeping out of it.

The sprawling canvas of the Gutiérrez play presented the librettist with the major difficulty of contraction, a difficulty faced by librettists with *Wilhelm Tell*, *Hernani*, *Don Carlos* and *Othello*, all plays turned into operas in the nineteenth century, three of them by Verdi.

To contract a five-act play to an opera of three or four acts (*Il Trovatore* has four, all rather short) generally means that if the musical interest is to be sustained, exposition and discussion must be reduced to a minimum. A complex story, however well articulated in the play, suffers a confusion of time lapses and motivations in the opera. In addition, since there is no opportunity to reveal or develop characters gradually they must be presented with an immediacy which, while causing no confusion whatsoever, obviates anything resembling subtlety of characterization. The primary emotions are present, but little else.

It is fortunate that the characters of *Il Trovatore* are straightforward, since the action, as contracted by necessity, is not. The story however, is not as involved as detractors have claimed. *Simon Boccanegra* is more confusing and *Figaro*, in its details, more complex.

In the Gutiérrez play, Doña Leonor (Leonora) has a brother, Don Guillén, with a function rather similar to that of another Verdian Leonora's brother in *La Forza del Destino*. It was wisely decided to dispense with him in *Il Trovatore*, although the lady's refusal to marry the count as her brother wishes enriches her character in the play. We may note, but not regret, the omission of the political background material. We have to accept, in the interest of forward motion, stereotypes for three of the four leading characters. We abandon ourselves with delight to the surging music, scarcely realizing that in addition to a collection of splendid tunes the work is an excellently organized set of contrasts in emotional expression. Offering vocal challenges to five singers, it does what conventional *opera seria* did before it but in a totally different way, demanding at the same time a histrionic involvement on the part of the singers and a more strenuous vocalism.

Il Trovatore is a musical drama, a continuous piece with all vocal numbers linked by expressive accompanied recitative and each, after the first, bearing an emotional and musical relationship to its predecessor and to the total continuum. Its organizational tightness makes it as different from an eighteenth-century *opera seria* or early-nineteenth-century vocal showpiece as a realistic Ibsen play is different from a Shakespearean chronicle play. Yet *Il Trovatore* is based upon a romantic tragedy and betrays some of the disorderly elements of that form.

Il Trovatore is transitional. It stands between the old-fashioned assortment of vocal numbers, varied only because variety displays the singers' talents, and the new-fashioned groping toward the *verismo* to come, the Italian *verismo* which corresponds to Ibsen realism, tightly constructed in spite of its attempt to seem as like life as possible, its vocal numbers contributing to the emotional continuity.

The work is also transitional vocally. *Opera seria* favored the direct relationship between singer and audience, the concert performance, with numbers perfunctorily linked by conversational continuity scarcely deserving of the description drama. The result was little more than a well-selected program, with costumes and scenery as visual decoration. The composer selected the program, but singers could alter it if in their judgment the composer had revealed his inability to organize it satisfactorily.

A new dimension of continuous vocal drama was demonstrated by Verdi, just as a new dimension of continuous orchestral drama was evolved by Wagner, the first leading to a more realistic drama with a concentration upon the outer manifestations, the second leading to a more naturalistic drama. The first is objective and extrovert, the second subjective and introvert. In both cases, for different reasons, the singer is now a character (even if a stereotype) rather than a personality in a stage costume, and the singer is furthermore the intermediary between the composer (or the dramatist and the composer) and the audience.

What is sometimes called the absurdity of *Il Trovatore* as performed can be better understood as the very serious problem that arises when a potent new wine is poured into a shabby old leather bottle.

We can readily accept bravura arias one after another once we are accustomed to Italian *opera seria*, just as in the work of the French Baroque we can accept the *divertissements*, the dances and the festive choruses, as a part of what the taste of the period considered a satisfactory whole. But while we readily accept the concert convention in a number of works before 1850, we are disturbed by it in many works written after that date. The Italian opera ballet, the remains of the series of divertissements, has been dropped from *Macbeth* and *Otello*.* What has not been dropped from many productions of Verdi is the method of performing the bravura arias. In the middle of a continuous musical dramatic performance, the concert performing style obtrudes itself, to the destruction of the dramatic continuity and the discomfort of the audience, a discomfort more often subconscious than conscious.

We are moved forward, as it were, on the crest of the drama and the music, only to be stopped for a demonstration badly out of key with the piece being performed. As recently as November 1968, in the Lyric Opera of Chicago, the tenor and soprano in *Un Ballo in Maschera* broke the third act to come forward and acknowledge audience appreciation of their impassioned duet, while Renato, the baritone, waited for his entrance. His difficulty, however, is not as great as that of Amelia, who after bowing and smiling must resume an anxious expression and sing "Ohimè! S'appressa alcun" ("Alas! Someone is approaching").

Only in works with a compulsive forward drive does this kind of behavior seem ludicrous in the extreme. In old-fashioned performances of *Il Trovatore,* when the imprisoned Manrico came out of his prison tower to take a bow with Leonora, some members of the audience must have wondered about her lines a moment or two before:

> Ahi! forse dischiuse gli fian queste porte
> Sol quando cadaver già freddo ei sarà.
>
> (Oh! Perhaps these doors will not be opened
> Until the corpse is already cold.)

Once again it is the baritone's entrance which is ruined. Fortunately, more recent productions have kept the tenor in the tower, and sophisticated productions have even discouraged the soprano from coming forward to take advantage of the fact.

Il Trovatore is a work poised uncomfortably between *bel canto* concertizing in costume and bloodcurdling *verismo*. It is easily made

---

* Verdi wrote ballet music for the Paris version of *Il Trovatore*, printed only in the French score. He also inserted four dances for the Paris production of *Otello*.

ridiculous. In itself it is not so, provided that we can accept the sudden Spanish jealousies, the convenience of the convent, and the ring containing a phial of poison. The convention of an aria instead of a soliloquy should be even easier to accept, even in the notorious case of "Di quella pira," which Manrico sings when, according to literalists, he should be hurrying to save his supposed mother from the flames.

It is unfortunate that for English-speaking audiences listening to the work in Italian, the explanation of events which have already taken place, offered in a florid bass aria in the opening scene, is not enough. Even if it were, the W. S. Gilbert gibes at mixed babies have made a laughingstock of Azucena's hysteria. Romantic melodrama in translation sounds worse than it really is. Witchcraft and frenzied vengeance seem old-fashioned and false unless they are offered in verse, or prose of better quality than a mediocre libretto translation. Unless the audience is given the necessary information, however, Manrico's relationship to Azucena is not clear, nor is Azucena's grim recollection in the firelight at all meaningful. The battles between the forces of Biscay and those of Aragon involve the two rivals for Leonora, but reference to the actual facts are of the sketchiest. At the end of Act 1 the Count and Manrico go off to fight a duel, but in the next scene, the opening of Act 2, when we might logically expect to discover what happened, we discover instead that there has been a lapse of time, that at the battle of Petillo, Manrico and the Count have once again faced each other, and that upon this occasion Manrico, hearing a voice from heaven, has spared the life of his rival. The *voix du sang*, or call of the blood, was a favorite motif in eighteenth-century melodrama. It is simply intuition provided with a supernatural charge.

In spite of these awkward connections or the lack of any, the main issues are simple enough and they are presented with astonishing vocal continuity, the numbers growing out of the texture in a manner quite different from the concert-placing of *opera seria*. Each of the four acts seems short. Each contains five or six numbers, but between the numbers in the connective recitative are *arioso* phrases of great beauty, phrases devoid of vocal ostentation but rich with emotion. Their very presence ennobles the recitative and makes the parading of an aria as a concert number a betrayal of that nobility.

The first aria, given to the bass Ferrando, is frank exposition, not very convincingly motivated. The servants of the Count di Luna who are falling asleep at their posts ask Ferrando to keep them awake by telling them the story of the bewitching of one of the old Count's sons, the burning of the witch, and the disappearance of the young child, together with the finding of a child's bones in the charred remains of the fire. Since this all happened twenty years ago it can scarcely be the first time the story has been recounted, but the servants at first seem to be ignorant of the facts. A little later they appear to have heard of the witch's daughter, who is suspected of having stolen the child and murdered it. Ferrando adds that even though it is suspected that the remains of the child are the remains of the Count's younger son, the Count on his deathbed had a feeling that the child was still alive, and enjoined his older son never to cease in his search for his brother.

The aria and the response of the servants serve a purpose beyond mere exposition. The themes of witchcraft and the terror of death by fire, violence, and vengeance are powerfully projected in this narration and are to be resumed in the famous scene in which we first meet Azucena. Between these scenes, however, is a contrasting scene in the palace garden, with a gentle beginning and a totally different kind of violent ending.

The acts in *Il Trovatore* are quaintly and old-fashionedly named The Duel, The Gipsy, The Gipsy's Son, and The Execution, an inconsistent set of descriptions made even more so by the fact that each act has two scenes. For four of the eight scenes these titles are wholly inappropriate.

The first, third, and fifth scenes are concerned with the gipsy and the second, fourth, and sixth with the love story of two brothers, unaware that they are brothers, in love with the same woman. At the end of the sixth scene, Manrico leaves his bride to go to the rescue of his mother. A reverse of the pattern follows in scene 7 which, like scene 6, is mainly about the lovers, and scene 8 joins the two stories for the denouement.

In the second scene, provided the audience does not applaud the prima donna, we hear only a few short phrases before Leonora's aria, but Leonora's are emotionally charged and arresting. For comparable involvement one would have to go back to Purcell's *Dido and Aeneas* and Handel's *Semele*, but old-fashioned *opera seria* had little of this emotional approach to the preparation of an aria. An aria prepared lyrically and dramatically produces a very different effect from one approached conventionally and perfunctorily.

Leonora's aria "Tacea la notte placida" begins serenely and gains in passion as it proceeds. The old-fashioned cadenza reminds us that old conventions take long to disappear, and the almost immediate addition of a sprightly *cabaletta*, the fast-moving contrast to the more slowly moving aria, reminds us of a convention at war with the dramatic urgency of a good story. The soprano must inform us that she can sing fast and elaborately decorated music as well as more languorous and impassioned music. "Di tale amor" describes her intoxicated heart, *il cor s'inebbria,* but it is unconvincing and we are better pleased with the return of the quiet night and the voice of the tenor, "Deserto sulla terra," punctuated by the baritone expostulations of the jealous Count. From this moment of lyricism we proceed to the headlong trio of jealous fury and defiance, which ends the act in an appropriately Italianate manner. It seems a short act, since the contrasts are frequent and the lyrical outbursts intensely functional.

There is still a question of what the singers do when they repeat the impassioned phrases and peal out their exciting high notes. It is the price paid by a transitional work poised between providing opportunities for vocal bravura and pressing on heatedly with a fast-moving story. With some inventiveness on the part of the stage director and considerable cooperation on the part of the singers, there can be a signal avoidance of stage center positions with much singing out front and no character relationships. The conventional production, unfortunately underrehearsed and often relying only upon voices, falls into stock patterns, concert stances, and outmoded gestures. This, combined with a reliance upon the conductor and the prompter, is likely to aim the bulk of the vocalism at the center of the auditorium so that parts of the opera not only look like a concert but also sound like a concert.

Act 2 proceeds from a spirited work song, popularly known as

"The Anvil Chorus," to Manrico's excited departure to prevent Leonora from entering the convent. Naively theatrical, a chorus which describes the characters the singers are assuming is the most primitive kind of musical-theatre device. Their costumes inform us clearly what they are. Their words and their music tell us the pleasure they take in being so. The situation is what in modern parlance could be described as a wine break. It is dawn and the gypsies are already at work. They strike their anvils in time with the music, ask for wine which the women bring them, and then gather around Azucena to listen to her song, in most productions, that is.

Once again we are faced with the irreconcilability of the old and the new. The framework is tawdry and unconvincing. Azucena's aria is subjective, not narrative. She is recalling a terrible experience which obsesses her. It makes no sense whatever to group the chorus about the woman. They hear nothing of it. Their only comment is "Mesta è la tua canzon" ("Your song is a sad one"), which they could have noticed if they had continued working, though for obvious reasons not quite as noisily as before. Stage time is shorter than real time, and if the gypsies have been working instead of idly listening to what is none of their business, their departure to find food is more acceptable. The scene is often a ridiculous one. They strike their anvils, they drink, they listen, though absorbing little of what they hear, they eagerly (*sollecitamente*) put away their tools and depart for the nearby villages.

Azucena's compelling self-communion ("Stride la vampa") fits uneasily into this hack scene unless something quite unusual is done with it. The more compelling her musing, the more terrifyingly suggestive (for a thoughtful actress) of a concentration camp memory which will not be blotted out of the mind, the more laughable the surrounding scene becomes unless the traditional approach is discarded. This musing is no more heard by Manrico than by the gypsies. He is fixedly contemplating his sword, the sword he was about to plunge into his enemy the Count when a voice from heaven, or an inner compulsion, prevented him. Manrico hears, however, Azucena's "Mi vendica" ("Avenge me!"), which as the stage direction informs us she sings directly to him.

An old-fashioned narration follows, but such an exciting description in words and music that it continues most effectively the nightmarish, vague outline of the aria. The librettist has erred in making Azucena's account so clear to us in this narration that we are not convinced by her quick denials and evasions when Manrico demands to know whose child he is. She pleads her own distractedness as an excuse for her ravings, and we forget that Manrico is preoccupied also and, as it happens, on the very same theme. It is not sufficiently stressed. There is something too mathematical in the disposal of the third child, Azucena's own, leaving us with the knowledge that the remaining two, the Count and Manrico, are brothers and that only Azucena and we in the audience know about it. But it is this uneasy wonder, this half-suspicion, which prompts Manrico to recount the story of the sword and the strange feeling that there is some mysterious connection between his rival and himself. The dramatic continuity is admirable and its musical realization equally so. They are in fact one, making music drama of a scene which begins with one of the worst conventions of old-fashioned opera.

A technique, to be repeated in reverse later, ends the scene. A messenger brings the news of Leonora's determination to enter the convent. In spite of Azucena's attempts to keep Manrico for her private revenge, he hurries off.

After the feverish excitement of this scene, the second scene gives us a beautiful and popular aria for the Count, "Il balen del suo sorriso," the only opportunity we have of appreciating the Count as a lover, the only hint we are given that the tempest in his heart (*la tempesta del mio cor*) is calmed only by Leonora. The aria has been criticized as being out of character for the villain, making us forget for a moment or two that he is violent and sadistic. His nature, however, is richer for this possibility of serenity in one so turbulent, and the scene is musically richer. In a contrasting *alla marcia* as a kind of *cabaletta* number, the Count restores the tempest to his heart as he informs us at the convent gates that he will wrest Leonora from his rival God if necessary. It is a brief exercise in savage joy, and if splendidly sung and enthusiastically applauded drowns a major part of the women's chorus which follows. The nuns, "chanting faint hymns to the cold fruitless moon," supply more conventional atmospheric music in order to restore, rather too carefully induced, the calm before the melodramatic storm to come.

Only the most careful staging will prevent the rescue at the convent gates from being a hilarious burlesque. Three choruses, the Count's men, Manrico's men, and a troop of nuns, all facing front, the nuns creaking down a short flight of steps and holding electric candles, showing so little real consternation that even their grouping is unchanged, soldiers hiding in full view like four-year-olds, a poorly rehearsed fight with token clashes of weapons and three or four characters instructed to run around aimlessly in order to provide the necessary confusion—all contribute to the degradation of *Il Trovatore* to casual provincial entertainment. It is admittedly difficult to handle this scene well. The music makes it worth the trouble, and on the few occasions when a stage director has shown imagination, and one or more singers conviction, the improvement has been so striking that one longs to see the work treated with full respect for its undeniable power.

The first scene of Act 3 presents fewer problems. An Azucena who can act and who does not mind being treated roughly can make a terrifying thing of being caught, interrogated, and recognized. Using the familiar technique of starting the scene with a jolly chorus of irresponsible soldiery, the librettist and composer change the mood abruptly for the main action. Ferrando, the bass who sang the expositional aria, has an opportunity to act in this scene if he will take it. The second scene begins on the strongly contrasting note of calm, although the characters know it will be only a brief respite from turmoil. Manrico and Leonora are to be married. At dawn the castle will be besieged. The aria-*cabaletta* convention serves a functional purpose most effectively. Manrico's love song "Ah si, ben mio" is followed by the rousing "Di quella pira" with its celebrated and interpolated high C's (unless transposed downward), and the only separation is the sound of the chapel organ, a tiny duet for the lovers, and the announcement of Azucena's capture.

It has been said that this aria shows more clearly than any other the absurdity of the operatic convention. A man is informed that his supposed mother is about to be burned at the stake. Instead of immediately rushing off to rescue her, he steps to the footlights and sings an aria to which spectacular high notes have been added in order to excite the audience further. In a play, it is said, a far more believable treatment would have been applied. In a realistic play, perhaps. In a romantic play, the hero would soliloquize, even if only briefly. How otherwise would we know exactly what he feels? In a romantic music drama, monologue or aria must take the place of spoken soliloquy, and this is the function of "Di quella pira." The drama is not realistic. Our appreciation of a character's reaction is of greater importance than the persuasiveness, realistically speaking, of the action. This aria is telling us excitingly of Manrico's fury and determination, and every phrase of it is replete with fury and determination. It is even motivated, with a genuflection toward realism, by having Manrico order Ruiz to summon his men together. After the solo passage, Ruiz returns with the soldiers. They join Manrico on the final phrases *All'armi*, and all go off in haste to rescue Azucena. Manrico succeeds (she is not burned), but both are taken prisoner.

The conflict here is once again between an old and a new approach. A Handelian aria at this point (for example, "With rage I shall burst" from *Saul*) would cause no trouble, provided that the rest of the work were in the tradition. The invitation to ridicule comes from the juxtaposition of a powerful expression of being about to burst with rage, and an applause-getting aria aimed directly at the audience, with that purpose only in mind.

Into the fourth and last act is packed an incredible amount of beautiful music. The tiny role of Ruiz is enriched with the sombre atmospherics of "Siam giunti; ecco la torre," and to have the first words in any scene is a challenge. The recitative preceding Leonora's florid aria is touchingly plangent, the aria itself being the poetic conceit of a sad sigh floating upward into the prison tower, finding Manrico there and calling to his memory the ecstasy of happier days. Suffusing the upward motion is the downward motion of Leonora's anguish:

> Ma deh! non dirgli, improvvido,
> Le pene del mio cor.

> (But do not heedlessly tell him
> of the anguish in my heart.)

The brilliant device of the famous *Miserere* has suffered from its having been a barrel organ favorite in the days when barrel organs were not rarities. Well staged, it can be very moving. The concert hall applause for Leonora's aria and for the *Miserere*, especially if acknowledged, make Leonora's pleading and bargaining scene with the Count less effective than it deserves to be. Her hysterical jubilation "Vivrà, contento e giubilo!" is believable until the Count joins her and the *cabaletta* convention becomes too apparent.

The final scene is pure music drama, with two particular dangers to its complete success in production: the familiarity of "Ai nostri monti," another barrel organ favorite, and the cliché of the jealous Latin who believes the worst of the woman who is giving her life to save him. A device which works superbly has Azucena, after her earlier hallucinations, dreaming aloud most poignantly, repeating "Ai nostri monti" and recalling the happiness of years ago as Manrico furiously accuses Leonora of betraying him. The speed with which the ending is handled accords with the economy of the whole—it is a lean, athletic work with astonishingly little which can profitably be deleted. Its rousing and tender music, with the most generous writing for the four main voices, is the substance which has ensured its popularity for well over a century.

The ambivalence of its position in the development of opera has made it a staging problem. It is neither old nor new. The old in it spoils the new with bathos; the new shows up the old. It is not easy to persuade an audience to respect it. There is no need to persuade an audience to enjoy it. One point of view urges us that the only way to stage *Il Trovatore* is to hire the four greatest singers in the four ranges, and let them go to it. This procedure certainly fills the theatres in the international capitals, but performances with far more modest singers than the four greatest can please and excite an audience in the theatre (especially in a theatre with a 1000 to 1500 capacity) and this often with only the most perfunctory consideration given the dramatic tension which lies beneath the music.

Familiarity with *Il Trovatore* has, regrettably, bred contempt. It is to be hoped that it is not too late for a new approach, one which will command the respect of an audience too accustomed to patronizing. Unless this happens, a new audience must be found. This can most readily be done by dropping the work from the repertory (if the public and Verdian performers will permit) and then discovering it years later as a neglected masterpiece, to the astonishment and delight of all. With the continuing popularity of this particular warhorse it will be many decades before *Il Trovatore* will be enough of a rarity for the experiment to be contemplated. (See Plate 14).

II

Comic Opera: Victorian

English comic opera was raised to distinction by W. S. Gilbert, the dramatist, and Sir Arthur Sullivan, the composer. Ballad operas and extravaganzas had been a staple of nineteenth-century theatre, and although James Robinson Planché's mythological and fairy-tale burlesques, familiar to British audiences acquainted with the Christmas pantomime tradition, now seem too arch for our taste, we can sense a mild sophistication, a way with words, and a satirical wit as early as the 1830s. In France in the 1860s Meilhac, Halévy, and Offenbach were purveying in such works as *La Belle Hélène* and *La Vie Parisienne* a satirical *opéra bouffe*, livelier and more pointed than the *opéra comique* of Grétry and Boieldieu.

W. S. Gilbert was studying stage direction at this time by watching Tom Robertson rehearse his so-called realistic plays. These plays no longer seem realistic, but in the middle of the nineteenth century the detailed business which the playwright-director insisted upon was novel enough.

Gilbert translated *Les Brigands*, one of the Offenbach works, for the London stage, and the style of the librettists Meilhac and Halévy was close to his own taste. Grafting the French *opéra bouffe* upon the English comic extravaganza, Gilbert astutely created an immensely popular British comic opera. Aggressively unmusical himself, he possessed a keen sense of the absurdities of romantic Italian opera. Sullivan, with his Leipzig conservatory education, matched this with a natural gift for melody and a skill at musical parody which charmed the sophisticated audiences of the 1870s and 1880s who knew their Bellini, Donizetti, Rossini, and early Verdi from performances at Covent Garden with Albani, Patti, Nicolini, and Maurel. In Leipzig also, where less than two decades before Albert Lortzing had acted, sung, and composed with success, Sullivan absorbed many of his characteristics. It is significant that a very usual reaction to a first hearing of Lortzing is "Why, it's just like Gilbert and Sullivan."

Gilbert's meticulous approach to stage direction contributed enormously to the success of the comic operas he wrote for Sullivan's music. They became a cult and a legend, they cornered the professional market in their day, dominated the amateur market in the Commonwealth for half a century, and enjoyed international publicity when the copyright expired. *H.M.S. Pinafore* is a happy but sharply pointed satire of British class distinctions.

H.M.S. Pinafore

Text by W. S. Gilbert. Music by Sir Arthur Sullivan. First performed at the Opéra Comique, London, 1878.

In addition to being lively and tuneful entertainment *H.M.S. Pinafore* is a literary, musical, and social satire. It laughs at the jingoistic attitudes which prevailed when the "Jolly Jack Tar" shows of the nineteenth century were popular and when the unfurling of the Union Jack (nearly a century before George M. Cohan unfurled the Stars and Stripes in New York) stimulated patriotic cheers in the audience. It laughs at the conventions of Italian opera, at recitative and aria, at the function of the chorus, at the melodramatic ensemble, at Verdian whispering conspirators, and specifically at the mixed-up babies of *Il Trovatore*. It examines with scrupulous delicacy the three main classes of society, the upper, the middle, and the lower, and makes the distinctions ludicrous.

Most of the British plays of importance during the nineteenth century dealt uneasily and evasively with the matter of marriage between disparate classes. Only in exceptional cases where there was great love on the one hand, a natural superiority on the other, and adaptability on both was it recommended. Some plays had dishonestly used the old cliché of a last-minute discovery that the lower class partner was really a duke, and at once rank solved every problem. It made no difference that the supposed commoner had had little education and that his companions had been of the lowest order. Blue blood could not be permanently hidden. A duke was by nature a gentleman, and even his speech contrasted unaccountably with the unacceptable speech of his associates.

What did Gilbert do with this sentimental nonsense? The three classes, covering the entire social spectrum, are represented in *H.M.S. Pinafore* by a self-made man, Sir Joseph Porter, at the top, a ship's captain in the middle, and a humble seaman, Ralph Rackstraw, at the bottom. Ralph's name, however, is pronounced Raif, rhyming with "waif," and this declares him at once, in England, to be of the upper classes.

"I lack birth," he confesses, but he expresses himself in Johnsonian periods, demonstrating that, for blue blood, education is quite unnecessary.

"In me there meet a combination of antithetical elements which are at eternal war with one another. Driven hither by objective influences—thither by subjective emotions—wafted one moment into blazing day—plunged the next into the Cimmerian darkness of tangible despair, I am but a living ganglion of irreconcilable antagonisms."

He is "the lowliest tar that sails the water," while Josephine Corcoran is a "proud maiden" and his "captain's daughter."

Josephine, in love with Ralph and about to elope with him, sings an operatic *scena* in which she contrasts "papa's luxurious home, hung with ancestral armour" with the life she will lead as Ralph's wife in "a dark and dingy room in some back street" where dinner is "served up in a pudding basin."

Yet Josephine is described, by Sir Joseph Porter, as appalled by his exalted rank, and Sir Joseph adds:

> Though your nautical relation [her father]
> In my set could scarcely pass,
> Though you occupy a station
> In the lower middle class.

At the conclusion of the opera matters are solved with delightful unconvincingness. The plump contralto Buttercup confesses "a long concealèd crime." As a baby farmer she was in charge of a "well-born babe" and "one of low condition." She declares Ralph to be the former and Captain Corcoran to be the common sailor.

How Josephine's father and lover could be of similar age is not explained. The two men have conveniently stepped offstage before the confession and they now reappear, properly dressed, Ralph as the Captain, the Captain as a common seaman.

In spite of the fact that "love levels all ranks" (as in sentimental plays and novels) Sir Joseph now finds Josephine too far beneath him in rank. He turns to Hebe, his cousin in the chorus, and takes her for his bride. Ralph, now higher than Josephine in rank, magnanimously marries her. Captain Corcoran, now a member of the lower classes, cheerfully marries his former nurse, Little Buttercup. (This floral name may have a mischievous origin in *Il Trovatore: azucena* is the Spanish for "lily.") The entire preposterous ending is literary satire of the first order. Even Shakespeare *(The Winter's Tale)* sometimes paired off his characters at the denouement with unseemly haste.

Audiences of today are mostly unacquainted with the Jolly Jack Tar shows, in the originals of which T. P. Cooke invariably danced a hornpipe. Ralph, it is observed, cannot dance one. Sir Joseph comments: "That's a pity; all sailors should dance hornpipes. I will teach you one this evening, after dinner."

Most audiences with any experience of melodrama can understand the embarrassment Dick Deadeye feels at having to be a villain because he bears a villainous name. "You can't expect a chap with such a name as Dick Deadeye to be a popular character—now can you?" asks the Boatswain. Dick Deadeye responds: "From such a face and form as mine the noblest sentiments sound like the black utterances of a depraved imagination."

Buttercup's remorseful recitatives are in the Verdian tradition both in words and in music. *Ernani, Macbeth, Rigoletto,* and *Il Trovatore* come clearly to mind when the chorus sings:

> Carefully on tiptoe stealing,
> Breathing gently as we may,
> Every step with caution feeling,
> **We will softly steal away.**

The chorus of female relatives dancing around the stage and singing:

> Gaily tripping,
> Lightly skipping,
> Flock the maidens to the shipping.

is Gilbert's direct invitation to Sullivan to burlesque Donizetti's numbers of inappropriate jollity, such moments as his chorus of young girls in *La Favorite*. Sullivan accepted the invitation readily.

The ever-obliging Italian opera chorus, echoing the tenor's last lines, is greeted with Ralph's response:

> I know the value of a kindly chorus
> But choruses yield little consolation . . .

The very necessity for the soprano-alto-tenor-bass vocal distribution is satirized by Sir Joseph's entrance accompanied by his female relatives. In Italian opera we are accustomed to courtiers in palaces and villagers in exterior scenes. On the quarterdeck of a ship tenors and basses are easily motivated, but what about sopranos and contraltos? Cousin Hebe offers the explanation and provides the solution:

> And we are his sisters, and his cousins, and his aunts.

The satire is generally good-natured, but in W. S. Gilbert imperialistic chauvinism received the early prods which later became the contemptuous thrusts of Bernard Shaw:

> He is an Englishman!
> For he himself has said it,
> And it's greatly to his credit,
> That he is an Englishman!

The bullnecked English chaplain John de Stogumber in Shaw's *Saint Joan*, with his "no Englishman is fairly beaten," his eagerness to burn the Maid, and his total lack of imagination, is the tragicomic prototype.

H.M.S. Pinafore is more than nonsensical fun, and a first-class production will have taken note of this fact.

12

Verismo and Viennismo

Just as romanticism punctured the pomposity of the Baroque, so realism cooled the excesses of romanticism by attempting, at least, to face the crude as well as the exhilarating aspects of life.

Realism on the stages of the nineteenth century affected the visual elements first. Real carpets, real tea in real china cups, and doors and windows which worked preceded by a number of years anything that resembled fidelity to real-life situations, characters, and dialogue. The musical stage, as usual, lagged behind the stage for the spoken play. Real things happening to real people on the musical stage presented difficulties of assimilation. For half a century many works claiming to be realistic were at least half traditional, and in many instances the conservatism of operatic production paid only lip service to realism and presented the works as if they were little different from operas of the romantic school.

Verismo is the expression applied to a certain kind of realism popular in Italy, and elsewhere, toward the end of the nineteenth century. It implies truthfulness to life as opposed to the excesses of the romanticism which preceded it, but the term *verismo* is imprecise. Romantic works may range from the highly imaginative but improbable to the easily believable, with a stress upon the splendor and beauty of life and a tendency to avoid the sordid aspects of it. Overenthusiastic realism, with its interest in the hitherto neglected ugliness of life, may distort actuality as violently in the opposite direction, but it is quite likely to claim more fidelity to the truth because it qualifies as *verismo*.

In the nineteenth century there are reflections in the theatre of a fresh interest in everyday occurrences, ordinary people, and life as it may be observed in the streets of the town or in the village square. This interest coincided with the increasing number of three-dimensional set pieces used on stage, the literal depictions on large surfaces by the scenic artists who deceived the eye and made some of the necessary flat surfaces look three-dimensional, and it also coincided with the kind of acting which was praised as seeming "natural" or "true to life," very difficult of achievement in a large theatre. The fact that what looked natural in the 1860s would not look natural today to us is immaterial. The new regard for the life-like in a period of broad strokes, poorly lighted stages (according to our present-day lighting standards), and melodramatic action is significant.

Musical theatre is frankly conventional, though there is wide variety and some musical theatre can partake of some of the lifelike or so-called realistic qualities associated with the more progressive kind of stage play in the nineteenth century. Such works were written. *Carmen* is one of them, originally planned as an *opéra comique*, a piece with spoken dialogue between the musical numbers. The librettists Meilhac and Halévy based their text on the Prosper Mérimée French novella. Georges Bizet, as French as they, managed to catch a strong Spanish flavor, at least for non-Spaniards, especially in the dances and songs based upon Spanish dance rhythms.

Romanticizing and glamorizing die hard, especially in opera. *Carmen* has been promoted to the larger opera houses and supplied with recitatives, written after Bizet's death, in place of the original spoken dialogue. It works well both ways, though the motivations are clearer in the version with dialogue.

In many productions prettification takes over. Mérimée's Carmen is described as a sleazy gypsy with copper-colored skin, coarse black hair, and wearing a black dress, but she is vibrantly, animally attractive. Some Carmens in the opera house have attempted something like authenticity, but the majority have allowed the general prettification to engulf them and many productions have become so "grand" that the original conception has been quite lost.

A production a few years ago in the Verona arena used huge crowds to fill the large stage, while Carmen herself, Giulietta Simionato in a pink skirt, found frequent opportunity to display a whipped cream thickness of frilly white petticoats, impeccably clean.

A Paris production of the same period mixed approaches by setting a sleazy black-clad Carmen, Jane Rhodes, in a "grand opera" setting involving horses, crowds, rolling oranges, and other picturesque impedimenta.

In 1943 in America the Billy Rose production of *Carmen Jones* managed a return to the basic atmosphere, but could not resist a Broadway prettification of a wholly different sort. When Bizet composed it, *Carmen* was a noteworthy move in the direction of sordid, savage realism as opposed to romantic grandeur. It is ironic that this, of all works, should have capitulated so frequently to the onslaughts of splendor.

Similar distortions have been imposed upon the most characteristic *verismo* operas, Mascagni's *Cavalleria Rusticana*, Leoncavallo's *Pagliacci*, and Giordano's *Andrea Chénier*. Mascagni placed his action in a Sicilian village square, but then interrupted his passionate sequences with vocally rewarding "numbers." Leoncavallo based his Calabrian melodrama upon an actual occurrence, but what audiences usually see is a clown in snow-white satin, picturesque peasant costumes, and a glamorous little stage for the play within a play. A Nürnberg production of the 1960s set the opera in a shabby Italian square with paper posters peeling from the walls. Bereft of prettiness, *Pagliacci* became real, and the faithless wife, instead of being a peasant for tourists, was a common little tart who clearly deserved what she got, a stabbing to death by her husband.

The *verismo* quality of *Andrea Chénier* is evident in the dramatic juxtaposition of extravagant aristocracy and servant slavery on the eve of the French Revolution. The opening sequence in which the son of a servant ironically addresses a gilded sofa can be striking if operatic attitudinizing is avoided, and the rumble of the impoverished rabble which impinges upon the prancing gavotte is an exposition in sound of the basic premise of the piece. Melodrama, however, and cloak-and-dagger stereotypes take over, and the piece turns into a singers' opera with applaudable "numbers" calculated to enthrall a typical operatic audience and destroy the last vestige of *verismo*.

Verismo works are best seen in small but good repertory opera houses where they may be intelligently directed and more than adequately sung. Spectacular voices are not necessary. Ironically, *verismo* loses much of its believability the moment we become aware of a performing personality. This kind of theatre is grounded in illusionism, whatever the composer may impose upon it. When an unknown singer portrays a suffering peasant, we are much more easily persuaded to the reality of the drama than when a celebrity, trailing clouds of audience approval, takes over. All celebrities were once comparatively unknown and may have participated in compelling productions of *verismo* operas. As soon as they become internationally famous, however, the audience attitude toward them changes. This is not the celebrities' fault, but it certainly shatters the illusionism.

It is not to be wondered at that the fruitful years of *verismo* should coincide with the fruitful years of operetta. The forms are opposite sides of the same coin, and there are times when the metal between is so thin that an element of one becomes blended with the other. For the most part, however, they are distinct, and while *verismo* leans toward the real, the sordid, the crude, the proletarian, and the poverty stricken, operetta is concerned with escapism, not so much the escapism of fantasy as an escapism linked nostalgically to a former reality, albeit wilfully distorted. Unpleasantness is avoided. Court life is presented with its masked balls and mischievous intrigues and with no emphasis whatsoever upon the underlying corruption. The middle classes are avoided unless to be presented as absurd provincials, awed by court splendor or pretentiously aping it. The working classes appear, anonymously, as bewigged footmen and scampering chambermaids, or, picturesquely, in peasant costume and merrily engaged in village festivities.

Operetta is sentimental rather than satirical, conventional rather than adventurous, old world and picturesque rather than up to date and realistic. While the music is less ambitious than that of operatic comedies, it is tuneful and graceful rather than dynamic, instrumentally more stringy than brassy, and in all expertly concocted to please. With gratifying solo work, a few ensembles, and generous opportunities for the chorus, with usually quite glamorous settings and colorful costumes, courtly elegant or peasantly pretty, operetta guarantees attractive entertainment. Its most criticized features, re-sulting from its reliance on music and on visual display, are its un-originality in story, its conventional and superficial characterization, and its flat dialogue, often sounding flatter after translation and the passage of years. In spite, however, of the offhand story treatment of many operettas, the clichés in the dialogue, the blandness of much of the music, the outmoded countesses in the ballroom scenes, and the antedeluvian jokes, the better operettas have an enviable staying power, and in Germany and Austria a tenacious hold upon a senti-mental public. The appeal exerted by Strauss, Lehár, and Kálmán is based upon nostalgia, and since they were never really up to date they date less disastrously than musical comedies, most of which last the two or three years of their first run if they are successful, but upon revival run briefly or are not revived at all. Indeed, the ones with the strongest operetta characteristics are the ones most likely to be revived with success.

Puccini and Lehár have been juxtaposed here not only to stress the relationship between *verismo* (in Puccini's case romanticized *verismo*) and operetta. The two musicians admired each other's work. Puccini, a composer of Italian opera, tried to write an oper-etta for Vienna and failed. The work, *La Rondine*, was turned back into an Italian opera, the form with which Puccini felt completely at home. Lehár, a composer of Viennese operetta, tried to write a senti-mental opera, *Giuditta*. It was performed at the Vienna Staatsoper, but in spite of the ambitious orchestration it remained an operetta, the form with which Lehár felt completely at home.

La Bohème

Text by Giuseppe Giacosa and Luigi Illica, based upon Scènes de la Vie de Bohème, *a se-ries of sketches by Henry Mürger (né Henri Murger). Music by Giacomo Puccini. First performed in Turin, Italy, 1896.*

La Bohème is recommended as an ideal work with which to begin a career of operatic theatregoing. A skilful blend of *verismo* and ro-mantic lyricism, it makes a direct appeal both to those who want their operas to resemble plays and to those who find operas resembling plays lacking in tunefulness. It is extremely difficult to be rewardingly tuneful through long stretches of musical conversation. Almost any tune sounds good after spoken dialogue or dry recitative. The composer of a through-composed work must be tunefully inventive throughout the opera, yet keep a kind of super-tunefulness in reserve for lyrical expansion and moments of splendor. If the composer lacks inspiration and inventiveness for the conversations, we are uncomfortably aware of the ambitious attempt to make something of musical importance out of what is rather ordinary dialogue. If he performs his task too well, he may not be able to rise to the heights demanded by the lyrical outpouring of his librettist. His Muse by then may be exhausted. *La Bohème* is an astonishing example of an unusually athletic Muse.

Each of its four acts has extended conversational passages, but passages so lively, melodious, and orchestrally piquant that few audience members find them unrewarding, even though many are looking forward to the two arias in the second half of Act 1, the duet which closes the act, Musetta's song in Act 2, the male duet in Act 3, Mimi's farewell and the quartet, and in Act 4, Colline's coat song and the scene of the lovers before the reentrance of the others and the poignant death scene. The rewards are considerable, even for those who are impatient with the subtleties of musical chatter. The rewards are even greater for those who take a musical interest in the conversational sequences.

Most English-speaking audience members are content to have only a rough idea of what is being said in song. Very few want *La Bohème* sung in English so that they can understand and enjoy the fun. Some years ago, in the 1952–53 season, an English *La Bohème* at the Metropolitan suffered defeat at the hands of the Italian *La Bohème* in the same theatre. (True, the Howard Dietz translation was severely criticized.) Most of the audience understood little Italian, especially at the speed of the *La Bohème* conversations, but it was clearly demonstrated that they preferred to listen to the music without troubling themselves much about the words.

While one may inveigh against the promusical, antidramatic approach, it must be conceded that the main dramatic issues in *La*

Bohème are clear enough and the verbal embroidery of scant importance.

If the sketches by Henry Mürger (he deliberately umlauted himself) had been faithfully dramatized, the verbal embroidery would have been all-important, but wit is difficult to musicalize, and happy turns of phrase which depend in their effect upon an actor's timing sound labored when uttered in fixed time to a conductor's beat. The fun is literary, and when quickly and silently read the size of Colline's hat brim upon which ten could be served tea and the elaborate devices used by Marcel to foist his canvas upon the jury at the Louvre are a delight. Turned into spoken lines, they might elicit some audience laughter. Turned into sung lines, the number of words and the length of the phrases would be out of proportion to the effect. The horse's saddlecloth in Marcel's painting, which he uses to try out strips of color, does not translate easily into stage terms, nor does Rodolphe's promise to make a dress for Mimi out of his writing. "One sleeve is done," he assures her, but Mimi wants pleats in the skirt, so Rodolphe must add more characters to prevent skimping the material. The whole tone of the Mürger sketches is playful, wry, quicksilver comment, and completely unsentimental. The cooing pigeon which finds itself cooked and sliced had a lovely voice. The lovers exchange glances, their eyes are full of tears, but the tears are caused by the onions which Juliette has been peeling to go with the pigeon. When Mimi is in the hospital news comes of her death but a ridiculous mistake has been made. Number 8 is dead, but it turns out to be another patient. When Rodolphe excitedly goes to the hospital after not seeing Mimi for days because he thought she was dead, he learns that she died at four o'clock that morning, without her Bohemians around her. His last sight of her whereabouts is the cart which takes unclaimed corpses to the common grave. Four lines later a year has passed and Rodolphe and Marcel are giving a party.

The librettists did with Mürger's sketches what the play by Mürger and Barrière had had to do for success in the theatre. It made Rodolphe and Mimi the hero and heroine, grouped Marcel, Colline, Schaunard, and Musette around them for Bohemian atmosphere, and stressed the sentimental appeal of the pathetic love story.

The opera which results has nothing of the dexterous wit of the Mürger sketches, but it skilfully projects an atmosphere of youthful jollity in poverty as a background to the loose narrative of the four acts: the first meeting, the celebration, the postponed separation of the lovers (an ingenious compromise requiring sadness tinged with joy and joy tinged with regret), and their reunion at the death of Mimi. Marcel's Red Sea canvas has a brief mention, although the drowning of a Pharoah and the brief reference to snow-covered forests are in need of scholarly footnotes if their meaning is to be understood. It is clear to everyone that a dramatic manuscript is burned in place of a stinking canvas, but the necessary speed of the ironic commentary "I find it brilliant," "But it doesn't last long," "Brevity's a great asset" makes it almost impossible to catch. The page which crackles to the comment that the crackles were kisses, and Rodolfo's "I want to hear three acts together" followed by Colline's admiration of the audacity of the integration, are literary conceits which in less skilful hands might have been heavily handled in music to match. The reckless speed of the orchestra and the lifelike *parlando* of the singers repair the damage to Mürger's original fabric by restoring the spirit at the expense of the letter. When Schaunard arrives, preceded by the feast he has provided, and tries to interest his friends in the story of the parrot poisoned with parsley, his friends take very little notice, and most of the audience take no more. It is not even clear to many of the audience why Schaunard puts away the food and insists upon dining out.

The jollity reaches its climax, unless overacted, in the scene of the landlord's ejection, the entire sequence leading to a masterly transition to the world of sentimental tenderness. In Mürger, Louise employs seductive attitudes, asks Rodolphe to unlace her boots, and then blows out the candle. Rodolphe, it might be added, is described as prematurely bald. In a later episode between the sculptor Jacques and Francine, it is Francine who pushes the key under the bed. In the Italian opera Mimi is not a hussy, except offstage and in the intervals, Rodolfo is not bald, or if he is, measures have been taken to conceal the fact, and it is he who pockets the key in order to further his intimacy with the girl.

Everything has been artfully arranged to blend the high spirits of irresponsible youth with as tender a Christmas Eve love story as was ever concocted, and the artfulness is responsible for much of the success. The music is responsible for even more, matching as it does the optimism and the hedonism with vigor, and the sentimentality with sumptuous lyricism. There are Victorian touches of tear-jerking in the action involving the earrings, the old coat, the bonnet, and the muff and, as in Gounod's *Faust,* the verbal and musical recollections of happier days are employed for the encouragement of tears. There is no denying the sentimentality, but there is no more denying the skill with which it is deployed.

In production, *La Bohème* often suffers from the unwillingness of the participants to blend the *verismo* and the lyricism, which makes them seem actors of a sort in the conversational sequences and operatic singers presenting concert numbers in the lyrical sequences. Audiences for Puccini do not object, since audiences for Puccini are among the least perceptive of operatic audiences. Indeed, it may be said that neither Puccini's considerable skills nor Illica's and Puccini's lapses attract much attention in the face of the emotionalism of the attractive music.

Stage designers are for the most part content to supply realistic scenery, and producers who search for ingenious methods of production for other works are curiously conservative with *La Bohème.* The attic is sometimes of an enviable spaciousness, and we occasionally get a glimpse of the roofs of Paris. The Café Momus and the Barrière d'Enfer are traditional, and scenery painted with snow in the old nineteenth-century tradition seems to be called for. The old settings at the Metropolitan lasted an astonishing number of seasons and were nostalgically missed when they were replaced in the 1952–53 season.

In Act 2 it seems to make very little sense that the Bohemians who have been complaining of the cold in the attic choose to sit outside the café on a chilly Christmas Eve. Colline the philosopher professes to hate the vulgar crowd inside and Schaunard claims to need room for his elbows when he eats, but the explanations do not convince us. We know quite well that the exterior, especially with an occasional hint of falling snow, is more picturesque. We also know quite well that European cafés take their chairs and tables inside and store them in the basement during the winter. Realism must here give way to romanticism. A partial exterior is necessary, since Parpignol the toy vendor is to push his barrow across the square and the children are to follow him jubilantly. Alcindoro, Musetta's elderly admirer, is the most sensible person present and is astonished at having to sit outside. Since Musetta, who is with him, play-acts for the benefit of her lover Marcello, the tables must be within reasonable distance of each other.

Some productions use a half-interior, half-exterior setting. Alcindoro's reference to sitting outside may easily refer to the outer room where the Bohemians are sitting instead of to the inner room where, perhaps, he customarily sits. Other productions cheerfully place the Bohemians and other Parisians outside as if it were a warm June evening. It scarcely matters. The scene is youthfully irresponsible and musically satisfying. Alcindoro, who is often Benoit the landlord in another costume (the roles being doubled), frequently overacts and makes much of his faint at the curtain when he receives the bill for the entire party. It is a typical stage meal, with no time to eat. The music is mostly ensemble, so there is very little opportunity to pay much attention to eating. The whole scene is theatricalism masquerading as realism and only the unobservant are deceived. The music is exhilarating, and the second soprano has her brief chance to outshine the first and sometimes succeeds. We hear comparatively little of the words. The music and the abundant action give generously of the atmosphere of an artists' gathering in a Paris café, and the result is most pleasing.

Music and atmosphere are at their best in the opening of the third act at the Barrière d'Enfer, with the cold music (open fifths in the harmony), the peasant women with their baskets, and the street sweepers stamping their feet to keep out the cold. The action makes very little sense; we immediately see through the device of Mimi not wanting to meet Rodolfo and therefore playing her scene with Marcello outside in the cold instead of inside where Rodolfo is sleeping. Rodolfo, although exhausted, wakes and comes out on cue, declaring without preamble: "Marcello, at last! Here no one can hear us. I want to leave Mimi." Mimi hides behind a tree and coughs pathetically. We are surprised to learn that Mimi, who in Acts 1 and 2 charmed us with her freshness and comparative innocence, is *una civetta*, a flirt, with eyes for any man of title she can lead on. This sounds more like Mürger's Mimi. Musetta's laughter calls Marcello indoors. The lovers must play a scene together, without onlookers. Rodolfo has suggested that Mimi go inside the tavern where it is warm, but Mimi replies that the atmosphere would suffocate her. Since it is full of tobacco smoke she is probably right, but it seems like an obvious device. Some of the most appealing music is heard in this scene, and we are advised to forgive the dramatic lameness. We should not forgive as readily the histrionic excesses to which we are sometimes treated by Marcello and Musetta, whose function it is to provide the earthy contrast to the other pair of lovers and their lyrical decision to part company in the spring, some three months later. The two duets are beautifully integrated into a quartet, and overacting spoils the musical effect.

Overacting is a temptation in the opening scene of the fourth act. Like the breezy opening of the first act, the references in Italian leave the foreign listener agape—Musetta's heart under the velvet, Musetta's dark eyes, Marcello's wilful paintbrush, the herring worthy of Demosthenes, parrot tongue for the Duke, the King summoning Colline—but by way of compensation much of the visual is overclarified, and we are pelted, as it were, with the four rolls and the herring, the water carafe in Colline's hat, the dance, the falsetto passage, and the fight with the firearms. The snatches of music from previous acts, now quite familiar, are blended in masterly fashion, and the separation of two sequences of chatter by the lovely nostalgic duet for Rodolfo and Marcello is in Puccini's best vein of lyrical outpouring. It demands subjective treatment and must at all costs avoid the vulgarity of facing front at the prompter's box. A similar danger comes moments later in the act, with Colline's little bass apostrophe to his coat. This, too, is a private moment upon which we are permitted to eavesdrop, and done this way it can be very moving. If it is performed as a concert number it tears the delicate texture of this last act in half, and the audience will contribute its share to the destruction by applauding the bass if he is celebrated, and quite often if he is not.

Joseph Kerman accuses Puccini of applying his melodiousness

indiscriminately, and of having "throughout his career skittishly borrowed and bowdlerized up-to-date techniques for his own conservative ends" (pp. 257–58). The criticism is valid. *La Bohème* remains, however, one of the most popular operas of our time. In less than thirty years it will be a century old. As the first opera in the experience of a listener or viewer it may, in a minority of cases, repel him with its sentimentality, or it may enamor him so that all other works seem cold and dull by comparison and the potential operagoer is forever embalmed in sweet amber. In most instances it is probable that its charm is instantly recognized, its obvious shortcomings forgiven, and an appetite for more and different musical theatrical experiences stimulated, in which case we may be grateful for its prodigious success. Whether we are grateful or not, the fact of its potency cannot be ignored.

The Merry Widow

Text by Viktor Leon and Leo Stein, based on Henri Meilhac's L'Attaché. Music by Franz Lehár. First performed in Vienna, 1905.

The two operettas which, almost incontestably, are the first favorites in Vienna and all the would-be Viennas of the world sprout from Parisian roots. Johann Strauss's *Die Fledermaus* was based on a German comedy which in turn was based on Meilhac's and Halévy's *Le Réveillon*. Franz Lehár's *Die lustige Witwe* was based on the French comedy *L'Attaché* by Meilhac.

This is not surprising. The Offenbach vogue in the 1860s was widespread, and the *opéras bouffes* of this composer, primarily to the texts of Meilhac and Halévy, were especially successful in Vienna. The establishment of Viennese operetta was a direct result of Offenbach's power and Offenbach's greed. The fact that Johann Strauss dethroned Offenbach, to some extent, by supplying a native form is responsible for the special character of Viennese operetta. Johann Strauss was already a celebrated dance band conductor when he turned to writing for the stage. Following him was a flock of other composers, some as Viennese as Strauss, others with a dash of

Bohemia or Hungary to flavor the waltz and the march with a touch of the exotic (Slavic or Ugro-Altaic) and to introduce the rhythms of the polka, the mazurka, and the czardas by way of contrast.

Lehár was a Hungarian by birth, Bohemian by family and education, and Viennese by adoption. He spent much of his time in a charming house on the river front at Bad Ischl. The house is now a museum, rich in memorabilia and associations, in which one can see, in addition to the bed in which Lehár died, the room in which he composed much of *The Merry Widow.*

The sixty-five-year-old work has the clichés of the operetta form. The glamorous setting is Paris, with an embassy ballroom setting for the first act. The glamorous leading lady is Hanna Glawari (Sonia in British and American productions), who is not only beautiful but vastly rich. This fact conveniently forms the hub of the plot and provides two further settings, one for the second act in the garden of her naturally splendid house, and one for the third in that same house extravagantly redecorated to resemble the interior of the famous restaurant Maxim's.

The basic premise of a titled man and a wealthy woman in love with each other but neither in a position to take the first step toward mutual understanding is ancient enough. The real love between Hanna and Count Danilo is sentimentally resplendent. The intrigue of Valencienne, wife of the Pontevidrinian ambassador, with a French officer provides a piquant contrast, fashionable flirtation with no intent to dishonor marriage. It adds a soupçon of cynicism to the otherwise sugary proceedings, and a touch of anxiety when Valencienne is compromised in the summer house, until her reputation is cleared by the big-hearted and resourceful widow herself. Crude sex, as crude as sex is permitted to get in operetta (which is more picturesque than tangible), is supplied by the girls from Maxim's.

Although the widow is wealthy and the little Balkan state which can be saved by her remarriage is on the verge of bankruptcy, there is no hint of the sleazier aspects of poverty. Everyone is superbly or appropriately costumed, according to social position. The guests, if not as rich as Hanna, are putting up a good show, and the grisettes from Maxim's, preying as they do upon the rich, cannot afford to disgrace their benefactors.

Act 2 opens with a number of guests in Pontevidrinian national dress, and an entire sequence in exotic costume is motivated into fashionable Paris, all in the interest of glamor.

The potential for satire which the era's preoccupation with money provides is not permitted to tarnish the radiance of *The Merry Widow*. The hypocritical, double-standard world of the turn of the century is accepted as it stands, without protest. The caste system is criticized only in the story's basic premise, that before the curtain rises on the operetta Count Danilo has been prevented from marrying the little nobody Hanna. The little nobody promptly married a millionaire and the millionaire as promptly died, leaving a merry widow and a problem for the Balkan state if the lady marries a foreigner.

Cynicism and acceptance are mixed with romance and tenderness. The best of both worlds, the world of frivolity and the world of sentiment, are artfully blended to create the exhilarating ambiance of *The Merry Widow*. The men pursue the women and sing lustily of "women, women, women, women, women," but real ladies are expected to remain within the bounds of virtue. "I am a respectable wife," sings Valencienne to the ardent French officer, advising him to get married. When later she meets the young man in the summer house, ostensibly to bid him goodbye, we in the audience are partly delighted to have her comic husband peer through the keyhole and learn of her apparent infidelity, and partly concerned for the lady's dilemma.

Taking a cue from Oscar Wilde's popular sentimental melodrama *Lady Windermere's Fan*, one lady takes the place of another and Valencienne escapes with her reputation. The trick at the end of the operetta is right out of the comedy of manners of the seventeenth century. Hanna, in declaring herself penniless if she remarries, rids herself of mercenary pretenders and assures herself of Count Danilo's genuine affection.

The music is equally eclectic. The French verve of Offenbach and the Viennese *Schwung* of Millöcker, Zeller, and Johann Strauss are easily detectable, though the observation is by no means intended to imply lack of originality on Lehár's part. Characteristic of Lehár, there are Slavic injections in the opening chorus mazurka, in Hanna's entrance, and in the second-act finale, while the second act begins with a hint of polonaise.

The Offenbachian galop has encouraged some producers in Europe as well as the United States to add the cancan music from Offenbach's *Orphée aux Enfers,* presumably because *The Merry Widow* takes place in Paris.

While the work qualifies as a waltz operetta, there is enough rhythmic variety to escape the accusation of monotony. The vocal variety is noteworthy, extending as it does from the sentimental lyricism of the celebrated waltz, through the soubrette sequences of Valencienne on the one hand and the patter sequences of the roving males and the grisettes on the other, to effective passages of *mélodrame* and *Sprechstimme.* The speaking across "music under" is designated in the score. The *Sprechstimme* is briefly indicated, but a comparison of the score with performance practice suggests that in some productions singers take more liberty with this *diseur-diseuse* technique than Lehár intended.

In its first production *The Merry Widow* was an up-to-date piece, almost what we would call a musical comedy. 1905 was not glamorous in 1905. The years have applied the glamor and the work has become more of an operetta with the passing of time, occasionally in self-conscious productions to be all but smothered in its cartwheel hats, ostrich plumes, and unmanageable trains.

In its first production, as in the case of its predecessor *Die Fledermaus, The Merry Widow* was not an immediate success in Vienna. These two most famous Viennese operettas were launched upon world fame in a critically more astute city, Berlin. When *The Merry Widow* came to New York in 1907 it captivated America and restimulated the popularity of European operetta in the new world. Was its phenomenal success attributable in part to the essentially musical-comedy character of its writing, a character now only faintly perceptible beneath the accumulation of nostalgia? (See Plate 19.)

13

Proletarian Music Drama

With *Der Rosenkavalier*, 1911, the most recent opera with an assured place in the international repertory, and *Wozzeck*, 1925, much too "modern" for the average theatregoing audience of the 1960s and early 1970s, the state of contemporary opera is discouraging.

A mixture of apathy, fear, and active dislike reduces potential audiences for works by Arnold Schoenberg, Alban Berg, Igor Stravinsky, Paul Hindemith, Serge Prokofieff, Ernst Křenek, Rolf Liebermann, Benjamin Britten, and Hans Werner Henze. Exceptions can be made for some of the works of these nine distinguished composers, but the popular response to performances of their works is not as wholehearted as to the operas of Verdi and Puccini, which are continuing to make money at the box office.

The apathy of potential theatre audiences makes a manager hesitate to stage new or rare works when he is sure he can fill the house with the old romantic warhorses or long-established comedies. Until the community shows its dissatisfaction and restlessness by demanding a chance to see and hear the unusual, the unusual is not going to be performed.

Much good, but some harm, is done by the excellent recordings which are now available for quite new and rare operas. While providing an opportunity to study a work before attending a performance of it, they tend to mislead listeners into regarding opera as something to listen to only, or worse, as background music to accompany whatever they happen to be doing. In addition, the high standard of singing and orchestral playing on good recordings makes public performances, even by the same professionals, seem inadequate by comparison. Lesser professionals compete against heavy odds, and amateurs can scarcely compete at all. A grave danger lies in the possibility that audiences may lose their capacity to look as hard as they listen, and that they may regard themselves as too sophisticated to attend performances by young professionals and talented amateurs. Yet these less-accomplished singers in America are to some extent providing the equivalent of the smaller professional repertory companies in Europe. Until America has as many of these for its size and population as, for example, Germany, it will have to adjust to a top and a bottom without a middle.

Wozzeck

Text by Alban Berg, taken almost verbatim, with deletions, from Georg Büchner's play Woyzeck, *1836. Music by Alban Berg. First performed at the Berlin State Opera, 1925.*

"Ladies and gentlemen—I beg you to forget all theory and musical aesthetics which have served my explanations, before you attend the Tuesday performance—or a later one—of the opera 'Wozzeck,' staged at this opera house!"

These are the last words of Alban Berg's lecture which preceded a 1929 production of the opera in Oldenburg, Germany. (The translation is by H. F. Redlich and the entire lecture is published in his *Alban Berg, the Man and his Music*, p. 91.)

The opera *Wozzeck* is almost as faithful to the text of Georg Büchner's play (allowing for cuts) as Debussy's *Pelléas et Mélisande* to Maeterlinck's and Strauss's *Salome* to Wilde's. Berg's arrangement of fifteen scenes, however, has imposed an order upon the chaos of the unarranged scenes of the play, between twenty-three and twenty-five of them, depending on separation and the passage of time. A few scenes are now included in the play text which were not available to Berg when he chose the play as the basis of his opera.

Georg Büchner, dedicated to representing the world as it was rather than as it should be, wrote *Woyzeck* in his early twenties. He never reached the middle twenties. In the 1830s, a period associated with romantic verse-plays for the upper classes and sensational melodrama for the lower, Büchner curiously foreshadowed the naturalism of the late nineteenth century, the expressionism of the late nineteenth century and early twentieth century (from Wedekind to Toller), the epic theatre associated with Brecht and Piscator, and to some extent the midcentury Absurdists.

The little man as protagonist of a play had been anticipated by George Lillo's *George Barnwell* in 1731, but Büchner's *Woyzeck*, a century later, instead of treating a humble 'prentice ruined in "a tale of private woe," treats an even humbler character, captain's orderly and doctor's guinea pig. Woyzeck finds himself an alien in a sick society, sick himself, as his aberrations and his pent up violence testify, without money and without morals, without morals because without money, and he destroys the thing he loves and himself. "But if I could be a gentleman and had a hat and a watch and a cane and could talk nice I'd like to be moral. There must be something grand about goodness, Captain, but I'm a poor fellow."

When we first see Woyzeck he has a razor in his hand. He is shaving his captain. When we first see Marie, his mistress, she is admiring another man, the tree-like, lion-like Drum Major. When the Drum Major first sees Marie it is between a fair-booth demonstration of a monkey with a sabre (a real soldier) and a performing horse, which, being animal, misperforms. When Woyzeck brings Marie his pay and his tip from the Captain, she has just been bullying their little boy to sleep by flashing a light from a piece of broken mirror into his face. Marie, conscience-stricken, ruminates on her badness. "I could stab myself," she declares.

Woyzeck, sighted in the street by the Captain, is described as "moving through the world like an open razor." With the Captain's sadistic teasing in his ears Woyzeck accuses Marie, and she spits back her famous line, "I'd rather have a knife in my body than your hand on mine." Thereafter the images of dancing, the hot whore, and the stabbing knife whirl in Woyzeck's brain. He buys the knife, Marie fumbles with her Bible and sees herself as the woman taken in adultery, as Mary Magdalen, as wholly unworthy, a scene of one line in an open field shows us Woyzeck stuffing the knife into a hole, and in the scene by the pond he stabs it into Marie. Returning from the dance where the blood on his hand and elbow has been noticed, Woyzeck looks for the knife, finds it, and throws it into the water, but not far enough. Partly to throw it farther and partly to wash himself of the blood, he pushes on. Either he is drowned or he is pulled out and arrested, depending on how Büchner's editors have finished the play. A scene in which the idiot Karl cries out "He has fallen in the water" is placed by some, prophetically, before the murder scene by the pond. By others, it is placed after it. The final one-speech scene in the play is spoken by a policeman: "A good murder, a real murder, a beautiful murder. As splendid a murder as you could wish for! We haven't had one like it for years." In Carl Richard Mueller's edition this scene is placed in the morgue, and in addition to the only speaking character there are the judge, the court clerk, the captain, the doctor, the drum major, the sergeant, the idiot, Woyzeck, and Marie's body. If the murder is described as beautiful, the capture of the murderer seems to be indicated. Berg chose the ending by drowning.

Among the scenes not used in the opera two are at the fair, one is at the doctor's and involves throwing a cat from a window, one is at the pawnbroker's for the purchase of the knife, one at the barracks in which Woyzeck is disposing of his property, and one, taking place in front of Marie's house, is the grandmother's story. She tells of the desperate condition of the world, with no one left in it but a little girl who went to the moon, the sun, and the stars, and disappointed by them, looked down, only to see that the earth was an upside-down chamber pot. All alone she sat and cried, and there she remains today, quite alone.

The juxtapositions, the telegraphic style of some of the scenes, the laborious lecturing of the doctor, the animal symbolism, the action symbolism of knife and blood, several scenes of extreme brevity, and the many characters, some of whom appear only momentarily, give the play an oddly jerky, disconnected quality not unlike a nightmare. Beneath the surface disconnectedness is a unity of idea as blatant as an obsession.

Alban Berg saw the play in the Vienna Kammerspiele in 1913, was immediately taken by it, and decided to set it to music. The style of composition to which, as a pupil of Arnold Schoenberg, he was accustomed had abjured tonality, a long-established method of constructing musical works. In his 1929 lecture on *Wozzeck* Berg draws attention to the harmonic device he employed for purposes of unity, the parallelism between the preseduction clash of Marie and the Drum Major and the sadistic clash between the Drum Major and Wozzeck at the end of Act 2, and the linking of the final bars of Act 3 to the opening bars of Act 1, closing the circle and going on forever.

In addition, the strongly organized central act, consisting of sonata form, fantasy and fugue, largo, scherzo with subdivisions, and rondo, is preceded by a more loosely constructed first act, the five scenes of which consist of a suite, a rhapsody, a military march with lullaby, a passacaglia and *rondo andante,* and is followed by a third act consisting of five inventions.

Berg's purpose was cohesion without the help of tonality, and the achievement of considerable variety by avoiding the Wagnerian approach of through-composing each scene similarly. Each of Berg's scenes is composed from a different point of view but with unifying principles in mind. He is anxious to have us understand that he had no antiquarian purpose in employing variations, passacaglias, fugues, pavanes, and gavottes, and he carefully informs us that his folk music is harmonized according to the principles of Viennese atonality, drawing it into the prevailing *Wozzeck* style instead of allowing it to have an intrusive effect.

It is unlikely that many audience members, even the professional musicians present, will be aware of this formal structure when they are hearing and seeing *Wozzeck* in the theatre. Berg himself begs us to forget his theories and his musical aesthetics before we attend performances of the work. *Wozzeck* is intended for the theatre and it is in the theatre that it performs its magic, if we permit it to do so.

A large theatre is not necessary, although a large stage is helpful. The Chicago Opera House seemed too large for it during the 1965 season, the first Chicago performance of the work, but the mere fact that it was done was a tribute to the ambition and courage of Miss Fox. More suitable to *Wozzeck* was the 1150-seat Stadttheater in Mainz, where a remarkably effective production was given in 1959.

The landmarks in American appreciation of *Wozzeck* are the premiere in Philadelphia under the baton of Leopold Stokowski in 1931 and the radio performance in 1951 under the direction of Dimitri Mitropoulos, the recording of which introduced thousands to Berg's music and helped to build at least some audience interest for productions to come. Erich Kleiber, who conducted the 1925 premiere in Berlin, revived it two and three seasons later in the same city, and by the early thirties it had been staged in a number of European countries. In Nazi Germany after 1933 *Wozzeck* was understandably expelled from the theatre repertoires, although in Mussolini-controlled Italy in 1942 Tullio Serafin conducted a production in Rome. After 1945, *Wozzeck* was restored to the German theatre and productions of it increased in number. A Salzburg Festival production was given in 1951. Covent Garden staged its first *Wozzeck* in 1952, under Erich Kleiber. The New York City Center presented it first in 1952. One major German city came thirty-two years late to *Wozzeck*, expectably Hitler's favorite city of Munich, which saw its premiere in 1957.

One of Rudolf Bing's ambitions when he came to New York to manage the Metropolitan was to stage *Wozzeck* there, and this he achieved in 1959 with a production staged by Herbert Graf, conducted by Karl Böhm, and with settings and costumes by Caspar Neher. Everything was done during its careful preparation to interest the theatre audiences and the radio audience in the work, so that their appreciation of it might be increased. Boris Goldovsky introduced it at the March 14 broadcast and analyzed the musical structure during the first intermission. Yet audience reaction in the theatre was disappointing. Many listeners, finding the musical style too unfamiliar, must have turned off their radios during the opening scene, and others, although more liberal and adventurous, may not have listened to the end.

Wozzeck received another broadcast from the Metropolitan on April 12, 1969. It may be that the recent well-publicized recordings of *Wozzeck* and the interest aroused by Sarah Caldwell's *Lulu* production have helped to build up an interest in Alban Berg's music. A willingness to be persuaded to a different kind of musical theatre is mostly what is necessary. A good production of *Wozzeck* will do the rest.

Each act of *Wozzeck* has five scenes, and interiors and exteriors are mixed with an unconcerned abandon foreign to those who are accustomed to think in terms of backstage practicality. If the scene designer can endear himself to the audience and to the technical crew at the same time, he is hailed as that phenomenon a practical visionary and no words of praise are too extravagant for him. Naturally any scene designer would prefer to accept the challenge of *Wozzeck* to slaving on yet another variation of Parisiana for *La Bohème*.

The scenes in the opera are short, but none is as short as some in the play. Interlude music carefully and integrally supplied by Berg, who objected to concocted scene-change music, makes the planning less difficult, but timed sequences between scenes are more nerve-racking than sequences permitting pauses or repetition, if anything technical goes wrong. Scenery which is quite literal is both unsuitable to the character of the work and impractical.

With every scene break a scene change is required. The forest path is used twice in Act 3, but the two scenes are separated by a tavern interior. The street outside Marie's house is used three times, once in each act. The interior of Marie's house is similarly used three times, once in each act. Some reduction can be made in the actual number of constructions by combining the interior and the exterior of Marie's house, often by employing a wagon with the appropriate hovel on it, with the fourth wall, as usual, imagined. A lamp post, separately placed, is the simplest and most usual indication of the presence of a street, and the space between the lamp post and the wagon is therefore the street. The tavern garden can similarly be situated in front of the tavern interior. That still leaves, however, the captain's room, the doctor's study, the open field, a street in the town which cannot be the street in front of Marie's house, and the guard-room of the barracks, each used only once.

Space staging has been used effectively, with wagons moving silently into and out of pools of light, with curtains between scenes in some productions, and with no curtains between scenes in others. The rising and falling of the curtain for the beginnings and ends of acts have been clearly established by Berg himself.

The abrupt localities given in Büchner's play—Room, the Town, At the Doctor's, Tavern, Barracks, etc., are somewhat softened and supplied with lighting instructions:

Act 1	The Captain's room	Early morning
	Open field, the town in the distance	Late afternoon
	Marie's room	Evening
	The Doctor's Study	Sunny afternoon
	Street before Marie's dwelling	Evening twilight
Act 2	Marie's room	Morning, sunshine
	Street in the town	Day
	Street before Marie's dwelling	A dull day
	Tavern garden	Late evening
	Guardroom in Barracks	Night
Act 3	Marie's room	Night, candlelight
	Forest path by the pond	Falling dusk
	Tavern	Night—dim light
	Forest path by the pond	Moonlight
	Street before Marie's dwelling	Sunshine

A different quality and intensity of light are demanded by each scene, and it may be noted that where more than one scene occurs in the same location, variety of atmosphere is established. In Marie's room it is respectively evening, morning with sunshine, and night by candlelight. In front of her dwelling it is respectively twilight, a dull day, and sunshine. The forest path is seen at dusk and at the rising of the moon.

There is variety, too, in the closeness to or distance from actuality in the scenes, although an astute designer will treat the near-realism with selectivity and control the non-realism so that the unifying principles which Berg applied to his musical treatment will be correspondingly applied to the visual elements. There is an understandable temptation to stylize exterior scenes for the simple reason that man-made interiors are easier to simulate without embarrassment. The interiors and the exteriors in *Wozzeck* belong to the same world of pity and protest, and two exteriors are physically attached to the interiors, making it easier to connect them but making it more difficult to draw the field and the forest path into the scheme.

The first three scenes of the opera set the breadth of style, first a one-sided conversation between two men of markedly different rank, a scene which would not be out of place in a realistic play. The second is a scene of violent contrasts: the simple cutting of sticks in a field opposed to Wozzeck's disordered imaginings, the extrovert songs of Andres opposed to the terrors of Wozzeck, and the two young men themselves similarly occupied and of equal rank but temperamentally so different. The third scene passes from street corner lust to solicitous motherhood, with Wozzeck's arrival to the images of all the heavens on fire, smoke rising from the land, and after he rushes out pursued by his delusions, to the darkness in which the terrified Marie is left.

The greatest difficulty in producing *Wozzeck* is in acquiring the cast for it. The six major characters, Wozzeck, Marie, Andres, the Drum Major, the Captain, and the Doctor, have problems of intonation and rhythm that are not encountered in the bulk of the operatic repertoire. In addition to being accurate and pliable singers, they must project character with far greater definition than is generally expected in the looser, more casual work of the romantic school. There are several smaller roles, the smallest of which, that of the child who rocks and sings "hopp, hopp," can ruin the production if it is poorly done, so tense is this tiny scene at the very end of the opera. It is little wonder that the premiere required one hundred and thirty-seven rehearsals.

The fifteen scenes are all short, but they range in style from the purely conversational opening scene in the Captain's room, a similar one in the Doctor's study, and a third, the teasing scene in the street, to the strongly charged atmospheric scene in the field, Marie's seduction by the Drum Major, the Guardroom scene, and the immensely difficult final scene. In short scenes of this kind every second must tell. Alban Berg succeeded superbly, which makes it very obvious when the interpretative forces, sonic or visual, fall short.

The interlude music is fixed in length, and rightly. Technical considerations must take second place to musical continuity. Except for the final interlude, called an *Orchester Epilog*, which is of more than adequate length, the interludes are too short for elaborate changes. They range from about eighteen seconds to sixty, time enough to lower scenic units and to roll wagons, preferably with properties in place and preferably with no swinging or swaying after the lights are fully up. This fortunately discourages a series of elaborate settings and encourages the ingenuity which usually produces striking rather than ostentatious results. A medieval *platea*, or acting platform, has been used, furnished with the few necessary properties, while either projected at the rear and sides or with set pieces rapidly and silently placed the surrounding locale is suggested rather than supplied, and often distorted to match the nightmare quality of the entire work. The Aravantinos setting for the forest path murder scene in 1925 has become famous—a bench with the hint of water behind it, four pollarded willows rising from the bank like monstrous caterpillars, the young branches forming a tangled circle of whips against the rising moon. Fortunately, few properties are required and a scene in cluttered realism would only unbalance the production, so that for practical purposes Berg's interludes are long enough if the production is dexterously planned and all goes smoothly. The tavern interior, which suggests the most clutter, can be mainly the clutter of moving people, which is the easiest kind of clutter to move on and off.

Technically, the most difficult scenes are the short scene in the open field and the scene of Wozzeck's death in the pond. Cutting sticks in a field and drowning in a stage pond ask for realistic action extremely difficult to adjust to stylized scenery, while wholly realistic scenery is not only impractical but downright inappropriate. The drowning scene has the advantage of being a night scene, and on a deep, well-trapped, European stage Wozzeck can descend either upstage or downstage and seem to enter the water without the assistance of unconvincing devices. The moon can conveniently go behind a cloud in order to furnish the desirable obscurity, and the music makes us think we see much that is totally invisible.

For *Wozzeck* every kind of vocal production is required, from the most singable passages to the freest *Sprechstimme*. Although this technique (see pp. 64–65) is difficult for the singer, it is easy for the audience to understand because it resembles speech itself. It needs, however, to be performed by singers who are also convincing vocal actors.

For audiences who find this extraordinary drama compelling and who prefer orchestral subtlety to vocal splendor a production of *Wozzeck* can be an exciting event. Those who are affronted by its departure from traditional tunefulness will be happier attending *The Merry Widow*. Most fortunate are those with a taste catholic enough to be moved by Wozzeck's poverty one night and enjoy the widow's wealth the next.

14

Musical Comedy

American musical comedy is the rebel child of European operetta, which reached American shores to become especially popular in German-speaking communities. In the emergence of American musical comedy can be traced the effort of a new country to shake off the shackles of the old. The efforts during the nineteenth century were feeble enough, but early in the twentieth George M. Cohan created, almost single-handed, a real American musical comedy, a form that has not yet died, even though it has had to struggle for its existence against the more musically pretentious operetta and the more dramatically pretentious musical play.

All that is loud, exuberant, swift, topical, and up to the moment in American musical comedy may be gratefully attributed to George M. Cohan's dominance over the form, brief as that dominance was.

In 1907, in the very middle of the Cohan era, Viennese operetta in America received a tremendous impetus from the success of Lehár's *The Merry Widow*. The discouragement of Austro-German works after 1914 favored a second emergence of a native form, and Irving Berlin, with syncopated music of verve and an American dance team (Vernon and Irene Castle), made an entirely individual thing of it. Ziegfeld's girls in the more pretentious musicals and Jerome Kern's dexterity in the intimate musicals strengthened it. When Rudolf Friml, a Bohemian, and Sigmund Romberg, a Hungarian, wrote their "American" operettas, English in text but European in setting (*The Vagabond King* and *The Student Prince*, respectively, in the 1920s) the contest was on, youthful American exuberance in the bourgeois vernacular on the one hand, and on the other a more elderly tradition from central Europe, bloodlessly aristocratic but graceful, and always demanding to be expertly sung by attractive, well-schooled voices.

The contest is still on, but the most familiar aspect of it is the compromise, the giving in of brash Americanism to refinement, the capitulation of nostalgic Europeanism to a democratic directness. The original designations become meaningless, and the pieces with the greatest staying power like *Oklahoma!*, *Kiss Me, Kate,* and *My Fair Lady* are an artful blend of operetta and musical comedy, and in some ambitious moments, the musical play.

One borderline, however, is seldom crossed and opera remains a form apart, if only because it is performed in repertory and in special theatres while the lighter pieces, in addition to being performed in repertory, can be exhibited in long runs to more people.

The more ambitious form going by the name of opera shows its debt to nineteenth-century solemnity by moving toward the spoken play in matter and in words. At the same time it shows an opposition to nineteenth-century pretentiousness by moving, in some of its manifestations, toward the frankly theatrical and actually bringing some operas close to the commercial offerings of Broadway, and conversely, some Broadway shows closer to opera. Menotti's *The Consul* and Loesser's *The Most Happy Fella* attempted this and succeeded on Broadway. Kurt Weill's *Street Scene* attempted and failed.

"Musical play" is not a satisfactory term, but to many it implies a weight of purpose, dramatic or musical, neither achieved nor even attempted by operetta or musical comedy. It can therefore be loosely applied to works which refuse to be classified as opera but which have something to set them apart from the standard "entertainment only" pieces. Such are the parodistic *Jonny spielt auf* of Ernst Křenek, the Brecht-Weill *Die Dreigroschenoper* (*The Threepenny Opera*), Gershwin's *Porgy and Bess,* Bernstein's *Candide* and *West Side Story,* and one or two of Menotti's "Broadway-opera" successes.

These more ambitious works have done little to discourage the lighter musicals, which to most audiences mean American musical comedies, zestful and vital and aggressively of the present even upon the less frequent occasions when, like *Fiorello* and *1776*, they are set in the past. So avidly of the present are most of these pieces that perhaps the excitement of seeing and hearing them during their first few months is tinged with the regretful knowledge that they will never look and sound quite the same again.

Oklahoma!

Text by Oscar Hammerstein II, based on
Green Grow the Lilacs, *a play by Lynn Riggs.*
Music by Richard Rodgers. First produced in
New York, 1943.

Oklahoma! was perfectly timed. It is easy to understand the decline of operetta in the 1930s depression period, and the impatience of audiences at that grim time with the frivolities of the idle and titled rich. It is not surprising, however, that during the more expansive war years it was possible to detect a fusion of lively musical comedy and escapist operetta.

The vitality of musical comedy and the sweetness of operetta are not incompatible. While the later *Guys and Dolls* is vital without being sweet and *The Sound of Music* is sweet without being vital, *Oklahoma!* may have owed its spectacular success to a blending of the two in well-matching proportions.

Not only were musical comedy and operetta wedded in this work, but with the improvement of sources and texts a certain literacy and seriousness of purpose displaced the traditional inanities. Seriousness of purpose must be distinguished from pretentiousness. In later years many applauded the sentiments in *South Pacific's* "You've got to be taught" while being made uncomfortable and embarrassed by so obvious a pill in such quantities of jam. Many, too, were appalled by the glib heroics of *Camelot,* and even more appalled by the placid rumination by millions of the muddled philosophy regurgitated therefrom.

Oklahoma! in 1943 had no pretentiousness. Its much-praised freshness and windswept wide-open-spaces quality may have been the freshness of the wind over the Hudson and the openness of the spaces of Westchester county, but in the middle of the war years the piece seemed an honest affirmation of values nearly forgotten and peaceful times longingly recollected. It was escape, but escape to something worthwhile. Without being blatantly patriotic it sang of America and its local customs, and it had the courage to kill off the villain, an unusual occurrence in operetta, making it as extraordinary as *The Student Prince* of 1925, which had actually permitted duty and commonsense to put an end to the love affair.

The play upon which *Oklahoma!* was based, *Green Grow the Lilacs* by Lynn Riggs, had so many songs in it that it could claim to be a musical play in its own right. In his preface to the published version, after the Theatre Guild production of 1931, Lynn Riggs stated that his play might have been entitled *An Old Song*. "The interest has been solely to recapture in a kind of nostalgic glow (but in dramatic dialogue more than in song) the great range of mood which characterized the old folk songs and ballads I used to hear in my Oklahoma childhood—their quaintness, their sadness, their simplicity, their hearty or bawdy humors, their sentimentalities, their melodrama, their touching sweetness" (p. vii).

Antedating the television western and the folk song surge, *Green Grow the Lilacs*, from its first song, "As I walked out one bright sunny morning," captures the atmosphere of the Southwest in 1900 with its rich, farmy dialogue, its earthy characters, and its direct handling of the shivoree in all its vicious ugliness. *Oklahoma!*, while retaining the colorful locale, simplified the language for the New York audience, reduced to brisk and functional musical comedy dialogue the Synge-like extravagances of Lynn Riggs (some of them very beautiful), enlarged the small role of the peddler to a bravura comedy role played by Joseph Buloff, and saddled him with a shotgun bride for the finale in a typically vaudeville routine.

Ado Annie was promoted to a leading comedy role, played by Celeste Holm, and given a partner, Will Parker, so that the pair could portray the traditional comedy pair of operetta (soubrette and tenor *buffo* in many European works) in contrast to the romantic leads, Laurey and Curly.

The original Laurey and Curly are more natural and earthy than their musical counterparts. Jeeter Fry (turned to Jud Fry in the musical, since the name Jeeter in the late 30s and early 40s meant nobody but Jeeter Lester of *Tobacco Road*) retains his vindictive jealousy but is not permitted to attempt to burn the hero and heroine on a haystack. Being an unregenerate villain, he is required to fall on his own knife and die on stage, an unusual event in a musical, though common enough in opera. The play's excellently written shivoree scene, far more realistic than the one of Offenbach's *The Grand Duchess of Gerolstein*, is reduced in *Oklahoma!* to a brief pantomime and a few harmless lines.

While an enthusiast for the folk song atmosphere and hearty dialogue of the original may regret the standardizing which was applied to the musical script, the astuteness of adaptor and composer in fusing the fresh and the conventional must receive the highest commendation. Unaware that the doubtful-looking *Away We Go* (the tryout title) would miraculously turn into *Oklahoma!*, one of the greatest musical successes of the first half-century, they presented the work in the terms most likely to appeal to the audience, without whose approbation the work could not continue to be performed.

The critics and the public were delighted by the freshness and vigor of the work and enormously pleased by the excellent music, the charming folk atmosphere, the gaily painted country settings, and the exhilarating choreography of Agnes de Mille.

Long runs in New York and in London's Drury Lane Theatre put *Oklahoma!* close to the head of the American "classics." If the musical had broken fresher ground it might easily have failed to enrapture the public of the 1940s. As it is, Oscar Hammerstein's book respects the style of the original while making it much easier to follow. The lyrics, witty and graceful, break out of the dialogue unselfconsciously, and the total result is one of the best musical comedy or musical play texts in musical theatre. One need only read the trashy text by Milton Lazarus for *The Song of Norway*, a success of the following year, to appreciate the novelty and the quality of *Oklahoma!*. (See Plate 20.)

Kiss Me, Kate

Text by Bella and Sam Spewack. Lyrics and music by Cole Porter. First performed in New York, 1948.

Many American musical comedies are welcomed in Europe, some to be staged for long runs in metropolitan theatres independent of the state, others to enliven the programs of the operetta theatres of the state system. Few outlast the two- or three-year period of novelty, to be accepted with affection in the German-speaking countries alongside the old favorites by Strauss, Lehár, and Kálmán. Two which seem to have been accorded this honor are *Kiss Me, Kate* and *My Fair Lady*. Since *My Fair Lady*, with its English setting and Shavian dialogue, is an unusual specimen of American musical comedy, *Kiss Me, Kate* has been chosen to represent this genre. It represents it most aptly. It has, in the main, an American locale, middle-class American characters speaking in the vernacular, modern speech, except in the Shakespearean sequences, and up-to-date banter, as opposed to the timeless and often witless interchanges of operetta. It has a simulation of realism in setting and in characters, with the contemporary American backstage milieu, topical jokes, and vaudeville and burlesque entertainment supplied by the two gangsters, by Paul and his friends, and by the low-voiced Lois-Bianca singing in a popular style and Hattie, the Negro maid, singing the opening song.

Kiss Me, Kate shrewdly blends the appeal of American musical comedy with some of the appeal of operetta. In operetta there is generally more emphasis on music than on the dramatic situation and the songs are often decorative rather than functional. The music of many songs is of an ingratiating character, often sentimental, gratifying to the singer, easily remembered, and subsequently treasured by the audience. Dances are decorative rather than functional. Comedy sequences in operetta are usually supplied by a second pair of singers, *buffo* male and soubrette female, less honeyed in their vocal equipment than the male and female leads. Operetta encourages prettiness of setting, often quite exotic and colorful, with prettiness of costumes; attractiveness is more important than appropriateness.

The operetta blandishments in *Kiss Me, Kate* are not excessive, and the basic atmosphere is unquestionably that of American musical comedy. Capital is made out of the juxtaposition of musical comedy topicality and operetta archaism. Capital is also made out of the juxtaposition in the "musical within the musical" scheme, with many of Shakespeare's own lines for the spoken passages of the *Shrew* scenes and for one song at the close, "I am ashamed that women are so simple."

The operetta fondness for romantic locale and colorful costumes is satisfied by the Padua and Verona scenes of the musical *Shrew*, which gain in glamor by their alternation with backstage, dressing room, and theatre-alley Baltimore scenes. Of the eight scenes of the first act, scenes 4, 5, and 8 are Italian. Of the eight in the second act, scene 2 is before the diamond-patterned show curtain and scenes 3 and 8 are Italian scenes.

Lilli-Kate and Fred-Petruchio must be respectively a soprano and a baritone of genuine vocal attainments. Lilli's cadenza with two trills echoed by the flute is burlesque coloratura, but unless she can sing it well she ridicules herself rather than the operatic cliché, and her high notes must be as assured as her dominant nature. Fred-Petruchio has three excellent songs, "I've come to wive it wealthily in Padua," "Were thine that special face," and "Where is the life that late I led," through which his voice must range confidently from low B flat to high F, not an especially demanding range but requiring a dash and a virility not all baritones can command, and certainly beyond the capacity of an average pleasant musical comedy singer.

In the 1953 first-edition text, an introduction by Sam and Bella Spewack describes four kinds of musical show, the play with music, the operetta, the musical comedy, and the spectacle or extravaganza with music. While the Spewacks say that in the play with music and in the spectacle, the songs do not carry forward the story, they make the surprising claim that in operetta the songs do. They add the contention that while in musical comedy the songs ought to serve a similar function, they sometimes serve a mood function instead. Cole Porter's lyrics in *Kiss Me, Kate* do more than that, and one of their charms is that they do what they do in different proportions. The same could be said of many songs in the better operettas and musical comedies. While it is possible to carry the story forward in a song, it is done quite seldom. More usually a point is reached in the forward movement of the story which makes the delaying action of a song advisable. The comment made upon the situation by the character who sings the song fixes the situation in our minds so that we remember it with pleasure later. The song may also delineate the singing character for us and may also, as the Spewacks suggest, create a mood which the nature of the music reinforces.

Hattie's opening song, "Another op'nin', another show," with a chorus of dancers in practice costumes, singers, and stage technicians, is sung against the brick and radiator background of the Ford Theatre in Baltimore. It is the sophisticated equivalent of the explanatory number of the we-are-gypsies, we-are-jolly-peasants, we-are-gentlemen-of-Japan type, but without the direct explanatory statement that the two dozen people on stage are show people it creates immediately the necessary background of tensions, hopes, and fears. The story is not even hinted at. Theatre atmosphere is the purpose and the song serves it admirably. Apart from establishing Hattie as a southerner ("show" rhymes with "Baltimo'e") it says little about her as a character, and as a character she is unimportant except for the fact that she brings the bouquet of flowers to the wrong recipient and acts as Lilli's confidante. She is important, however, as the spokeswoman for stage folks who are saying "Hello" and introducing themselves.

"Why can't you behave?," a sentimental song sung to a gambler by the girl who understandably finds him irresponsible and incorrigible, might have had some point if Lois and Bill had continued to be what they began by being, the second pair of operetta, the song-and-dance contrast to the leading couple but with an intrigue interest of their own. An actress of Lisa Kirk's personality was able to make this low-lying plaint effective out of context, but in context it seems altogether out of character. Bill's interpolated "Gee, I need yuh, kid" is more embarrassing than anything in *Madam Butterfly*. Lois drops out of the play at this point, to return ten scenes later with a mercifully brief variation of "Why can't you behave?," this time without dredging the low F sharps. This leads into the much more believable "Always true to you in my fashion," which Miss Kirk made very much her own. Between these two appearances Lois has appeared in her other character of Bianca in *The Shrew*, to sing in "We open in Venice" and "Tom, Dick, or Harry" and to dance a tarantella with Lucentio (Bill) and the ensemble.

This brings us to one of the enormous difficulties in organizing this work. The Spewacks have explained that of necessity most of the Lois-Bill story had to be deleted. It is difficult enough to handle two pairs of characters in dialogue and song, but the structure of *Kiss Me, Kate* turns these four characters into eight, since they become the Shakespearean characters in the musical *Shrew* for five scenes out of the sixteen. Considering the difficulties, the Lois-Bianca role came off surprisingly well. The Bill-Lucentio role was less successful. Lucentio sings in three ensemble numbers, has four dances, and according to the biography of Cole Porter by George Eells, a song written in the elevator of the Waldorf between the first and the forty-first floor mainly to satisfy Harold Lang, who desperately wanted a solo in addition to his dances.* The song "Bianca" is undistinguished and remains an afterthought. It does not advance the story one jot, it sheds no light on Bill's character and establishes no particular mood, unless it is the pleasant one suggested by the old-fashioned soft-shoe tempo. It provides a song and a dance, however.

"Wunderbar," introduced by an intentionally dreadful snatch of stale dialogue, makes fun of European operetta clichés, but, ironically, as soon as the music of its operetta tune is heard the satire crumbles, and the number, now an established favorite, has taken its place without a blush beside *The Merry Widow* waltz.

"So in love," the lyric of which comes perilously close to burlesque itself, follows "Wunderbar," and it was either daring or dangerous to follow the ridicule with that risk. The music saves it, however, and the tune has become an established favorite. It serves the important function of declaring the genuine affection which underlies the bickering between Lilli and Fred. Lilli sings it in the third scene of Act 1 when she receives the flowers intended for Lois,

* *The Life That Late He Led*, New York, 1967, p. 248.

and Fred sings it in the sixth scene of Act 2 after Lilli has been freed by the gunmen. It is the equivalent of the sentimental interchanges in Noel Coward's *Private Lives*.

Cole Porter's music in these moments, however, is far superior to his words, and two dominant personalities, necessary for any performance of *Kiss Me, Kate*, can easily avoid mawkishness. They are helped by the fact that elsewhere in the work their music is of considerable vigor, Fred's in particular. They both sing in "We open in Venice," as catchy a tune as Porter ever wrote. Lilli has the comedy song "I hate men," and in the final scene the only passage setting the words of Shakespeare, "I am ashamed that women are so simple" with its tongue-in-cheek mock solemnity. Fred has the virile "I've come to wive it wealthily in Padua," and shortly after "Were thine that special face," a broad and expansive tune, warm without sentimentality, lightly handled with a dancing chorus, and effectively placed between the first meeting of Petruchio and Kate and the famous Shakespearean encounter scene, acted with much of the original blank verse dialogue. With the splendid "Where is the life that late I led?" the leading man acquires what is almost an embarrassment of riches. Fred's music is as rewardingly superior to Lilli's as Lois's to Bill's, so that the pairs are reversed. Lilli, however, as Kate, has acting rewards to compensate for the commonplaceness of "I hate men." This song is a successful *tour de force* and has the potential of supplying the shrewish Kate with the appeal of humor. In Shakespeare Kate's vitality is offset by Bianca's wan gentleness, but in *Kiss Me, Kate* Bianca is a lively flirt with an attractive vibrancy, and Kate's hidden charm must be powerful indeed if she is not to be thought tiresome.

The ensemble "I sing of love," performed by Bianca, Lucentio, and the singing ensemble, is admittedly a delaying device for the scene change to the finale of Act 1, but stretched with a patter sequence and followed by the tarantella. The patter sequence does nothing to advance the action and only a shred to develop character, but in front of the *Shrew* show curtain it serves to keep up the expectancy for the finale in a colorfully appealing way.

The scene outside the church, as befits a musical comedy finale, is sumptuous looking and, in an extremely brief ensemble "Kiss me,

Kate," comic, dramatic, and full-sounding. It does not need the interpolated device of the girl carrying a bird which will fly up with
Kate's coloratura passage and be shot by a gunman, to fall, as directed, on Baptista's hat. A somewhat similar device, though not used
in the same place, appeared in the Lunt-Fontanne production of the
Shakespeare play in 1935.

The novelty of hearing Shakespearean blank verse in an American musical comedy gives the impression that a considerable amount
of the original play is used, and *Kiss Me, Kate* is sometimes called a
musical version of Shakespeare's play. Comparatively little of the
play has been used, only enough to set the story going and to make
capital of such good scenes as the encounter, the wedding, the teasing, Petruchio's soliloquy "Thus have I politically begun my reign,"
and a brief snatch of the reformation leading to Kate's "I am ashamed
that women are so simple."

The selection was most skilfully done. Many scenes had to be
omitted and the loss of the sun and moon scene is a considerable one,
but for an audience likely to be awed or bored by Shakespeare, unless there are celebrities in the cast to assure them that it is not as
dull as they had supposed, the most functional and the most entertaining passages were employed to excellent effect. The fact that
the illusion of having seen much of Shakespeare's comedy obtains
at the end of a performance of *Kiss Me, Kate* is a tribute to the
shrewdness of the Spewacks.

A good production fosters this illusion of the play going on
even when we are not seeing it but are instead being entertained
during an intermission with "Too darn hot," and while the performance is going on, "Always true to you in my fashion" and "Brush up
your Shakespeare."

"Too darn hot," in addition to evoking the atmosphere of late
summer or early fall in Baltimore, is lively entertainment and in 1948
was thought rather daring. Breaking into a jazz session, it can easily
stimulate the audience to demand encores until the dancers are exhausted. The placing of this exhilarating number at the very beginning of Act 2 is enough to save *Kiss Me, Kate* from the possible fate
of many musical comedies which, having shot their bolt in a long
first act, usher in the decline too patently with the first number of

the second. Not only does Cole Porter triumph in this, but he follows it with "Where is the life that late I led," a rousing number for the leading man. Lois's "Always true to you in my fashion" shows no hint of abandoning the *brio*. The dangerous moment in Act 2 is the rather long scene introducing the stereotype character of Harrison Howell, the millionaire bore. This is further lengthened by the insertion of "Bianca." A reprise of "So in love" for Fred restores at least our sentimental interest, but the most potent restoration is the presence of the gunmen and their song, "Brush up your Shakespeare," which was written after Bella Spewack had asked Cole Porter not to write any more songs. A low-comedy number of this brilliance immediately before the exuberant final scene is as well placed as "Too darn hot" at the beginning of the act. *Kiss Me, Kate* owes most of its effectiveness to Cole Porter's musical inventiveness, variety, and tuneful charm. It owes almost as much to the placing of its songs and the skill of the Spewacks in splicing in the Shakespeare text, always careful not to let a passage run too long without a song of contemporary appeal. The topical slang cheek-by-jowl with blank verse in the songs which appear in the *Shrew* musical within the *Kate* musical is on a more conventional and less original level, but at its best in "Tom, Dick, or Harry" it has a tangy pertness. Projected by attractive personalities, the device can be very winning.

In spite of the excellence of more than half the lyrics and of almost all the songs, *Kiss Me, Kate* must have these attractive personalities to scatter its charm and ebullience successfully. In the Broadway production of 1948 the choice of Alfred Drake contributed greatly to the buoyancy which earned the production its enthusiastic notices. The choice of Patricia Morison was preceded by a consideration of Jarmila Novotna, Mary Martin, and Lily Pons. It would have been interesting to hear what a *Rosenkavalier* Octavian, a *One Touch of Venus* Venus and a *Rigoletto* Gilda would have done with the role of Kate.

Cole Porter's lyrics and music and his whole approach to the theatre have been dubbed "sophisticated." Porter himself detested the sobriquet and disclaimed it with justification. *Kiss Me, Kate* is astutely bourgeois entertainment. Not only does it delight the

American musical comedy audience and foreign audiences with a developed taste for the genre, but it delights an operetta audience, whether conscious or unconscious of the fact that that is what they are. In addition, it deftly adds the easily digested best scenes from a Shakespeare farce, blending the entire mixture with uncommon skill to please American and British audiences, and in translation, the middle-class audience of Vienna's Volksoper as well as audiences in a score of other countries.

It makes no sense to praise a work for what it is not when it so richly deserves praise for what it is.

Contemporary Opera

A Midsummer Night's Dream

Text, almost verbatim from Shakespeare's play, cut and rearranged by Benjamin Britten and Peter Pears. Music by Benjamin Britten. First performed at Aldeburgh, Suffolk, England, 1960.

Unlike *Kiss Me, Kate,* which uses a few portions of one of Shakespeare's least poetical plays in five out of sixteen scenes, Benjamin Britten's *A Midsummer Night's Dream* relies entirely upon one of Shakespeare's most enchantingly poetic comedies, using virtually nothing but Shakespeare's own words for a three-act opera based upon the original five-act play.

All the characters, with the exception of Egeus and Philostrate, appear in the opera. The text has been necessarily shortened, and a major rearrangement of scenes has sensibly relegated Theseus and Hippolyta to the final scene. Thus the opera can have a more immediate beginning in the wood, where it remains until the transformation to the palace of Theseus for the performance of the play by Bottom and his fellow artisans, or mechanicals. The opera simply has them first meet in the wood, by no means the only time this alteration has reduced trouble and expense for a production of the Shakespeare play.

If the play is to be a marriage play and the mechanicals' performance before the duke in the fifth act is to be retained, the palace scene is necessary. The play uses it twice, once for the exposition to explain the flight into the wood and once for the entertainment. The story takes place in the wood. The palace scenes are a framework only.

Britten could have lopped off the first act, which prepares for the flight into the woods (much as Boito lopped off the expositional first act of *Othello* for *Otello*), and he could have finished the opera at the end of the fourth act, when the lovers wake and are happily restored to each other. There is no more story. Act 5 in the play and Act 3, scene 2 in the opera both present antimasque and masque, a farce performance by enthusiastic mechanicals followed by the lyrical masque of hymeneal blessing.

A Midsummer Night's Dream, however, is too well known to have its last act omitted. Besides, the mechanicals' play is far too entertaining and must therefore be retained. If it were not, the preparation scene and the rehearsal scene would also have to be omitted, and with the excision of the mechanicals, the ass's head sequence linking the Oberon-Titania story with the lovers and the mechanical world would also have to be excised. Cutting Shakespeare is invariably more difficult than it seems at first sight.

Britten and Pears were extremely skilful, not only in their cutting of the play but in reassembling the parts. Many scenes and many speeches do not come in the original order but the essentials of the play are there. Those who know the text intimately (scholars, teachers, and those who have recently acted in or read the play) will immediately notice the changes. The bulk of the average audience will scarcely be aware that changes have been made. Even those who *think* they know the play well will not notice the changes once the omission of the expositional Egeus episode has been observed, to be reminded perhaps at the opening of the final scene that they are hearing the very first words of Shakespeare's first act.

The opera opens with the fairies and Puck, but instead of giving Puck the first line and having him wait and listen to a single fairy describing the service to the queen, the fairies and four elves sing the "Over hill, over dale" passage and Puck makes a sudden appearance. His lengthy description of himself is cut. In Shakespeare's play, the meeting of Oberon and Titania and the little scene about the herb treated in dialogue between Oberon and Puck run one hundred and thirty lines. Forty-two are retained for the opera. The classical allusions of jealousy are omitted, together with the descriptions of the votaress and the fair vestal, but the essentials are there. The Hermia-Lysander plan to flee (from the first act of the play) now follows, but the two are already in flight. This scene of one pair of lovers is almost immediately followed by the first Helena-Demetrius scene, to have the dramatic advantage of juxtaposing the two couples much earlier in the opera than in the play. Few audience members, when they meet the mechanicals for the first time in the opera, will recollect that in the play their appearance precedes that of the fairies and that of the Helena-Demetrius flight.

A mixture of affection for the Shakespeare text and full knowledge of the need to compress were the guiding principles in a work which ranks with Boito's Italian texts for Verdi's last operas, both based upon Shakespeare. For *A Midsummer Night's Dream* the task was easier in that the English needed no translation, but much more difficult in that Shakespeare's English, even with minimal alteration, is likely to invite comparison with the original. Not only are passages missed in the theatre likely to be regretted upon rereading the play, but the substitution of Britten's music for Shakespeare's music (the beauties of sound and meaning in speech) will for some listeners invite comparison.

A composer who sets any play to music immediately imposes an interpretation upon it. Britten's is the traditional one, unlikely to offend anyone who has known and loved the play for years. The magical beauty of the wood, the excessive yearning and its peevish counterpart in the music of the teenage lovers, the bouncing eagerness and outright incompetence of most of the mechanicals are all there as expected, together with the pardonable burlesque of romantic opera in the final scene, to parallel the burlesque of flamboyant Renaissance fustian. It is all a far cry from Jan Kott's interpretation of brutal eroticism ("Titania and the Ass's Head" in *Shakespeare Our Contemporary**), although it need not be a matter of "tunic-clad lovers and marble stairs" nor "flowing transparent muslin and ropedancers." (See Plate 21).

* Trans. Boleslaw Taborski, Garden City, N.Y., 1964.

A certain latitude in interpretation prevails. John Gielgud's production at the Royal Opera House, Covent Garden, was full of charm, marred only by a strong element of preciosity. On the other hand, Walter Felsenstein's 1961 East Berlin production, using the Negro singers William Ray and Ella Lee as Oberon and Titania, tried to project the other-worldliness of the play in an outer-space atmosphere of exploding atoms, satellites, and spacecraft. It was made recognizably earthy with a gigantic spider's web for Titania's bower, but Oberon flew through the air like a fiery comet, in marked contrast to Puck's satyr appearance. To have gone the full distance toward Kott's views would have done too violent a rape upon the music, but Felsenstein's taste led him in the direction of the harsher, more animal values of the play. They can be found, but Kott is so fascinated by them that for him the play is an exercise in Goya-like bestiality. The fact that there is a deal of fun and high spirits in it eludes him. The Pyramus and Thisbe sequence he describes with much solemnity, summing up the scene with the observation that " the world is cruel for true lovers." Although Jan Kott's essay is immensely stimulating, one cannot help feeling that an important quality of *A Midsummer Night's Dream* is wholly foreign to him.

Response to music is so intensely subjective that one cannot confidently describe one composer's music as strongly sexual and another's as somewhat sexless. There are responsible listeners who hear evil incarnate in the arias of the Queen of the Night. Others hear little more than bravura pieces for Mozart's sister-in-law. Genuine emotion and burlesque are difficult to distinguish from each other in *Così fan Tutte*. There are differences of opinion on the matter of the musical sexuality in Verdi, Wagner, Puccini, and Strauss. For some listeners Britten's countertenors, harps, and treble boys provide such an aura of sexlessness that Kott's interpretation of the play, if applied to the opera, becomes inadmissible for them. Oberon (Oberon and Alberich are philologically cognate) may be dressed in black and sufficiently removed from his original association with the dawn *(aube)*, but for these listeners the disembodied purity of the countertenor voice, while it easily projects otherworldliness, seems inappropriate to the dark realm of unbridled lust. Peaseblossom, Cobweb, Moth, and Mustardseed, sung by boys whose voices have not broken, assuredly sound closer to the "winged goblins" or "German dwarfs" so despised by Kott who, for the play, recommends toothless, wet-lipped, sniggering old courtiers. Their names are "love pharmacy" names, but their eggshell vocalism is altogether of another quality.

Kott's views supply an admirable antidote for bloated farce and bespangled Mendelssohnianism, but it is to be wondered whether, if Titania's court is as repulsive as Kott describes it, the punishment of animal intercourse is as much of a punishment as Oberon intends. If the ass is clearly the lover Titania wanted without wishing to admit it, she is, as Kott states, released from her inhibitions during the night. Oberon is thereby reduced to a self-cuckolding character like Mr. Pinchwife in Wycherley's *The Country Wife*, whose own stupidity reveals to Mrs. Pinchwife that there are better men than he and better sport to be had than he can provide.

Britten states his views in the music written for Titania's wooing:

> I pray thee, gentle mortal, sing again,
> Mine ear is much enamour'd of thy note;
> So is mine eye enthralled to thy shape,
> Thou art as wise as thou art beautiful.

This music may, to some ears, plumb the dark comedy depths of bestiality, but to most it will probably sound more beguiling than abhorrent.

It would be possible to detect repulsive tones in the passage "Be kind and courteous to this gentleman," and evil in the soprano filigree, but once again most ears will hear the daintiness and not be offended by it. The "Hail, mortal, hail!" sequence, with the boys' flutelike tones, would be difficult to make in any way disgusting.

It should be urged that Kott is writing only of the play and makes no mention of the opera, even though the Felsenstein production was first seen in 1961 and Kott's book appeared in 1964. A movement toward Kott's interpretation is a great deal simpler in the play, as was demonstrated at the Shakespeare Festival at Stratford, Ontario, during the summer of 1968. For a play, the director may choose his music in accordance with his interpretation, and he is

unlikely to choose music which for the majority of listeners contra-
dicts it. For an opera with the music already composed, a stage
director is obliged to listen to it before coming to ineradicable
conclusions.

A conductor's or a management's decision to use a tenor, a baritone, or a contralto for Oberon changes the conditions to some
degree. Some countertenors sound effeminate rather than other-
worldly, and movements which are more mincing than regal will
reinforce this unfortunate effect.

Puck is written as a speaking role and usually cast with a boy
whose voice has recently broken. The husky, uncertain quality of a
voice in this state has great appeal and the kind of "fourth form"
prankishness to which a somewhat traditional production is favorable. There is little that is sinister or spidery in this quality of voice.
Together, the countertenor, the trebles, and the husky adolescent
who in one scene sings an imitative passage or two on definite pitch,
form a contrast group of six against the assured voices of Titania
and the four lovers, and yet another contrast with the rough, in-
delicate voices of the six mechanicals.

The handling of the comedy sequences of *A Midsummer
Night's Dream* presents a number of problems. The fixed timing of
the musical lines makes a comedian's fine-adjustment timing to the
audience far more difficult, and many of the comedy lines tend to
fall flat even in the charge of obviously gifted comedians. Much of
the comedy is in the orchestral touches, which for the most part are
to be enjoyed in delighted silence. In as sophisticated a musical piece
as this, too much and too loud laughter is destructive. The slower
pace of many sung lines reduces the laughter response in some instances, but the pleasure afforded by Helena's breathlessness, Snug's
groping hesitations, and the mockery on the syllable "moon" is more
than compensation. Rather more obvious are the dove and lion
phrases for Bottom, but perfectly appropriate to character and scene.
The expression of the comedy has changed to a marked degree but
its basic nature has not. The wise singer will realize that his comedy
is shared by the orchestra and will therefore be content to do only
his part and no more. The unwise singer, recollecting and competing
with performers of his role in the spoken play, will strive for similar

effects and in all probability overact. The mechanicals are not a sophisticated half dozen, but in many instances sophisticated means are employed to present them musically-dramatically.

The most difficult scene of all, because it seems the easiest and because audiences respond to it so ebulliently, is the final scene of the performance before Theseus and Hippolyta. Critics of Britten have found this scene out of harmony with the remainder of the opera. The same criticism might be applied to Shakespeare's play. In play and opera it is outrageous burlesque. Underplaying it and overplaying it are equally disastrous. Only a pedant would object to the burlesque of Italian opera, which provides as hilarious a commentary on pretentious devices as the inflated rhetoric of the Elizabethan dramatists of the 1580s read now by no one but specialists. Since Britten's music is mid-twentieth century, the popular bombast of the nineteenth century musical theatre is as fair game as Shakespeare's immediate predecessors were to Shakespeare. Meaningless melodic embroidery for Thisbe cheek-by-jowl with piled-on passion for Pyramus combine to furnish a scene that will gain greatly by earnest singing and acting, losing its point in direct proportion to the performers' overt sharing in the joke.

Unless Oberon and Titania are the company's best speakers and Puck is outstanding, the scene following the departure for bed is, in the spoken play, something of an anticlimax. Britten's blessing on the house, sung by the disembodied voices of a countertenor and the fairies and threaded with the silver gleam of Titania's high soprano, is extraordinarily beautiful, and there is little danger of anticlimax in the opera. In its very different way it is as triumphant a crown upon the work as Verdi's exuberant fugue at the close of *Falstaff*. Music can remain exclusively music and yet serve a dramatic end, when the composers are so superbly confident of what they are doing.

Britten's *A Midsummer Night's Dream* has no need of extravagant scenery. John Gielgud's production at Schwetzingen (a visit from London) was unpretentious. The woodland scrim revealed the mysterious depths which in turn became the familiar, much clearer and rather lovable wood. A pleasing perspective on a central screen was all that was necessary for the palace scene, and the scrim wall was later pierced by the little lights in the hands of the fairies, who were never far from the proceedings.

An orchestra of less than two dozen and a small theatre (and for that reason high ticket prices) are essential to this work. A revised version in Italian with a larger orchestra was a failure. Shakespeare is easily turned into good German, but not easily into passable French or Italian. *A Midsummer Night's Dream* is as delicate as cobweb and peaseblossom. It is not conventionally melodious, and its exquisite touches are fleeting. A single payment of a high ticket price is not enough. A minimum of three is recommended, preferably within a short space of time, so that one may have the sobering pleasure of realizing what one's ears missed the last time they were listening to the same notes. Dedication is expensive but its rewards are beyond price.

REFERENCE MATTER

Glossary of Terms

A vista. In view, referring to changing scenery in full view of the audience rather than attempting concealment by use of a stage curtain.

Affective memory. In Stanislavsky's system, the use by an actor of a remembered incident in his own life in order to participate fully in the experiences of the character he is playing. Incidents which have moved him deeply are essential, and those of long standing are preferred to recent ones.

Alla marcia. In the style of a march.

Apron (forestage, open stage, platform stage). The part of a stage to the front of the proscenium. In a *thrust* stage without a proscenium, this is the main stage of action. Placing an orchestra between stage and audience discourages use of the apron stage much used in play performance.

Arc spotlight. Extremely bright, bluish-white spotlight used in musical comedy, burlesque, and vaudeville. The electric arc between two carbon electrodes produces an exhilarating but crude brilliance.

Aria (air, English and French, *ariette,* French). A formal song sung by a single vocalist. It may be in two parts (binary form), or in three parts (see *da capo*) with the third part almost a repetition of the first. A short aria is an *arietta* in Italian, *ariette* or *petit air* in French.

Arioso. Adjectival description of a passage less formal and complete than a fully written aria, but sounding like one. Much recitative has *arioso,* or songlike, passages.

Aside. A brief statement in play or opera intended to be heard by the audience alone. A useful but artificial device, avoided by those writing realistically.

Atonality. Lack of a definite tonal focus, all sharps and flats being applied in the score when necessary. With no key and therefore no sense of finality, such music sounds odd to the conservative ear, but with practice the listener can find pleasure in it.

Backdrop. A large, painted surface at the rear of the stage, associated with old-fashioned stage settings. Two-dimensional, but often striving with painted shadows and perspective to suggest a third dimension. The commonest exteriors are trees against a sky with clouds, or a street of houses. An old term is *back scene* (not lowered from above, like a drop). A *roll drop*, associated with nineteenth-century melodramas, is a drop rolled around a wooden pole, useful in theatres with no fly space.

Ballad opera. A play with many songs; the number has ranged from fifteen to seventy-five. In the early eighteenth century its music was drawn from popular folk song or quite sophisticated songs appropriated from successful operas. Later the term ballad opera was often applied, incorrectly, to the work of a single composer. The French equivalent of ballad opera is *opéra comique*, and the German equivalent *Singspiel*.

Baroque. A style of art and music characteristic in particular of the Louis XIV period in France and the Charles II period and after in England. In architecture and sculpture the high priest of Baroque was Gian Lorenzo Bernini (1598–1680). Baroque pictorial art is associated with theatrical energy and much decoration but nevertheless respects classical principles. The musical theatre of the Baroque, highly pictorial, developed the *opera seria*, with comic *intermezzi* between the acts.

Basso buffo. Comedy bass (or as frequently baritone), especially in Italian *opera buffa;* for example, Leporello in *Don Giovanni* and Dr. Bartolo in *The Barber of Seville*.

Basso cantante. Literally a singing bass. A bass-baritone with a voice more suited to lyrical than *buffo* singing.

Bel canto. Although meaning simply "beautiful song," the term is usually applied to the school of singing prevalent in the eighteenth and nineteenth centuries (Baroque and Romantic) which gave much attention to vocal purity, control, and dexterity in ornamentation.

Berliner Ensemble. Acting company in East Berlin specializing in Brecht's plays and in the Brechtian techniques of acting calling for alienation, a nonillusionistic approach suitable to the didactic nature of the plays.

Biedermeier. The period in Germany and Austria between 1815 and 1848 associated with cozy, pleasant, unpretentious middle class family life. A state of mellow well-being between social and political upheavals. The art and theatre of the period, at their worst, betray escapism into stagnant *Gemütlichkeit*.

Bravura. Implying brilliance and dexterity (bravura singing, a bravura aria, etc.). Intended for display and the technical execution of difficult passages.

Brio. Animation or sprightliness.

Buffo (feminine, *buffa*). Comic, as in *basso buffo* and *opera buffa*.

Cabaletta. A fast, contrasting short aria sung at the close of or shortly following a slower aria, often for vocal effect only but sometimes dramatically motivated.

Cadence. A resting place or close of a passage of music, clearly establishing tonality.

Cadenza. An elaborate passage, originally for singers, intended to display vocal agility just before the final phrase of an aria. Familiar also for instruments in the concerto form.

Camerata. Society of artists, scholars, and musicians in Renaissance Italy. The most famous camerata was Count Bardi's in Florence, associated with the attempted rebirth of classical drama and the actual birth of opera.

Cantabile. A singing style, flowing and lyrical.

Cantilena. Originally a little song, but now generally referring to smooth cantabile passages.

Castrato (also called *evirato, musico*). A type of singer of the Renaissance and Baroque periods associated especially with *opera seria,* a male soprano or alto. See pp. 182–83. See also Angus Heriot's *The Castrati in Opera.*

Cavatina. Originally an aria without a repeated section. Later used casually in place of aria. There are three in *Figaro,* all short.

Claque (a member of which is a *claqueur*). A group attending performances in the larger opera houses and paid by leading singers to encourage and direct applause. Associated with *Stagione,* seldom with true repertory. For the most thorough and entertaining account see Joseph Wechsberg's *Looking for a Bluebird* (Boston, 1945).

Coloratura. Referring to the singer or to the music sung. Music with embellishments or the singer who specializes in it. Originally all singers strove to perfect their coloratura. More recently the association has been with soprano singers with spectacular high notes, dexterity in passage work, and an acceptable trill or shake.

Comédie à ariettes. A development of the simple French vaudeville which used popular songs, the "little airs" now often written by a single composer.

Comédie en vaudevilles. The most primitive kind of French musical theatre, resembling English ballad opera. A play with a number of short songs, most of them popular.

Comic opera. Very loosely used to cover light musical theatre pieces, Italian *opera buffa,* French *opéra comique,* German *Singspiel* and anything from a play with songs to a through-composed opera on a comedy subject.

Commedia dell'Arte. Masked comedy or improvised Italian comedy of the sixteenth, seventeenth, and eighteenth centuries. A popular theatrical form with a sketched-out plot and stock characters, a pair of lovers without masks surrounded by comedians—Arlecchino, Brighella, Pantalone, Dottore, etc. Some of Mozart's and Rossini's operas retain the vestiges of these characters. Strauss, Busoni, and other recent composers have deliberately used them.

Comprimario. Literally "with the principal singer." A singer specializing in character roles, some small, some quite large. A *comprimario* is generally characterized by musicianship, reliability, and acting skill rather than by a sumptuous voice.

Confidant (feminine, *confidante*). In French classical drama, the male or female companion to whom the hero or heroine, respectively, relates past events and describes emotions. These roles in opera are generally sung by *comprimari*.

Constructivism. A method of stage setting and production opposing realism and naturalism and making no effort at concealment. Ramps, steps, ladders, swings, etc., provide places for action. Platforms show only the necessary structure.

Countertenor. The highest natural male voice, not a *castrato*. True male altos may be heard in choirs. The term *falsettist* is sometimes used but disputed. Alfred Deller and Russell Oberlin are celebrated countertenors. Rarely used in musical theatre, but Britten wrote the role of Oberon (*A Midsummer Night's Dream*) for this voice.

Couplets. French for verses. In *opéra comique* and *opéra bouffe* the couplets are strophic songs, sounding less formal than arias.

Cyclorama. Commonly abbreviated to *cyc.* A tautly stretched canvas sky-cloth, usually off-white, taking blue light well and giving the illusion of limitless distance. A canvas cyc is mounted on a pipe frame and flown when not in use. A plaster cyc, a solid background useful for small stages with no fly space, provides a similar illusion.

Da capo. From the top, or back to the beginning. A familiar direction in music. A *da capo* aria of the Baroque period repeats the first part of the aria, with different embellishments, after the singing of a contrasting second part.

Décor. French term for stage decoration or a designed setting.

Deus ex machina. God out of the machine, a Latin term for a Greek device in classical drama, when a divinity was swung out in a basket to settle the dramatic problem and provide a conclusion. The term now refers to any device of the sort, especially the playwriting technique of settling problems unexpectedly by use of a character who has hitherto not appeared in the play.

Diorama. Used interchangeably with panorama. A moving backcloth, working on the principle of two spools of typewriter ribbon, so that effects of motion may provide a realistic background for marches and sea voyages. Popular in the nineteenth century.

Divertimento. Generally, a light instrumental piece in several movements, but also the Italian equivalent of *divertissement* and as such meaning the same as the French term. Such insertions, except for the traditional ballet, are less common in Italian works however.

Divertissement. Scenes of dance and spectacle inserted in a musical dramatic piece for the sake of variety and for the display of other than musical talents.

Divisions. Popularly called *runs* or more formally *roulades*. In the Handelian type of bravura vocal line, notes are divided and subdivided to make pleasing passagework. See p. 184.

Downstage. The part of the stage closest to the audience. When in the Baroque period stages were sloping the description was literal.

Dramma per musica. Seventeenth-century Italian term for opera.

Durchkomponiert. See *Through-composed opera.*

Elevation. Sketch of a stage setting viewed from the front. Viewed from above it is a ground plan.

Embellishment. Decoration or ornament. A grace-note addition to the vocal line (also instrumental) of any kind, a four-note turn, or a two-note *appoggiatura* or *acciaccatura.*

Ensemble. A musical passage sung by several people. Meaning "together," an ensemble, strictly speaking, is anything from a duet to a chorus. Also means a performing group (e.g. Berliner Ensemble).

Evirato. See *Castrato.*

Expressionism. An approach to writing, acting, and staging which attempts to express the inner truth of a dramatic work by avoiding outward realism and using, instead, exaggeration or distortion. Writing may be telegraphic, repetitive, and angular, characters may be numbered instead of named, the actors' vocal delivery and movements may be mechanical, and set pieces may be exaggerated in size, distorted, or leaning.

Falsettist. Sometimes used synonymously with *castrato*. The possibility of uncastrated falsettists is treated by Angus Heriot in *The Castrati in Opera*, pp, 10–12.

Falsetto. The falsetto voice is of high pitch and produced by the vibrations of only one part of the vocal folds. The normal male voice sounds strained and effeminate in falsetto, but a natural alto or high tenor can produce effective vocal sound by this method. It is a singing mannerism to produce high tenor notes in falsetto. The term was originally used to describe a method of female voice production, and also to refer to the upper extension of an already castrato male voice.

Fermata. A sign (dot under a curve) indicating that a note or a rest (usually a rest) may be held at the will of the performer or conductor.

Festival. A special set of performances, often annual, sometimes commemorative, occasionally distinguished by excellently prepared performances but more often characterized by a list of celebrities guaranteed to sell out at high prices and stimulate tourist traffic. Some famous festivals are those at Berlin, Vienna, Edinburgh, Glyndebourne, Munich, Florence, Aix en Provence, and Schwetzingen.

Flat.   A unit for stage scenery consisting of canvas stretched and tacked upon a wooden frame and then painted. Most realistic scenery consists of flats of regular size.

Flies or Fly space.   The space above a stage where scenery is flown when not in use. A counterweight system simplifies raising and lowering flats, larger set pieces, and backdrops.

Follow spot.   A stage light swivelled to follow actors as they move about the stage. Especially in use on dimly lighted stages to pick out the soloist against the scenery. Usually equipped with its own dimmer. See also *Arc spotlight.*

Footlights (abbr., *foots*).   Traditional English *floats.* Not intended primarily to light the actors, these front and floor strip lights are useful in blending and toning the stage areas and setting, which might otherwise look spotty. Used poorly, foots cast unwanted shadows on the rear wall.

Footlight spots.   Small spotlights of low wattage mounted in the footlight trough for special purposes.

Formalism.   A unliteral method of using a single scenic background or set of units to do duty for a variety of locations. The audience is expected to use its imagination and accept a slope for a hill in one scene and a stairway in another, for instance.

Forestage.   See *Apron.*

Fourth wall.   The convention accepted in the use of realistic interiors displaying three walls of a room and omitting the fourth, through which the audience looks and sees the action.

Fugue (also *fugato*).   A contrapuntal form of musical writing in which a short theme in one voice is pursued by another and another until a web of statement, answer, and echo is created. Rare in musical theatre, but note the fugal finale to Verdi's *Falstaff.*

Fugato.   More frequently met than fugue in musical theatre. In fugal style but not as complete. See third-act introduction to *Rosenkavalier.*

Gaslight.   Succeeded oil lamps as a method of lighting the stage, as oil lamps succeeded candlelight. The year 1817 is usually given for the introduction of gaslight in London.

Gavotte.   French dance in 4/4 time. A second gavotte, often called a *musette,* usually follows the first, and then *da capo.*

Gesamtkunstwerk.   Unified art form, referring to Wagner's theories concerning the integration of the arts.

Grand opera.   An unfortunate and misleading term used by many to denote any work of the musical theatre which is neither musical comedy nor operetta. Strictly speaking the term should apply only to large-scale works written with spectacular production in mind, like those for the Paris Opéra in the 1830s. Later examples are Verdi's *Aida* and Puccini's *Turandot*.

Grid. Gridiron. Framework from which lines are hung and battens attached for the "flying" of scenery. The grid is situated high in the flies just beneath the ceiling of the fly loft.

Groundcloth. A functional, neutral-colored stage floor covering, itself covered with carpeting when necessary.

Ground plan. A sketch of a stage setting viewed from above.

Illusionism. Term implying the creation of an illusion of reality whether in dialogue, acting, scenery, costumes, or lighting. Related to representational, realistic, and naturalistic as opposed to presentational, stylized, impressionistic, and expressionistic.

Impressionism. An imprecise term, borrowed from the more precise use of the word in painting. Used in music to imply more concern with mood than with form, and with suggestion rather than direct statement. In both drama and music separately the work of Maeterlinck and Debussy come readily to mind. Their *Pelléas et Mélisande* is often cited as an impressionistic music drama.

Intendant. The general manager of a German state or municipal theatre, controlling programs and policies and responsible for the quality of the company and its productions.

Intermezzo. Short topical comedy interlude inserted between the acts of an *opera seria* in the eighteenth century. Pergolesi's *La Serva Padrona* was made from two *intermezzi*. Supposedly the origin of *opera buffa*. Also an instrumental interlude between scenes, as in *Cavalleria Rusticana*.

Intonation. Strictly, the inflection immediately preceding Gregorian chant. In general usage intonation means pitch. Correct intonation is therefore in tune or on pitch.

Jugend Abonnement. A German term, though *abonnement* is French. Performance of a standard work with low prices for young students and schoolchildren. Most subsidized theatres accept this as a responsibility. The Stratford, Ontario, school performances are similar in purpose, as are also the New York Metropolitan Opera junior performances.

Largo. A slow movement or aria. The most famous is Handel's in *Xerxes,* a reposeful song sung to a plane tree, actually a *larghetto*.

Legato. A smooth, flowing line. In vocal music it demands steadiness of emission and a sensitivity to phrasing.

Madrigal. A contrapuntal vocal piece, unaccompanied, usually secular in character in contrast to the motet, which is usually religious.

Masking. A scenic frame or device to prevent the audience from seeing into the wings of the stage. Door and window openings are usually masked, often with realistic backings.

Masque. An entertainment popular in the late sixteenth century and throughout the seventeenth. A form of "total theatre," it combined music, scenic splendor, poetry, and some drama. Milton's *Comus,* with music by Henry Lawes, is the most celebrated.

Melodrama. A basically serious play, frequently using comedy for relief, it only outwardly resembles tragedy. The conflicts and calamities are more interesting in themselves than are the characters, who tend to be stereotyped, good and bad. Passion, excitement, and action, often unmotivated, are emphasized. Intended for undiscriminating audiences, it uses much music to stimulate the emotions and much scenic effect to please the eye.

Mélodrame. In addition to being the French word for melodrama, this term refers to a technique, which became popular during the eighteenth century, of playing orchestral music under or between the phrases of spoken dialogue. Mozart used it twice in *Zaide,* and Beethoven in the prison scene of *Fidelio.*

Melodramma. *Dramma per musica* (drama for music) and *Melodramma* (sung drama) antedate by many years the term *opera,* now in general use for works of this kind.

Method acting. A popular and often misunderstood term. Used accurately, it refers to the American use of Stanislavsky's theories of acting (Group Theatre, New York, 1930s) now associated with the Actors' Studio and its director Lee Strasberg. Popularly, the opposite of technique acting.

Mezza voce. Half-voice, with reference to a passage required to be sung softly throughout. A similar term, *messa di voce,* has the different meaning of beginning a tone softly, swelling it gradually, and then softening it again.

Modulation. A change of key in the middle of a piece of music. Regular classical modulations to related keys may be heard throughout the second-act finale to *Figaro.* In Verdi, Wagner, and Strauss, modulations are more daring and associated with an abrupt change of mood or thought. Synchronized with a light change, a slight movement, or a change of facial expression, it can be an enriching device in musical theatre.

Monologue. In a play, a long speech, sometimes a soliloquy, at other times performed with others listening. In a musical drama, a long solo lacking the formal construction of an aria. There are examples in *Boris Godounov* and *Der Rosenkavalier.*

Multiple setting. Originally the presentation, as in medieval theatre, of diverse localities (Heaven, the Garden of Eden, and Hell, etc.) on a single stage. Later used to describe fairly realistic settings arranged to permit successive scenes in different but closely placed locales without a change of setting: an outside porch, a downstairs interior, a staircase, a landing, and an upstairs bedroom, all exposed at once and contiguous, for instance.

Music drama. A convenient expression describing ambitious, through-composed musical theatre works not easily described as opera, a term which Wagner used for the older-fashioned pieces with numbers interrupting the musical and dramatic continuity.

Musical. The adjective used as a noun, a term used loosely and mainly for convenience to designate the more popular genres of lyric theatre without drawing fine distinctions between operetta, musical comedy, and the musical play.

Musical play. A convenient but inexact designation which has become popular in English-speaking countries to distinguish the more ambitious works in the popular field of lyric theatre from (a) European operetta or imitations thereof, (b) musical comedy of the vaudevillian sort, and (c) opera, especially in New York where the form is supposed to belong to the Metropolitan and the New York City Opera Company and is somewhat provincially considered "poison at the box office." David Ewen regards *Show Boat*, 1927, as the first work of the new genre, the musical play. By the 1930s the term had become a catchall.

Musico. Formerly used as a synonym for *castrato* or *evirato*. Now, in its plural, *musici*, simply referring to a musical group, with no implication of castration.

Naturalism. An imprecise but unavoidable term, first referring to the early nineteenth century scientific naturalism of Darwin and Spencer and the spirit of questioning which succeeded their studies, second, to the detailed and lifelike naturalism associated with Zola and Antoine. Elements of literal naturalism appear in all ages of theatre, the simulated blood of martyrs in medieval theatre for example.

Open stage. See *Apron.*

Opera. A term now used to cover musical-dramatic pieces of all kinds except musical comedy and operetta, although comic opera comes very close to these forms. The seventeenth-century Italian term for opera was *Dramma per musica* or *Melodramma.*

Opéra bouffe. A precise French definition, meaning almost exclusively the series of satirical works with texts by Meilhac and Halévy and music by Offenbach. There are other works in the genre but few with international reputation. In a similar tradition are the Gilbert and Sullivan works, more often designated comic operas, or even operettas.

Opera buffa. A precise Italian definition, meaning Italian comic opera of the eighteenth and early nineteenth centuries. Musical numbers are strung along a continuum of dry recitative.

Opéra comique. French light opera of the eighteenth and nineteenth centuries. Strictly speaking, any theatre piece written with spoken dialogue between the musical numbers (*Faust, Carmen,* and *Manon*) whether a comedy or not. The Paris Opéra Comique is also called the Salle Favart and was originally the home of all works using spoken dialogue, while the Opéra confined itself to through-composed works. In recent years these distinctions have virtually disappeared.

Opera seria. A seventeenth- and eighteenth-century form of Baroque musical theatre, generally with many arias for display purposes, little or no ensemble singing, and a functional continuum of dry recitative. Always of interest vocally, often of interest musically, and seldom of interest dramatically.

Operetta. A loosely used term, often used interchangeably with comic opera, *opéra bouffe,* and musical comedy. In Italian it originally meant "little opera," a short, light musical work (e.g., Weber's *Abu Hassan*). It has come to mean a full-length theatre piece on a light subject, with musical numbers and spoken dialogue, and characterized by ingratiating tunes, decorative dances, colorful settings, social irresponsibility, a slender dramatic line, and the requirement of at least two well-trained voices.

Oratorio. A musical-dramatic work originating in the twelfth century, now generally performed, in contradistinction to opera, without action, costumes, and scenery. Invariably associated with sacred subjects and often constructed with little regard for possible acting performance, though some of Handel's oratorios have received full stage treatment.

Orchestra. Originally, the dancing place in Greek theatre where the chorus accompanied the action of the drama with a commentary for the benefit of the audience. Now, the band of instrumentalists who accompany the drama's action and are situated in the same place, between actors and audience. Their commentary is wordless and ranges from a simple functional pitch and rhythm control to a complex musical continuum of high emotional potency.

Overture (prelude). An orchestral piece played before a musical-dramatic piece begins its action. An overture is a separate piece and comes to a formal close. A prelude generally leads into the opening scene with no separation, though some preludes are given a formal close for concert performance, sometimes by the composer himself.

Panorama. Term often used interchangeably with *diorama.* Wagner calls for the device in a walking scene in *Parsifal.* Now replaced by moving projections.

Parlando (parlante). In speaking style. An informal and realistic technique occasionally used in Italian opera, bringing singing close to speaking. The German *Sprechstimme* is a highly complex form of parlando.

Passacaglia. A musical form, originally a dance, in which a repeated

bass line forms the basis of the structure. Easily detected in seventeenth-
and eighteenth-century scores by observing the same few bars repeated
from beginning to end. For the listener, the decorations above disguise
the regularity. Dido's lament in Purcell's opera is a famous aria built
on this model. Act 1, scene 4 of Berg's *Wozzeck* is a passacaglia, but
not as easily detected. In instrumental music often called a *chaconne*.

Pastourelle. A song or a short musical-dramatic piece of a pastoral
nature. Also, the fifth of six movements in an eighteenth-century
quadrille or square dance.

Pavane (Italian, *pavana*). A dance of a dignified nature in simple common 4/4 time, probably originating in Padua.

Perspective settings. The wonder of the Renaissance, giving the illusion
by painting on wings and a backscene of far greater depth and vista
than the actual space available. Sebastiano Serlio in his *Architettura*,
volume 3, published in Venice in 1540, describes the methods used.

Piccola Scala. A small opera house in Milan, situated at the rear of the
famous La Scala (Teatro alla Scala). In the small theatre are staged
intimate and experimental operas, especially of the Renaissance, Baroque, and Rococo periods.

Pièce bien faite. See *Well-made play.*

Platea. The open platform of the medieval stage upon which much of
the action took place. Some of the quality and function of the *platea*
was retained by the platform stage of the Elizabethan and Jacobean
theatre.

Platform stage. See *Apron.*

Portamento. An Italian singing term, asking the voice to glide from one
note to another at some distance. An authentic and effective device,
to be distinguished from the mannerism of scooping.

Prelude. See *Overture.*

Presentational. As opposed to representational, acting or production
which strives for lifelikeness. Presentational staging uses a variety of
means, but never naturalism. Nonillusionistic, it accepts established and
new conventions.

Projection. A two-dimensional design thrown upon a neutral surface
by a projection instrument. The instrument consists of a light source
with a frame in front of it, into which a slide is placed, black and white,
colored, focussed or unfocussed, according to the designer's wishes.

Prompter. In spoken drama the prompter was considered necessary
when repertory, with frequent changes of play, placed a great strain
upon actors' memories. For a single production no prompter is necessary and actors are trained to improvise. Opera houses retain the
services of a prompter, generally downstage center under a hood, since
most opera is produced in repertory and is more complex than a play.

Proscenium. The stage opening, resembling a three-sided picture frame.

Immediately behind it and concealing the acting areas is the curtain. Of classical and Renaissance origin, production behind a proscenium is more distant and less involving physically than the thrust stage.

Rake. Raked stage. Partly to improve the perspective illusion, stages in the seventeenth and eighteenth centuries were sloped, or raked, from the rear down toward the audience, the customary slope being about one foot in nine. Early in the present century the Russian director Meyerhold repopularized the device, and rakes and ramps are much used today, often steeper than one in nine.

Ramp. A set piece of scenery with a sloping platform. The German *Rampe* means this and also means the stage apron which often does not slope at all.

Realism. An imprecise term, sometimes meaning reality outside a theatrical form, at other times something close to naturalism. Realism is generally more selective than naturalism. The term is most often applied to the literal and external devices of the nineteenth-century stage which aimed at the illusion of reality. The term is worse than useless unless carefully qualified.

Recitativo accompagnato. A sung passage with orchestral accompaniment, lacking the formality of an aria, yet more declamatory and agitated than *recitativo secco.*

Recitativo secco. Dry recitative. A sung passage so close to everyday speech that although the pitches and time values are respected, a conversational quality prevails. A keyboard instrument generally supplies the sketchy accompaniment. Commonly used in Italian *opera seria* and *opera buffa.*

Régisseur. A French term, but used widely in Europe to mean stage director. A one-man overseer of the entire production. Max Reinhardt was the most celebrated early twentieth century régisseur.

Repertory. A system of stage production in which a number of works are played, virtually in rotation, by a resident company, throughout a season which may last from September to June. *Modified repertory* avoids the prodigious difficulties and costs by offering four or five works only, rather than the twenty to forty of genuine repertory. The *short run* system of summer theatres is not repertory at all. The *long run* of Broadway and London's West End is the antithesis of repertory. See pp. 41–46.

Representational. Illusionistic, usually with reference to scenery. Its opposite is *presentational.*

Reprise. The repetition of a song already heard earlier in a stage work, a device most common in operetta and musical comedy.

Revolve. Revolving stage. Turntable. A section of the stage floor (permanently established) or a circular construction on a central pivot which revolves, to change scenery or supply movement of objects as well as people.

Revue. An entertainment involving dance, music, and drama, but generally more a series of sketches than a unified whole. Some elements may resemble dramatic skits, others scenes from operetta, and yet others ballet or popular dance sketches. Elements of revue have been used in American musical comedy.

Ritornello. A short instrumental piece, literally meaning repetition or refrain. In Monteverdi's work it usually consists of a few bars played between the verses of a strophic song. The term also means an Italian folk song, though for this *stornello* is more usual.

Rococo. In art, associated with the late Baroque period and the late eighteenth century. In contrast to the dignity, heaviness, and occasional pomposity of Baroque, Rococo art is playful, lighter in tone and color (pastel shades were popular), and adorned with scrolls, acorns, and shells. While Baroque is associated with courts and palaces, Rococo takes us into upper-class drawing rooms and is rich in minor domestic art works, coffee pots, trays, snuffboxes, etc. At its worst, Rococo art is fussy, mawkishly pretty, and extravagant. At its best it is sophisticated and graceful.

Romanticism. The movement strongly associated with eighteenth-century Germany, but felt through all Europe and responsible for far-reaching changes in all forms of art. Rebels against the establishment (which was founded on a deep respect for the classics), the romanticists opposed authority and advocated freedom from formal regulations. They encouraged a subjective, strongly emotional approach as an antidote to classical decorum. At their worst the romanticists fostered disorderly sensationalism, sentimental excesses, and excited frenzy.

Roll drop. See *Backdrop*.

Rondo. A musical form alternating a main theme or subject with contrasting material, but always with a return to the main theme. This early and simple rondo form is the one applied to vocal music. The mature instrumental rondo encountered in sonatas and symphonies is more involved, but the persistent recurrence of the main theme remains characteristic.

Scena. As a theatrical term simply a scene, with the division of an act into scenes marked by either a change of setting or the entrance of a new character of importance. As a musical term *scena* refers to a set piece, usually a solo, consisting of accompanied recitative followed by an aria.

Schlamperei. An untranslatable Austrian term suggesting the British "muddling through" and the American "let George do it." A sloppiness or carelessness associated with an easygoing nature, a characteristic of many but by no means all Austrians.

Schmalz. Literally, the German word for "grease." Excessive sentimentality in tune, accompaniment, or singing style. "Wien, Wien, nur du allein" with much *portamento* in the voice and *glissando* in the orchestra exhibits all three at once.

Scooping. A mannerism of undisciplined singers; sliding from one note to another with little discrimination. See *Portamento.*

Scrim. A curtain made of theatrical gauze. It is used like a drop to produce a misty effect or the effect which softens outlines and encourages an atmosphere of unreality. When the stage behind is brightly lighted, a good scrim is itself invisible but provides a hazy quality. When strong light from out in the auditorium strikes the scrim and there is no light at the rear, the surface seems solid and scenes painted on it look convincing. When the front light is reduced and the light behind increased, the scrim scene seems to dissolve and the stage setting gradually assumes visibility.

Set piece. Originally a two-dimensional and usually small piece of scenery (a rock or a bush, for example), intentionally lessening the formality of wing and drop scenery. Set pieces at the rear of the stage, painted to represent walls, hedges, or distant hills, are generally called *ground rows*. Since the advent of three-dimensional scenery, the term set piece has been more loosely used to refer to any scenic object or structure which occupies a position in front of the scenic background.

Shutters. A seventeenth- and eighteenth-century device, using painted scenery, which slid into place from the sides of the stage. With a back scene at the rear and wings at the side, shutters provided conventional but swift scene changes.

Sight lines. The lines of vision in a theatre. Center seats usually have good sight lines. Side seats near the front have poor sight lines, since one section of the stage is invisible. High balcony seats often have poor sight lines, with characters at the rear of the stage visible only from the knees down.

Singspiel. German for "song play," or a play with songs between spoken dialogue. Early eighteenth century *Singspiel* was popular and unsophisticated, but Mozart's *The Seraglio* is a *Singspiel* written for bravura singers. *The Magic Flute* and Beethoven's *Fidelio* are similarly intended for gifted, trained singers.

Soliloquy. In a play, a speech addressed to the audience, usually with no one else on stage. In musical theatre the soliloquy frequently takes the form of an aria, or to use a term current in spoken and sung drama, a monologue.

Sprechgesang (Sprechstimme). Used synonymously but also with different meanings (see pp. 64–65). A form of declamation halfway between speech and song. Instead of exactly notated pitch an approximation is given. The time, however, is given exactly and the singer is not allowed absolute license. Notations up and down are also meant to be respected. The form is used in Schoenberg's *Erwartung* and Berg's *Wozzeck,* though by no means throughout *Wozzeck.* A special sign in the scores makes clear which passages are intended to be given this treatment.

Stagione. A system of opera presentation customary in the larger opera houses of the world. Celebrated singers are imported for the major roles, and after a specified number of performances they depart to other opera houses. See pp. 41–46.

Strophic song. A song consisting of a series of verses, each with basically the same tune, though there may be slight variations. See also *Couplets.*

Surrealism. A nonillusionistic art form employing the disconnectedness of dreams and irrational thought. Büchner's *Woyzeck* antedates the surrealist movement of the early twentieth century by nearly a century but contains elements of surrealism, as does Berg's *Wozzeck,* which followed the Paris-dominated movement.

Tarantella. A fast dance of Neapolitan origin. Dancing it with vigor supposedly counteracted the poisonous bite of the tarantula.

Teaser. The horizontal upper part of the proscenium arch. Also, a piece of scenery or a frame constructed to adjust the height of the proscenium to prevent the audience from seeing into the fly loft.

Technique acting. A popular term used to describe the opposite of Method acting. At its worst, an actor's "bag of tricks." The term, in its more dignified sense of well-preparedness, came to be used when some actors devoted to the Method clearly demonstrated that they had not followed Stanislavsky, who had sensibly insisted upon the perfection of the vocal and physical instrument *before* making the psychological approach.

Through-composed opera. Continuous music drama uninterrupted by spoken dialogue or obviously recognizable recitative. In German, *Durchkomponiert.*

Tormentors. The upright sides of the proscenium arch, or constructed pieces immediately behind these sides, to mask the stage wings.

Thrust stage. In contrast to a proscenium stage, a thrust stage, with its origin in the medieval *platea* and the Elizabethan-Jacobean platform stage, brings the play closer to and even into the audience, thereby increasing its involvement. Thrust has been repopularized for Shakespeare and other dramatists with the construction of midcentury theatres like the Guthrie Theatre in Minneapolis, the Stratford Ontario Festival Theatre, and the Chichester Playhouse.

Tragédie lyrique. A French term associated mainly with Lully and Rameau. *Tragédie lyrique* comes somewhat closer to the spoken play in dramatic expressiveness than does the Italian *opera seria* of the same period, which may exceed it in vocal expressiveness.

Trap. A removable section of stage floor which allows actors to appear from below or properties to be raised to stage level. Erda in *Das Rheingold* sometimes rises on a trap.

Trill. A musical ornament requiring the rapid alternation of two adjacent notes. Vocally difficult to acquire, taking about two years to perfect. The term *shake* is synonymous but now less often used.

Trouser role. Informally called by some of its performers a *pants part.* The role in opera or operetta of a young man, usually in his teens, played by a woman singing soprano, mezzo-soprano, or contralto. Obviously unrealistic, since a boy's voice breaks usually between the ages of twelve and fourteen, but useful for vocal contrast to the mature male voice. The dissociation of sex from the singing voice was probably fostered by the *castrati.* Trouser roles were especially frequent in the nineteenth century after the decline of the *castrati,* for example, Siébel in *Faust,* Niklaus in *Tales of Hoffmann,* and Orlovsky in *Fledermaus.* The twentieth-century von Hofmannsthal and Strauss operas give us Octavian in *Rosenkavalier,* the Composer in *Ariadne,* and Zdenko in *Arabella.*

Truck. See *Wagon.*

Unit set. Seldom realistic, a unit set provides an acceptable playing space and background for more than one locale in a drama. For that reason, avoiding a literal depiction of reality, it is close to formalism. A different kind of unit set may use a single basic structure, relying on changes of curtains, lighting, set pieces, and properties to establish locales.

Upstage. The part of the stage farthest from the audience. To be distinguished from backstage, which refers to the area unseen by the audience.

Verismo. Italian for naturalism. A realistic movement paralleling literary naturalism and similar movements of the nineteenth century. Usually applied to Italian opera, and most frequently to Mascagni's *Cavalleria Rusticana* and Leoncavallo's *Pagliacci.* Not very realistic (music drama can never be quite realistic), *verismo* nevertheless counteracted romantic prettification by stressing the sordid, ugly, and crude aspects of life.

Wagon. Truck. A platform equipped with wheels or casters, facilitating the shifting of scenic units. Several wagons placed together can quickly assemble an entire setting.

Well-made play. A play constructed according to formula. The French *pièce bien faite.* The term generally refers to the expertly written plays of Eugène Scribe, many of which were intended for transformation into operas. Among his best are the texts for Rossini's *Count Ory* and Auber's *Fra Diavolo*. An expert television scriptwriter today works in a different medium but with the same goal, popular success at great speed.

Wing and Shutter. A seventeenth- and eighteenth-century device, occasionally revived today for period operas. The painted shutters meet and part in the center, and when drawn aside form wings or are drawn past a series of permanent wings. A back scene completes the setting.

Wings. The offstage areas to the sides of the stage.

Selected Bibliography

ONLY THE BOOKS MOST USEFUL FOR THE
GENERAL READER ARE LISTED. FOUR ES-
PECIALLY USEFUL AND THOROUGH
BOOKS ARE STARRED

Abraham, Gerald, ed. *Handel: A Symposium*. London, 1954.
Arnold, Denis. *Monteverdi*. London, 1963.
Ashbrook, William. *Donizetti*. London, 1965.
Austin, William. *Music in the 20th Century, from Debussy through Stravinsky*. New York, 1966.
Barzun, Jacques. *Berlioz and the Romantic Century*. Boston, 1950.
* Brockway, Wallace, and Herbert Weinstock. *The World of Opera*. New York, 1941. 2nd ed., 1962.
Burney, Charles. *A General History of Music*. London, 1776–1789. Reprint ed., New York, 1935.
Burnim, Kalman A. *David Garrick, Director*. Pittsburgh, 1961.
Burton, Jack. *The Blue Book of Broadway Musicals*. New York, 1957.
Crosten, William L. *French Grand Opera*. New York, 1948.
Culshaw, John. *Ring Resounding*. New York, 1967.
Dean, Winton. *Bizet*. London, 1948.
———. *Handel's Dramatic Oratorios and Masques*. London, 1959.
Dent, Edward J. *Mozart's Operas, a Critical Study* . . . London, 1913.
Donington, Robert. *Wagner's 'Ring' and Its Symbols*. London, 1963.
Eaton, Quaintance. *Opera Production: A Handbook*. Minneapolis, 1961.
Einstein, Alfred. *Gluck*. Translated from the German by Eric Blom. London, 1936.
———. *Mozart, His Character, His Work*. Translated by Arthur Mendel and Nathan Broder. London, 1946.
Engel, Lehman. *Planning and Producing the Musical Show*. New York, 1957. Rev. ed., 1966.
Ewen, David. *The Book of European Light Opera*. New York, 1962.
———. *Complete Book of the American Musical Theater*. New York, 1958.
Goldovsky, Boris. *Accents on Opera*. New York, 1953.

———. *Bringing Opera to Life.* New York, 1968.
Graf, Herbert. *Opera for the People.* Minneapolis, 1951.
*———. *Producing Opera for America.* Zürich, 1961.
*Grout, Donald J. *A Short History of Opera.* New York, 1947.
Heriot, Angus. *The Castrati in Opera.* London, 1956.
Hope-Wallace, Philip. *A Picture History of Opera.* London, 1959.
Hughes, Gervase. *Composers of Operetta.* London, 1962.
Hughes, Patrick. *Famous Mozart Operas: An Analytical Guide for the Operagoer and Armchair Listener.* New York, 1958.
———. *Famous Puccini Operas: An Analytical Guide for the Operagoer and Armchair Listener.* London, 1959.
Hussey, Dyneley. *Verdi.* London, 1940.
Kerman, Joseph. *Opera as Drama.* New York, 1956.
Kolodin, Irving. *The Metropolitan Opera.* New York, 1936, 1953, 1966.
Lubbock, Mark, and David Ewen. *The Complete Book of Light Opera.* New York, 1963.
Mann, William. *Richard Strauss: A Critical Study of the Operas.* London, 1964.
Marek, George. *Opera as Theater.* New York, 1962.
*Martin, George. *The Opera Companion: Guide for the Casual Operagoer.* New York, 1961.
Matz, Mary Jane. *Opera: Grand and Not So Grand.* New York, 1966.
Moberly, R. B. *Three Mozart Operas: Figaro, Don Giovanni, The Magic Flute.* New York, 1968.
Pleasants, Henry. *The Great Singers.* New York, 1966.
Redlich, H. F. *Alban Berg, the Man and His Music.* New York, 1957.
Rosenthal, Harold. *Two Centuries of Opera at Covent Garden.* London, 1958.
Seltsam, William H., ed. *Metropolitan Opera Annals.* New York, 1949.
Skelton, Geoffrey. *Wagner at Bayreuth.* New York, 1965.
Smith, Cecil. *Musical Comedy in America.* New York, 1950.
Toye, Francis. *Giuseppe Verdi: His Life and Works.* New York, 1931.
Turner, W. J. *Mozart, the Man and His Works.* New York, 1938.
Volbach, Walther R. *Problems of Opera Production.* Fort Worth, Texas, 1953. 2nd rev. ed., 1967.
———. *Adolphe Appia, Prophet of the Modern Theatre.* Middletown, Connecticut, 1968.
Weinstock, Herbert. *Donizetti and the World of Opera in Italy, Paris and Vienna in the First Half of the Nineteenth Century.* New York, 1963.
———. *Rossini, a Biography.* New York, 1968.
Westrup, J. A. *Purcell.* New York, 1947. Collier Books ed., 1962.

Index of Stage Works Cited

Index of Persons

ACTORS, COMPOSERS, CONDUCTORS, DESIGNERS,
DRAMATISTS, IMPRESARIOS, LIBRETTISTS,
SINGERS, AND STAGE DIRECTORS